William Henry Simcox

The Language of the New Testament

William Henry Simcox

The Language of the New Testament

ISBN/EAN: 9783743393684

Manufactured in Europe, USA, Canada, Australia, Japa

Cover: Foto ©Lupo / pixelio.de

Manufactured and distributed by brebook publishing software (www.brebook.com)

William Henry Simcox

The Language of the New Testament

THE
THEOLOGICAL EDUCATOR.

Edited by the

REV. W. ROBERTSON NICOLL, M.A., LL.D.,

Editor of " The Expositor."

REV. WILLIAM HENRY SIMCOX'S
THE LANGUAGE OF THE NEW TESTAMENT.

NEW YORK:
THOMAS WHITTAKER,
2 AND 3, BIBLE HOUSE.
1890.

THE THEOLOGICAL EDUCATOR.

EDITED BY THE
REV. W. ROBERTSON NICOLL, LL.D., M.A.

Foolscap 8vo, 2s. 6d. each.

A Manual of Christian Evidences. By the Rev. C. A. Row, M.A., Prebendary of St. Paul's. Fourth Edition.

An Introduction to the Textual Criticism of the New Testament. By the Rev. Prof. B. B. Warfield, D.D. Second Edition.

A Hebrew Grammar. By the Rev. W. H. Lowe, M.A., Joint-Author of "A Commentary on the Psalms," etc., etc.; Hebrew Lecturer, Christ's College, Cambridge. In Two Parts. Part II. preparing. Second Edition.

The Prayer-Book. By the Rev. Charles Hole, B.A, King's College, London.

A Manual of Church History. In Two Parts. By the Rev. A. C. Jennings, M.A., Author of "Ecclesia Anglicana," etc.

An Exposition of the Apostles' Creed. By the Rev. J. E. Yonge, M.A., late Fellow of King's College, Cambridge; and Assistant Master in Eton College.

An Introduction to the New Testament. By the Rev. Prof. Marcus Dods, D.D. Third Edition.

The Language of the New Testament. By the Rev. William Henry Simcox, M.A., late Fellow of Queen's College, Oxford, etc.

Outlines of Christian Doctrine. By the Rev. H. C. G. Moule, M.A., Principal of Ridley Hall, Cambridge. Third Edition.

An Introduction to the Old Testament. By the Rev. C. H. H. Wright, D.D., late Bampton Lecturer, etc. Preparing.

BY THE LATE REV.

WILLIAM HENRY SIMCOX, M.A.,
Rector of Harlaxton.

NEW YORK:
THOMAS WHITTAKER,
2 AND 3, BIBLE HOUSE.
1890.

PREFACE.

THIS little book does not profess to be a complete grammar of New Testament Greek. It may be a question whether the great works of Winer on a large scale and Buttman on a smaller leave room for a competitor. What is attempted here is both something less and something more: to indicate, not exhaustively but representatively, the points wherein the language of the New Testament differs from classical and even post-classical usage: to classify such differences according to their origin: and thus to vivify the study of purely verbal grammar, and bring it into connection with wider intellectual interests and sympathies.

Moreover, while it is true that we can talk about New Testament Greek, as one form of the language which has a real existence, and while the Greek Testament, or even the whole Greek Bible, forms but a small body of literature, it is true at the same time that every biblical writer—at least every New Testament writer—has a style of his own, and often grammatical peculiarities of his own, so that the works of one biblical writer may differ from the rest quite as much as from those of secular writers. The study of these individualities brings us, more perhaps than the study of the Hellenistic language generally, into contact with the minds of the evangelical writers, and so gives real assistance to the comprehension of their writings. An attempt has been made to distinguish how far each writer (or each school or group of writers) shares in the special characteristics of Hellenistic or biblical Greek, how far he has marked linguistic features of his own, and thus to give the student some notion of the extent and importance of purely grammatical questions in dealing with the New Testament. It is hoped that, if he desires to pursue the study of pure grammar further, he may here find an introduction to the subject that will relieve its apparent aridity and want of interest; and that if he does not, he will gain a just notion of the amount of deference due to grammatical specialists, and will be able to judge on what questions this decision must be accepted as final, and on what questions any careful and sensible reader has a right to think for himself.

It will appear that I take a large view of this liberty of the non-grammarian, that I look for little gain to theology, and hardly any to devotion, from the minute verbal study of the language of the New Testament. Even were it otherwise, a book like this is intended, of course, neither as a theological nor a devotional manual. Yet it would be wrong to treat, or to encourage students to treat, even a study subsidiary to theology otherwise than reverently: and it is impossible, and hardly desirable, to form a judgment on points of verbal criticism that shall not be coloured by the opinions and feelings on deeper subjects of the person forming it. While I had no call to enter on controversial topics, I have not been careful to avoid expressing an opinion where one seemed called for, even if it had a controversial bearing, or rested on grounds open to controversy.

The books that I have made most practical use of, and had most constantly in my hands, were Winer's "Grammar of New Testament Greek," in Dr. Moulton's Translation, and Grimm's "Lexicon of the New Testament" in Professor Thayer's version. Winer has never been superseded, though his work is, to some extent, obsolete in form, as when he first wrote, it was necessary to prove that the Greek of the New Testament was a real language that had a grammar, not a jargon in which any construction, any case or tense, any particle or preposition might be used instead of any other. I have found more use in Professor Thayer's own Indices, than in what the Lexicon, as such, adds to ordinary Greek Lexicons on the one hand, and to a concordance on the other. But I have given, as a rule, greater proportional attention to points that struck me in my own reading, than to such as I only noticed when my attention was called to them by grammarians. I believe this to be right in principle, especially when it was less my object to expound the subject exhaustively than to rouse a living interest in it. The student will know grammar best who does most to construct a grammar for himself; and it was by doing this that I could best help others to do it. For this reason, among others, I have rarely quoted authorities. I will ask critical readers to believe that it was neither because I spared the labour of consulting them, nor because I desired to conceal obligations to them; but, apart from the necessity of economising space, I sometimes made out from my own notes what I could have taken ready-made from a pre-existing work, and sometimes could ill distinguish how much was taken from one and how much from the other.

On the other hand, I have not the advantage of an idiomatic knowledge of modern Greek. When, therefore, I have occasion to make a statement about modern usage, unless it be something quite obvious and notorious, I generally refer to my authority.

I ought perhaps to apologise for an inequality in different parts of the book, in the fulness with which illustrative references and quotations have been supplied. There are subjects where a complete enumeration of all relevant passages seems essential; there are others where a few typical examples will suffice: and in the latter case, if much more than the sufficient minimum be supplied, there is a risk that any but the most painstaking students will feel that they cannot see the wood for the trees. I have therefore, deliberately, sometimes tried to give exhaustive lists, and sometimes left it to painstaking students to find parallels to one or two typical passages. But I feel no confidence that my judgment has always been right, or my practice consistent with itself in treating a subject by one or other method.

The above was written by my brother, but not finally revised for press, at the time when the MS. was sent to the publishers. It has been necessary to make one or two verbal alterations and omissions. One or two sentences on p. vi refer to a Second Part, describing the characteristics of New Testament writers and comparing specimen passages of New Testament and Hellenistic Greek, which, though completed for press, was reserved for subsequent publication, as it exceeded the limits of the series.

At the time of his death the author had passed two sheets for press; he had also practically completed the revision of four more; for the remainder I am responsible. The very few alterations and additions I have ventured to make are almost all marked by square brackets. It only remains to acknowledge with thanks the valuable assistance received from the kindness of Mr. F. E. Thompson, M.A., of Marlborough College, who has found time to read every sheet carefully.

G. A. SIMCOX.

September 1889.

CONTENTS.

	PAGE
PREFACE	V
INTRODUCTION.—THE GREEK NATION AND LANGUAGE AFTER ALEXANDER	1
CHAP. I. THE LANGUAGE OF THE JEWISH HELLENISTS	11
,, II. CHARACTERISTICS OF NEW TESTAMENT GREEK IN THE FORMS OR INFLEXIONS OF—	
(i) NOUNS—	
(A) PROPER	23
(B) APPELLATIVE . . .	30
(C) ADJECTIVE	32
(ii) VERBS	33
(iii) PARTICLES, AND COMPOSITION OF VERBS	42
,, III. CHARACTERISTICS OF NEW TESTAMENT GREEK IN THE SYNTACTICAL USE OF ARTICLES AND PRONOUNS	45
,, IV. CHARACTERISTICS OF NEW TESTAMENT GREEK IN THE SYNTACTICAL USE OF NOUNS—	
(A) SUBSTANTIVE	74
(B) ADJECTIVE	91

CHAP. V. CHARACTERISTICS OF NEW TESTAMENT GREEK
IN THE SYNTACTICAL USE OF VERBS AND
PARTICIPLES—

  (A) THE VOICES 95
  (B) THE TENSES OF THE INDICATIVE . 97
  (C) THE SUBJUNCTIVE AND OPTATIVE
    MOODS, AND THE INDICATIVE IN
    RELATIVE SENTENCES . . 106
  (D) THE IMPERATIVE AND INFINITIVE
    MOODS 114
  (E) THE PARTICIPLES . . . 122

" VI. USES AND MEANINGS, CHARACTERISTIC OF
THE NEW TESTAMENT, OF PARTICLES—

  (A) PREPOSITIONS 136
  (B) CONJUNCTIONS 160
  (C) RELATIVE ADVERBS—CONDITIONAL,
    FINAL, ETC. 169
  (D) NEGATIVE AND INTERROGATIVE
    PARTICLES 181

" VII. MISCELLANEOUS FEATURES OF NEW TESTA-
MENT GREEK 194

INDEX OF TEXTS CITED 205

INTRODUCTION.

THE GREEK NATION AND LANGUAGE AFTER ALEXANDER.

CONTEMPORARY opinion was divided, and posterity has disputed, whether the conquests of Alexander the Great are to be regarded as the ruin of Greece or as the triumph of Greece. The answer will depend on what we understand by "Greece"—whether we regard the true glory of the Greek nation as lying in its civic liberties, or in its intellectual influence on the world. The "victory at Chæronea" was no doubt "fatal to liberty" in one sense: but it is not therefore self-evident that it must have been a "dishonest victory"—one that the world, or even an enlightened Greek patriot, ought to regret or lament. In the eyes of contemporaries, the character of the Macedonian conquest turned, to a great extent, on the right of the conquerors to be regarded as Greeks themselves. A modern historian is tempted to treat this question as a meaningless piece of superstition: but so far as it has a meaning, the true answer is that the Macedonian kings were Greeks, though the Macedonian people were not. Whether the legends of the Temenids Caranus and Perdiccas be at bottom historical or no, the fact that they were told and believed was a real historical influence. There is no appeal from the judges at Olympia (Hdt. V. xxii) to modern criticism, but Philip must be allowed to be a Greek by descent, for three generations if for no more.

Philip was indeed, like Peter the Great, the king of a barbarous people; and, like Peter, he was a brutal barbarian in his personal habits. But he was as far-sighted a statesman as Peter, and as sincere in his appreciation of the culture of his civilised neighbours. Having spent much of his youth as a hostage at Thebes, he may be called a Greek by education as well as by blood: and he earned by war and diplomacy a title to the most sacred privileges of a Greek, when, after the so-called Sacred War against the Phocians, he was admitted to their forfeited place in the Amphictyonic Synod of Delphi and Thermopylæ. It was the possession of these common sanctuaries, the right of common worship there for Dorians, Ionians, Achæans, Thessalians and the rest, that gave to all Greeks a centre and a sanction for the sense of a common nationality, though they belonged to independent and often hostile states. If there ever was a king of all Greece after the time of Agamemnon, it was the Delphian Apollo. A human "king of Grecia" (Dan. viii. 21) only became possible, when an earthly king was able to enlist on his side the loyalty of Greeks to their god.

In Alexander's character, barbarism and high genius were even more strangely mixed than in his father's. Scratch the Macedonian, and you found the Thracian: but the overlaying was of gold as pure as adorned the image of Olympian Zeus. The man was as extraordinary as his deeds. A hero of romance, he was one of the three or four greatest generals of history; an adventurer, and by no means an unselfish one, he was the devoted champion of the cause of human progress; a conqueror in the name of a national fanaticism, he was the first of men to conceive the unity of the civilised world as something higher than nationality. From different points of view, we may compare him with Mahomet and with Charlemagne: and it would be hard to deny that the armed apostle of Hellenic culture was as sincerely devoted to his cause as the armed apostles of monotheism a thousand years later. We are told by contemporaries (Aesch. *de Fals. Leg.* 42. 47, etc.) that Philip, with all his brutality, exercised a singular charm over men who came into personal contact with him. Alexander's personal charm is so much greater, that it has almost won condonation for his faults and crimes, which were not slight, from every generation for two thousand years.

Worn out between the violent exertions of his active life, and the intemperance which was more and more his chief relaxation from them, Alexander died at Babylon in the twelfth year of his reign. As an empire, his empire all but died with him. His half-brother and his infant sons were mere puppets in the hands of his generals, and were before long murdered, and the royal family exterminated. But his twelve years' reign had sufficed to change the face of the world, and to modify the inner spirit of its life, more than any other equal period in history, unless it be that from the Edict of Milan to the Council of Nice.*

* Posterity must judge, if the period from the meeting of

Henceforth, Greek political life had no longer the interest that it had had for the world. Agis and Cleomenes, Aratus and Philopœmen, were not necessarily inferior men to Pericles or Epaminondas; but they had no longer a chance of such great careers. What political life there was flourished mostly in the cities whose past history had been least conspicuous: and there it was a necessary and difficult condition of political success, to secure the non-intervention, or if possible the friendliness, of the dominant Macedonian dynasty of the moment. It was a century and a half before, under Roman pressure, the politics of Greece became merely municipal: but, from the end of the Lamian war, the vital interest of Greek history lies elsewhere. For the literary greatness of Athens hardly outlasted its political greatness. The last eminent Athenian writers—Menander, Epicurus, Demetrius of Phalerum—belong to the generation that were children at the time of Chæronea or of Crannon.

For more than twenty years after Alexander's death —for eight or nine after the extinction of his dynasty —a confused and purposeless struggle went on between the various Macedonians who had gained distinction or influence, either as officers in his army, as satraps in his empire, or as regents, more or less legitimately authorised, for his heirs. At the battle of Ipsus in Phrygia, B.C. 301, Antigonus, who alone of these pretenders appeared to have any chance of securing the

the States General to the establishment of the Consulate be worthy to be ranked with these. The changes of the Renaissance and the Reformation, certainly, were spread over a greater length of time.

united empire, was defeated and slain; and a partition was agreed upon among the victors, which made some approach to a permanent settlement. Ptolemy the son of Lagus—or, as some said, an illegitimate son of the great Philip—became king of Egypt. Lysimachus reigned in Thrace and the north-western part of Asia Minor, and for a time occupied Macedonia itself; but he did not found a dynasty of any permanence: Macedonia soon passed into the hands of the descendants of Antigonus. The greater part of the Asiatic territory—the main body of the conquered Persian empire—was held by Seleucus, the son of Antiochus and Laodice, the seat of his rule lying first at Babylon, afterwards in Syria. Asia Minor partly belonged to the Seleucid empire, but in it were various kingdoms of lower rank, under princes Greek or Macedonian, native or even Persian. And while none of these could rank as co-ordinate with the kings of Macedonia, Egypt, and Syria, a fourth power of still greater extent and longer endurance grew up in the further East. At first, there existed a Greek kingdom in Bactria; but this was first isolated and at last overthrown, and the eastern half of the Seleucid kingdom detached, by the independence and growth of the Parthians under the native dynasty of Arsaces. And in each of these more or less Hellenised kingdoms there was a continuation, if not of the vigour of political life, at least of the civilisation and literary cultivation which in "Greece proper" had run its course. It seems that the native language of Macedonia itself, which, though very likely cognate with Greek, was never recognised as a Greek dialect, now died out more or less rapidly and completely, and was replaced by Greek.* The Macedonian kings, at any rate, could no longer be regarded as mere barbarians, as had been not unreasonable when Perdiccas aspired to hold the balance between Sparta and Athens, and not impossible when Demosthenes confronted Philip. In Egypt, the able kings of Ptolemy's race and name had on the one hand succeeded in identifying themselves in the popular mind with the ancient religion and the ancient national monarchy: on the other hand, they made their Greek capital Alexandria the home of Greek learning—of a progressive Greek science, such as had hardly existed before, as well as of a Greek literary revival, which holds a respectable place among renaissance literatures. In the kingdom of Asia or Syria, in like manner, though native languages continued in use, they were overspread by a stratum of Greek culture. The numerous cities named Antiochia, Seleucia, Laodicea or the like, overshadowed or rivalled the older capitals: and Greek proper names became common, at least as duplicates, even among men who kept their old language and a good deal of their old national spirit.† Even among the Parthians, though the strength of the monarchy and the origin of the dynasty itself were barbarian, Hellenic influence was by no means absent. Its

---

* It is doubtful whether Polybius would have considered the Macedonians a Greek people, in a sense that the Latins were not. But certainly the diplomacy of his day regarded them as a Greek power: and Liv. XXXI. xxix. 15 shows what was the character of the people in the historian's day at any rate, if not at the time he writes of.

† An extreme instance is furnished by the Hyrcanus, Aristobulus, Alexander, etc., whom we find in the Hashmonean dynasty, of which the very *raison d'être* was the championship of the national spirit against Hellenism.

existence, and at the same time its shallowness, is well indicated by the grim story of the performance of Euripides' Bacchæ at the wedding-feast of Pacorus.

And thus the Greek language, which had been a group of dialects spoken, and sometimes written, in the cities and districts on the two sides of the Ægæan and Ionian seas, became henceforth the language of at least half the civilised world—the language of government, commerce, and literature throughout the eastern half of the Mediterranean basin. A change like this could not take place without a certain amount of change in the Greek language itself. Until now, the literary Greek of every community had been, as a rule, the spoken dialect of that community itself; or if not, then the dialect of the community in which that form of literature had first flourished. But the mere existence of a literature tends to fix and stereotype the hitherto plastic usages of language, and to render obsolete, or to brand as incorrect, the divergences of dialect. Only four or five * of the Greek dialects had been used, to any important extent, for literary purposes; and only one of these, the Attic, had been used for a variety of purposes, both in prose and poetry, and had continued in active literary use down to the time we speak of, the time of the world-wide diffusion of Greek influence.

In consequence, it was a modified form of the Attic dialect which became the prevalent Greek of the new period. Some of the most distinctively local Atticisms

---

* Besides the Attic and the Ionic of Asia Minor, we have the Æolic of the early lyric poetry, the Doric of that form of choral poetry known to us by the chorus of the Attic drama, and the Bœotian of Pindar, which is hardly quite identical with the last of these, and still less with the third.

were dropped more or less completely. Certain words varied more or less from the Attic standard in pronunciation or in meaning: tendencies to the simplification and softening of the sound of words, and of grammatical forms, which had declared themselves in the later Attic itself, were carried further, or became universal: while a few forms and usages characteristic of other dialects were more or less widely adopted. Still the "common" or "universal dialect," the literary language of the new Greece coextensive with the Alexandrine empire, is substantially a form of Attic.

But while this conventional language came into universal use as the language of prose literature, and of intercourse among educated men, it was impossible but that, in a language so widely spread, a tendency to dialectical variation should assert itself afresh. There are some traces of such a tendency even among purely Greek communities: for instance, of distinctively Alexandrian grammatical forms, which are not likely to have been native, and are not proved to have existed, in any of the Greek or Macedonian communities from which the citizens of Alexandria were derived.* But still wider variations necessarily arose, when Greek came into use as an official or commercial language among nations still using their native languages—languages often of quite different genius and structure from Greek. The *Lingua Franca* of the Levant, the *Pigeon English* of the Chinese ports, and the dialects of English and French spoken by negroes

* The 3rd pl. of preterites in -οσαν was said to be originally Bœotian or Chalcidian, though inscriptions fail to prove it. Anyhow, it was probably from other causes than Bœotian or Chalcidian settlement that it was popu'arised at Alexandria: see pp. 36-7.

in the West Indies, show how utterly a language may be disguised and disintegrated when it comes to be used under such circumstances.*

In these instances, no doubt, the transformation of the language is carried further, because those who use it are uneducated men, and acquire it only for worldly purposes, without any intellectual interest. But liberal education and intellectual purpose will not always suffice to secure to men a perfect and sympathetic insight into the spirit and usage of a language not their own. It is doubtful, but it is from the nature of the case impossible to ascertain, whether the purest Latin of an elegant modern scholar would have passed muster in a Roman literary circle. But there is no doubt that what is called "Baboo English"—the English spoken or written by the first generation of natives of India well trained in British literature—has sometimes been almost as grotesque as the colloquial dialects begotten between uneducated Englishmen and uneducated foreigners. We may suspect that there were in ancient times Hellenised Orientals whose language, though it seems fairly correct to us, was felt by contemporaries to be either incorrect, or pedantic in its correctness. There are one or two extant writers,† on whose

---

* One may guess that it was from the observation of similar cases, that grammarians thought it plausible to derive σόλοικος (a word in tolerably early use) from the name of the town of Soli in Cilicia. There had been an early Greek settlement there, far from Greece in the geographical sense; and it seemed natural to suppose accordingly, that that must have been an early home of bad Greek.

† It may have been this kind of pedantry that prevented Josepus, despite his laboured classicalism of style, from gaining the attention of the classical world; though even

style we should be glad to have the judgment of a competent contemporary critic.

These circumstances—the modernising tendencies of the Greek language itself, the stiffening of literary Greek into something distinct from the spoken language, and the greater or less modifications of its form, when it came to be spoken and written by "barbarians"—are real justifications, apart from the prejudice of a narrow "classical" education, for our regarding the Greek writers after Alexander as less "classical" in style than those of earlier date. But it does not follow that their matter is of less value. Certainly there is one form of the post-Alexandrine or post-classical Greek, and that one in which the non-Hellenic element is largest, which deserves and will repay careful verbal study, from the unique intrinsic importance of the writings embodied in it.

pre-Christian historians were not able to ignore his subject. Dr. Abbott has suggested (in three papers in the Expositor, 2nd Series, vol. iii), that the Second Epistle of St. Peter is written in "Baboo Greek:" and as Professor Salmon has pointed out, the view is rather favourable than otherwise to its genuineness.

CHAPTER I.

THE LANGUAGE OF THE JEWISH HELLENISTS.

ON the frontier between the empires of the Ptolemies and of the Seleucidæ lay one or two * small communities, whose national religion had enough internal vigour at once to resist assimilation or fusion with the common Hellenic polytheism, and to inspire its adherents with energy and genius that prevented their forcible extinction or dissolution. Yet while maintaining an unbroken national life in their own country, they already were diffused or dispersed in, at least, all the adjoining lands. In Egypt, especially, they had a large and important colony. Various legends, incredible as they stand, yet point to the fact that the early Ptolemies regarded the Jews as loyal and valuable subjects, and granted

* We know very little of the real religious life of the Samaritans: but, from what seems to be authentic in our accounts of the teaching and career of Simon Magus, it would seem that religious thought with them had a history of its own, quite distinct from that of the Jews, and by no means without intellectual interest. In the curious description of Alexandria ascribed to Hadrian (ap. Vopisc. *Saturn.*) Samaritans are mentioned with Jews, Christians, and worshippers of Serapis, among the proselytising sects of the city. If (as the best authorities hold) the letter is spurious, its evidence of the vitality of Samaritan religion is even stronger, as its statements will apply to a later date.

them exceptional privileges.* It is generally admitted as credible, though the story comes to us in an untrustworthy form, that about B.C. 280 the reigning king of Egypt took sufficient interest in the nation and its national or religious life, to desire a Greek translation to be made of their sacred law. Our accounts differ as to whether this is to be ascribed to the first or the second Ptolemy; if there be any truth in the story that it was done by the advice of Demetrius of Phalerum, the first is likelier. But whatever the date, the royal patronage proves thus much, that in Egypt at least the Jews were not treated as enemies of the human race, but, like the native Egyptians,† as a nation of respectable antiquity, whose origins had an interest for Greeks. In the course of the next century and a half, the whole of the books ‡ reckoned as sacred or canonical by the Jews of Palestine had been translated into Greek, probably at Alexandria. So were other works which did not secure a permanent § place in the Hebrew canon; and some originally composed in Greek were regarded with equal or nearly equal honour. Hence

---

* See Mommsen's *History of Rome*, Book VIII. c. xi ad init. (vol. vi. pp. 162-5, English translation).

† It was certainly under Ptolemy II. (Philadelphus) that Manetho wrote his Greek chronicle of Egyptian history.

‡ Whenever the Book of Daniel was *written*, it was certainly *translated* after the event of its predictions about Antiochus Epiphanes.

§ It is held by some authorities, that the Wisdom of the Son of Sirach was at one time regarded as canonical, even in Palestine. It is implied in the Prologue, that the translator knew of the whole of what he regarded as the Hebrew Bible as existing in a Greek translation at his date—probably soon after B.C. 132, though the meaning of his language is disputed.

arose a literature, mainly if not exclusively religious, of *Hellenists* or Greek-speaking Jews: of men sincerely and thoroughly loyal—sometimes if not always thoroughly consistent—in their faith and obedience to the Jewish religion, but Greek, often exclusively Greek, in language, and often more or less influenced by Greek thought.

And though this Hellenistic literature was mainly of Alexandrian origin, its influence was by no means confined to Egypt. The same century and a half that witnessed its growth witnessed also a great extension of the Jewish "Dispersion." The effect of the Maccabean wars of independence was not to make Judaism again, what it had been in the days before the Captivity, the religion of a single nation inhabiting Palestine. Rather, the freedom of Jerusalem served to furnish a centre of loyalty, and a title of national legitimacy, to the Jews who carried their religion throughout the world. It may be true, as commentators on the Prophecies are wont to say, that the case of the Jewish Dispersion since Titus and Hadrian is absolutely unique—a nation without a country, but kept alive by a religion. But if it is since the Roman conquest that they have come into this state, in the interval between Ptolemy and Titus they had reached a state like that of the Armenians of modern times—a nation more attached to their religion than to their country, never forsaking the first, but thriving best away from the other. In every large city from Mesopotamia to Italy, there were large organised Jewish communities: in every country from Mesopotamia to Greece, and at some points both further east and further west, the smaller towns had smaller Jewish communities, generally organised like the larger. These Jewish communities were mostly poor, often turbulent, and increasingly unpopular: but they were so far assimilated to the population they lived among, that everywhere to the west of their own land they spoke and understood Greek. Many of them never, except for ritual purposes, spoke any other language.

These Hellenistic Jews of the Dispersion were very possibly affected by the tendency already mentioned to dialectical variation in the neo-Hellenic language: Cilician and Alexandrian Jews might talk more like other Cilicians and other Alexandrians than like each other. And at Alexandria, at least, there arose a school of what may in the widest sense be called Hellenistic literature, but of which the literary character is far more Alexandrian than Jewish—a school of which the Wisdom of Solomon, the works of Philo, and the Epistle to the Hebrews are specimens.

Still, all Jewish writers—at least if they wrote, as almost all did, on subjects connected with the Jewish religion—were subject to one common influence, which could not but give their style a common character. It could not but affect their language, that the writings which they treated as of the highest authority—which even a diligent classicist like Philo is compelled to take as text for his comments—were not native Greek works, thought out in Greek, but translations, and mostly slavishly literal ones, from a language of a totally different genius. In later times, all the languages of Christian Europe have had their phraseology, sometimes even their grammar, affected by that of the Latin or Greek Bibles with whose use their intellectual cultivation was inseparably connected. Still more, the modern English and perhaps the modern German language has been modified by the vernacular translations of the Bible that supplied them with their earliest classics. But to a Jew the received text of the Bible was more than to a Catholic, more than to any but the most fanatical Protestant, the one source of truth, wisdom, and enlightenment: and the influence of that text on the forms of thought and language was proportionately greater. Thus it is that there came to exist a Hellenistic dialect, having real though variable differences from the Common or Hellenic: a dialect in which any Greek-speaking Jew would naturally think and talk, and in which he would naturally write, unless, like Philo or Josepus, he could by a self-conscious effort or acquired habit eliminate the Hebraising element from his style.

But besides this Hebraising element, introduced from without, the Hellenistic dialect shows certain characteristics of the later Greek in a higher degree than more purely Hellenic writers of the same date. "Modern Greek," said Mr. Geldart, "is ancient Greek made easy:" and late Greek is, in general, "easier" to a modern reader than earlier Greek. It is very natural that it should be so, because the Greek language, in the course of time and of events, began to assume the character of a modern language. From the age of Thucydides to the age of St. Chrysostom, Greek style was more moulded by rhetorical art than is the case in most modern languages: but from the age of Plato onward it had been realised that rhetoric defeats its own end if it overrides grammar: and so, as in modern languages, and as increasingly in their most modern periods, it had been felt to be of the first necessity to write clearly—to write forcibly, or even elegantly, was an object secondary to this.

And if the comparatively pure literary Greek of the post-classical period showed this tendency to value simplicity and lucidity above all other qualities of style, this was likely to be still more the case with the language of less educated men, or with half-foreign idioms like the Hellenistic. Here the influence of rhetorical art and education, which as we have said was strong among pure Greeks, was almost entirely absent. Oratory had been the latest form of literary art in which independent Greece had displayed genius: it was the one in which it was hardest to draw the line between the old works of genius and the artificial productions of their imitators. But the Jews had never been orators nor men swayed by oratory:[*] the desire to be telling, which moulded the antithetical periods of the early sophists, and of their pupil Thucydides, had little or no weight with them: and they had only this in common with Demosthenes and his contemporaries, that they wished to make sure of being understood by men who heard their words once.

Thus the tendency of later Greek to simplification of construction and idiom was intensified when the

[*] The only passages in the Old Testament which can be called orations—addresses to assemblies on secular topics with a view to persuasion—are Isa. xxxvi. 13-20, and Neh. v. 8-11. The second passage is earnest and effective, but it is Nehemiah's deeds rather than his words that are eloquent. The first (which is not the work of a Jew) is clever enough: but we see that it fell utterly flat on the Hebrew mind, in contrast with the two words of "the king's commandment."

language was used by Jews: most especially was this the case, when the Jews, though able to speak and write in Greek, retained their own Semitic language in more or less habitual use. It is not very hard to learn to speak or write in a language not one's own. But to learn to think indifferently in either of two languages is much harder: and it is perhaps impossible so to think, as not to have the form of thought modified by the language in which it is natural to embody it. Now if you think in one language and translate your thoughts into another, your mastery of the second language is, almost *ex hypothesi*, incomplete: at any rate, your command of its idiom will be limited by your acquired knowledge of it—you have not the instinct that will enable you to speak or write freely and boldly, knowing that your words will be in harmony with the genius of the language, even if you do not know of precedents or technical rules to justify them. Therefore the man who can speak or write in a language, but cannot think in it, is obliged to confine himself to constructions and idioms for which the rules are few and simple.* And as with an individual, so with a community who adopt a language not their own: only in this case they will be aided by one another in adapting thought and language to each other, and the result will be completer and more systematic. When there are alternative ways in which a thought can be expressed, one will be selected—either as the easiest intrinsically, or as likest to the native language—and the other will drop out of use. And thoughts for

* Compare Westcott on St. John's Gospel, Introduction, II. 5. b, c.

which the native language supplies expression, but the acquired one does not, will find utterance either by importations from the native language, by imitations of it from the unused resources of the new one, or by modifications in the use of some words native to the latter. The biblical uses of Ἀμήν, προσωπολημψία, εἰρήνη are illustrations of these three methods respectively.

Thus we are able to describe the language of Hellenistic Jews, spoken and to a less extent written in the first century of our era, as a form of the post-Alexandrine or "common dialect" of Greek, modified partly by the local or dialectical peculiarities of Alexandria and its neighbourhood, but more extensively by a simplification of grammar and idiom, by an abandonment of the antithetical and rhetorical form of sentence usual in classical Greek, and by some adoption or imitation of Semitic idioms, or at least the choice of such Greek idioms as resembled the Semitic most.

It is in this language, whose origin and characteristics we have been tracing, that the books of the New Testament were written. And if there be any point in which the designs of Providence are obvious to man, it is that this language, with all its characteristics and with all the historical events that gave rise to them, was specially designed as an instrument for making the New Testament known to the world. It is generally recognised, how the purely political effects of Macedonian and Roman conquest had prepared the world for the reception of the Gospel. Alexander had raised the Hellenic spirit from the mere national pride of a gifted nation into the sense of an intellectual culture and civilisation which might be, and which tended to become, world-wide. On the other hand, he had failed to embrace the civilised world in one empire: and his successors had failed to make the common world-wide civilisation include the confession of Hellenic or syncretist Paganism as the common world-wide religion. The Romans, in their turn, first made their way into the world of Hellenic culture, and then took possession as heirs to Greece of its remaining intellectual life: and at the same time they succeeded where Alexander had failed, in embracing in one imperial polity the world of social and intellectual enlightenment. They too, like the Seleucidæ, felt their empire imperfect unless it extended into the regions of the soul and of the conscience: and against them, no doubt, it would have been, humanly speaking, impossible for one nation to maintain the cause of spiritual liberty, even had it had as worthy champions as the sons of Mattathias. But Rome did not precipitate the conflict with the People of the God of Israel, until His People had grown from the one nation of Israel into a Catholic Church. The Stone that was hewn without hands did not smite the feet of the image of the world-empire, until it was ready itself to become a mountain that should fill the whole earth.

And subordinate to this historical preparation of the world for the Gospel, but not unconnected with it, nor of too little importance to be worthily coupled with it, was the formation of the language in which the Gospel was to be conveyed to the world. Just as Greek is superior to most if not all other languages as a vehicle for poetry, so, Christian Hebraists tell us,

Hebrew is superior to other languages as a vehicle for devotion. Just as one gains by reading Homer in the original, so one gains by reading the Psalter in the original, though the nature of the gain be different. Still, even the Old Testament probably loses less in translation than most other literatures of high rank or influence; and when the Hebrew outline of religious language was copied in a Greek framework, the result can be reproduced without loss for every nation under heaven in their own tongue wherein they were born.

Thus we see the true answer, on the one hand to the sneers of half-pagan classicists who despised the New Testament as "bad Greek," on the other to the theories of Christian scholars, who held themselves bound to defend the purity of its language, because they felt the language not to be unworthy of its subject-matter. It is true that the half-Hebraised Greek of the New Testament is neither a very elegant nor a very expressive language; but it is a many-sided language, an eminently translatable language. It may be called, in the words of one of those who used it, "rude in speech, but not in knowledge": like Him Whom it reveals, it "hath no form nor comeliness, no beauty that we should desire it." But this very plainness fits it for conveying a plain message to plain men. "It was not God's pleasure to save the world by logic;" neither was it His pleasure to save the world by eloquence or poetry. The Gospel, starting from the meeting-point of East and West, was so expressed from the first as to be able to travel both eastward and westward. All round its earliest home it was intelligible as it stood: its Semitic base made it easy to introduce it to the nations of the further East: its superficial Greek structure made it equally easy to reproduce it in the kindred tongue of the great West. It reached the capital of the world in its original form; perhaps in Italy and Gaul, certainly in Africa, it was translated in a form closely resembling the original, for the Italian or Latinised population of the empire. Then, in modern times, the fact that it belongs to a late stage of language has made it easy to reproduce it in languages which themselves are in a late state: as Tyndale truly said, there are some characteristics of Greek which it is far easier to express in English than in Latin.

This characteristic of the language of the New Testament, that it is an eminently translatable language, may warn us not to expect too much from the minute study of New Testament grammar. Just as there is hardly any grammar in English as compared with other languages, so there is very little grammar in New Testament Greek compared with other Greek. There is something that the diligent scholar can learn from study of the Gospel in the original: but he must beware of overrating its importance, which is but slight compared with what any diligent reader can learn from study of any decently faithful translation. There are cases, though few, where a passage has its beauty and significance heightened by a shade of language that vanishes in translation: one may instance the use of φιλεῖν and ἀγαπᾶν in the last chapter of St. John. Again, there are cases where Greek idiom defines what another language gives no means of defining without cumbrousness: *e.g.*, a Latin version cannot express the force of an article, nor can an English one express (at least elegantly) a present participle passive like σωζόμενος, to which neither "saved" (σωθείς or σεσωσμένος*) nor "such as should be saved" (σωθησόμενος) is a real equivalent. For things like these, those who are not Greek scholars must depend for guidance and control in interpretation on those who are: and those who are will have a greater freshness, perhaps a greater keenness of insight into the processes of the minds of the inspired writers. This, and not any new or transforming light on the general teaching of the New Testament, is what may be gained from the study which we are approaching.

* St. Paul however is not afraid to say ἐστὲ σεσωσμένοι (Eph. ii. 5, 8): so that even here our lesson is only one of grammar or at most of exegesis, not of general theology.

CHAPTER II.

CHARACTERISTICS OF NEW TESTAMENT GREEK IN THE FORMS OR INFLEXIONS.

I. Nouns.—(a) *Proper*.

HERODOTUS observes (I. cxxxix. 2), that all Persian proper names of men ended in the letter *s*. This was true of all such names *as known to the Greeks*, but in the native Persian forms, known to us from contemporary inscriptions, while some end in a sibilant, others end in a short vowel. Now to a Greek it seemed impossible that a masculine name should end in a vowel: so while names of the former class were transliterated with approximate fidelity, those of the latter were Grecised by adding the termination -ας, -ης, or -ος; the choice of a vowel being determined partly by euphony, partly perhaps by an instinctive sense of philological analogy, just as Greeks and Romans saw the equivalence of -ος and -ον with -*us* and -*um*, when they had occasion to transliterate proper names or other words from one language into the other.

Thus, from the earliest days of Greek prose literature, a precedent was established for the Grecising of Oriental proper names, and this precedent was extended, in time, to names belonging to languages which had not, like the Persian, any affinity or analogy to Greek declensions. Herodotus himself has several pure Phœnician names with Greek terminations: two are recognisable as compounds of *Baal*, and a third is apparently the same as the Biblical *Hiram* (VII. xcviii).

Several non-Hellenic or non-Aryan names, however, were accepted by Greek writers for use as they stood. If their terminations made them capable of Greek declension, they were declined, at least in some cases; Plato has (*Phædr.* 274, D, E), Θαμοῦ and Θαμοῦν as gen. and acc. of Θαμοῦς. On the other hand, he uses (*ibid.*) Θεῦθ as indeclinable: and so Herodotus had done with the Arabian divine names Ὀροτάλ and Ἀλιλάτ (III. viii. 4). Similarly Clearchus (ap. Josep. *c. Ap.* i. 22) gave the accurate transliteration Ἰερουσαλήμ* for the city whose name was usually supplied with a Greek termination and a Greek etymology in the form Ἱεροσόλυμα.

Of course in the LXX. there was more frequent need than in any purely Greek work for the insertion of "barbarian" proper names. And as a rule, the names of persons and cities are not supplied with Greek terminations, but simply transliterated, and used as indeclinable. A certain number, however, lent themselves to Greek declension as they stood. Both in Hebrew and in Greek a long *a* (followed, it

---

* In discussing the form of these "barbarian" proper nouns, it seems best to omit the breathing. The MSS. that mark it are too late to embody a tradition of any value; words like Ηλίας, Ησαίας, as to which one would think ecclesiastical use must have embodied a tradition, are among the forms as to which MS. use is most variable.

is true, in Hebrew by a mute *h*), is a common termination of fem. names; and so we find Εὖα, Σάρα or Σάρρα, Σεπφώρα regularly declined in the LXX.

Now not a few masc. names have the same termination: in particular, the many compounds of the Divine Name, which in the older biblical language ended in -*jahu*, were in later Hebrew apocopated to -*jah*. These and other names of the same ending were treated as analogous to the fem. names in -*ah*, and were represented by names in -ας of the first declension: sometimes barytone, as Ἰούδας, Ἠλείας,* but oftener with a circumflex on the last syllable, which regularly had the accent in Hebrew.

And for these names in -ας representing -*ah*, the late Greek had a suitable declension ready. Pure Greek nouns in -ας formed their genitives in -αο (Homeric), -εω (Ionic), or -ου (Attic): but there had arisen a large class of pr. nn., including the Persian ones already mentioned, for which the only gen. in use was the (originally Doric) form in -α. We get Οἰδιπόδα in the tragedians for the Homeric Οἰδιπόδαο, Γωβρύα and the like in Xenophon for the Ionic Γωβρύεω, besides the Syracusan Γνωσία (*Hell.* I. i. 29): Herodotus himself has Σίκα in VII. xcviii, and the verses (apparently not new in Plato's time) in *Phædr.*, 264 D, have Μίδα.

And if this was a recognised declension for names either purely Greek or naturalised in the best Greek period, there were two influences that made such names commoner in later Greek. Roman masc.

* In the Books of Kings, what seems to be the oldest text of the LXX. has the indeclinable form Ηλιού to represent *Elijahu*.

names in -α were represented by names of this form, e.g., Σύλλας, gen. Σύλλα, for *Sulla, -æ*: and names in common use of pure Greek derivation had colloquial abbreviations, such as Ζηνᾶς for Ζηνόδοτος or Ζηνόδωρος, Δημᾶς for Δημήτριος. Every one will remember that these names occur in the N. T. : in circles where they were familiar, we see there was an analogy ready for the treatment of Hebrew names like Ἰωνᾶς, or Aramaic ones like Θωμᾶς. Words in -ας pure however (and therefore the large class in -ίας), generally but not universally take -ου in the gen., e.g., Οὐρίου, Matt. i. 6; Ἡσαΐου, iii. 3; but Ἠλεία, Luke i. 17, is the better attested form.

But the usage of the LXX., and even of the New Testament, does not proceed quite consistently, in deciding what names are or are not capable of Greek inflexion. Several names, both personal and local, are treated as indeclinable, though they have terminations admissible in Greek nominatives: we have Βηθφαγῆ, not -γῆν in Matt. xxi. 1; Κανᾶ, not Κανᾶς or Κανῶν in John xxi. 2; Ἀαρών, not Ἀαρῶνος, in Heb. vii. 11, ix. 4. In the LXX. Σαλωμών is indeclinable, though the final ν, not existing in Hebrew, looks as if it were added to Grecise the word.* But in the N. T. we have the dialectical variant Σολομών, which is declined—the gen. being, according to the best MSS., Σολομῶνος not -μῶντος, except in the two places where it occurs in the Acts (iii. 11, and perhaps v. 12).

Comparatively few names are Grecised in the N. T. by simply sticking on the termination -ος, as Josepus does to all names—e.g., his own—which could take

* Apparently, however, the Ν really belongs to names in kindred languages supposed to be identical with this.

no Greek inflexion otherwise.* We have, however, Ἰάκωβος very often, Ἰάειρος in two parallel passages of the Gospels (St. Matthew, though having the story, omits the name), and Σαῦλος usually of St. Paul—Σαούλ only in our Lord's words at his conversion, which we are expressly told were spoken in Hebrew, and in those of Ananias, which presumably were so likewise. In all these cases, the inflected forms are used only of contemporaries. The patriarch is always Ἰακώβ, the king of Israel Σαούλ: similarly we have Λάζαρος of the two N. T. characters, but Ελεάζαρ in Matt. i. 15 (note the MS. reading *Alazarus . . . Lazarum* in Tac. *Hist.* V. xiii. 4, 5). But the prophet is Ελισαῖος (so, with one σ, the best MSS.), in Luke iv. 27. Ἀγαβο:, Αλφαῖος, Θαδδαῖος and Λεββαῖος are on a somewhat different footing, not being names derived from biblical Hebrew; and Τίμαιος is no doubt the pure Greek name borrowed, though the form Βαρτίμαιος shows how entirely it was naturalised in Aramaic.

Some of the names sufficiently Grecised to be habitually inflected are yet so far felt to be foreign words that there is some uncertainty and irregularity about their inflexion. Thus Μωυσῆς (so we ought apparently always to read) makes the gen. Μωυσέως, but dat. Μωυσῇ oftener than Μωυσεῖ, acc. Μωυσέα in Luke xvi. 29 only, elsewhere Μωυσῆν. Ιωσῆς has gen. Ιωσῆτος in Mark xv. 40, 47 in the best MSS.: but Ιωσῆ in Matt. xxvii. 56, unless we there read Ιωσήφ. Here we have an assimilation to the already described declension of names in -ας: we get something of the

* He almost apologises for the practice, *Ant.* I. vi. 1 fin. As to the way that we should write his name, it seems fair to follow his own usage in spelling it with a π not a φ.

sort too in the case of the contracted name Ἀπολλώς, which is all but indecl., having Ἀπολλώ even for acc., Acts xix. 1. And lastly, some names seemed capable of inflexion in some cases but not in all. To this class we may almost refer the name Ἰησοῦς, which in the nom. and the acc. Ἰησοῦν is fairly regular, but has always in the N. T. Ἰησοῦ for dat. as well as gen. and voc.—not the more regular Ἰησοῖ, which according to MS. evidence is used in the LXX.; doubtless because it was felt that the υ was radical.* In regard to this name it is to be remembered, that in *all* extant MSS. it is habitually abbreviated, $\overline{IC}$ or $\overline{IHC}$, $\overline{IY}$, $\overline{IN}$.

The name of the sister of Moses and of the mother of Jesus, which Josepus lengthens into Μαριάμμη, is in the N. T. one of these half-inflected names. In the nom. and acc. there is almost always a v. l between Μαριάμ and Μαρία, -αν: the gen. is always Μαρίας: the dat. occurs only twice, viz., Luke ii. 5, where Μαριάμ is almost certain, and Acts i. 14, where B and a few other MSS. have Μαριάμ against the majority for Μαρίᾳ. In the nom. and acc., the evidence preponderates for the form in -άμ in most places where the name belongs to the Mother of Jesus, for the inflected form in most where it is used of other women. But on MS. evidence it seems impossible to say that there is any constant distinction observed— still less is there evidence of the existence of two names, like our *Mary* and *Maria*.

The O. T. name *Levi* takes, according to MS.

---

* The declension of Θαμοῦς in Plato, already referred to, is as far as it goes identical with this: he does not use the dat. at all.

evidence, the form Λευίς or Λευείς* in the nom., in Heb. vii. 9, where it is used of the patriarch; but in ver. 5, as well as in Rev. vii. 7, and in the genealogy of Luke iii. 24, 29, the uninflected form Λευεί or Λευί is used as a gen. In the Gospels where the name is used of the publican, the gen. does not occur: the MSS. are all but unanimous for the nom. in -ίς and acc. in -ίν in St. Luke, and the evidence predominates for -ίς in St. Mark.

For the city Jerusalem, the Grecised form Ἱεροσόλυμα is almost exclusively used by SS. Matthew, Mark, and John: the indeclinable Ἱερουσαλήμ occurring only in Matt. xxiii. 37, and in the T. R., but not in the best authorities, in Mark xi. 1. But the latter form predominates decidedly in SS. Luke and Paul—contrary to what might have been expected in their more Hellenised style—and in the Apocalypse. It is always fem.; but Ἱεροσόλυμα is treated as a fem. in Matt. ii. 3 only—elsewhere it is a neuter pl. As to the breathing, Latin usage surely proves that people who used the declinable form pronounced it with an aspirate. Very likely they were led to do so by a false etymology (Tac. *Hist.* V. ii. 4), so that it throws no light on the correct breathing for Ἱερουσαλήμ: but in ecclesiastical Latin the *H* was admitted there also.

* For the uncertainty of readings involving the use of the simple ι or the diphthong ει see p. 40. In this name and several others, the best editors are nearly unanimous in preferring the diphthong. But Westcott and Hort are alone in reading Ἐλεισάβετ, after B, in St. Luke i.

(b) *Appellative.*

The chief change from classical usage in the declension of ordinary nouns is the result of the tendency of the later stages of a language to greater simplicity and uniformity. Just as in modern English exceptional forms like "brethren" have given place to "regular" ones like "brothers,"* so in Greek there was a tendency to reduce the three distinct declensions to two, one for masc. and one for fem. nouns, and to obliterate the distinction between the subordinate groups comprised under each of the three. But in Greek, even to the present day, the assimilation has not been carried as far as in English: in the N. T. we only observe it in a few isolated cases. *E.g.* though the Latin forms *tetrarcha*, *patriarcha*, show that the nouns usually, in the Greek of the first century and even earlier, had the termination -άρχης, we find the older forms in -αρχος not infrequently. These two words indeed have always the η (the former being, according to the preponderance of MS. evidence, spelt τετραάρχης). But we have χιλίαρχος always, and ἑκατόνταρχος sometimes, unless we are to assume uniformity in spite of MSS. In Acts indeed the last word always has -ης except in xxii. 25:† but in the Gospels usage varies. Certain fem. substantives in -ρα form their gen. and dat. with η instead of ā. According to the best MSS.,

---

* In the fifteenth century, according to a well-known story of Caxton's, "eggs" was only used in some local dialects, instead of "eyren"—a form exactly analogous to "brethren."

† In xxviii. 16 the best MSS. omit the sentence: but of those that have it, nearly all read ἑκατόνταρχος, and the best στρατοπεδάρχῳ.

σπεῖρα, μάχαιρα, πρῷρα, πλημμύρα have η in all or most of the places where these cases occur: so perhaps the pr. n. Σαπφείρα or -ρη and the ptcp. συνειδυίης in the passage relating to her.

Certain substantives in -os, which in classical Greek are always or generally masculine and of the second declension, are in the N. T. always or commonly neuters of the third—πλοῦτος, ζῆλος, ἔλεος, perhaps ἦχος in Luke xxi. 25 (but not Heb. xii. 19; elsewhere the word occurs only in the nom.), as well as σκότος, where the neut. form occurs in classical if not in Attic writers.

The declension of the contracted substantives νοῦς and πλοῦς is, by a false analogy, assimilated to that of βοῦς.

The dual number has altogether disappeared: even the word ἄμφω has been superseded by ἀμφότεροι. Thus δύο is left without any word analogous to it, except the higher numerals, and tends to become, like them, indecl. It serves for gen., as well as nom. and acc.: but the dat. is δυσί[ν], like τρισίν, τέσσαρσιν. (In this word the omission and insertion of the final ν appear to be equally frequent: in most dat. pl. forms in -σιν, and in the similar 3rd pl. of verbs, it is, according to MS. evidence, general but not universal.)

Lastly, the tendency shows itself which has prevailed more widely in modern Greek, to make all sing. acc. forms (except of course neuters) end in ν. Thus χεῖραν, ἀστέραν, and again συγγενῆν and the like, are in some places very strongly attested. Conversely, we twice (Acts xxiv. 27, Jude 4) have χάριτα instead of the usual χάριν: one MS. has the same in Acts xxv. 9.

(c) *Adjective.*

It is not worth while to discuss the cases where usage varies, in the N. T. as in other Greek, as to whether an adj. belonging to a fem. subst. shall receive a distinctive fem. termination, or retain that of the masc. Both classical and late usage being variable, the details of variation can hardly be significant, even where, according to the evidence now known, they varied in different directions. For instance, ἀργός, "idle," is in the classical period of two terminations; but the fem. form is found as early as Aristotle. In the N. T. we have it in Tit. i. 12 as well as in 1 Tim. v. 13: and though St. Paul was not a critic of Epimenides' text, it would be rash to say that Epimenides did not write ἀργαί. Again, ὅσιος is usually of three terminations, but of two, not only in 1 Tim. ii. 8, but as early as Plato.

In the comparison of adjectives there is little divergence from classical use. Of course the later forms, which are usually the more regular, are found: *e.g.* the adv. "quicker" is always τάχιον, not θᾶσσον.* But μειζοτέραν in 3 John 4 is the only case where we have a double comp. termination, such as becomes common in the later stage of a language, where forms of expression are losing their force, and have to be accumulated if it is to be retained. In the ἐλαχιστοτέρῳ of Eph. iii. 8, of course the sup. and comp. terminations have each their proper meaning: the formation of the word is a licence, but not a symptom of decay.

---

* Περισσοτέρως, used by St. Paul and in Heb., has classical precedent (at least, Isocr. *ad Nicocl.* p. 35 fin. has περιττο-

II. Verbs.

In the rich and varied inflexions of the Greek verb, there are many forms as to which literary usage was, perhaps, at no period of the language strictly uniform. There are some that occur so rarely, that there never were precedents enough to fix usage:* there are others whose formation is so exceptional that, when its history was forgotten, the impulse was at once felt to assimilate them to more regular types: others, again, that were familiar enough to be noted as anomalies, so that it was felt as a solecism to assimilate them. *E.g.*, the pluperfect active of most verbs was a cumbrous form, and the cases where the aorist did not sufficiently express its sense were few: no ear therefore learnt to be shocked at the omission of the augment,† while many ears were shocked instinctively by the stuttering noise of an ἐτετ. or ἐπεπ. Again, ἴσμεν, ἴστε ‡ gave place to οἴδαμεν, -τε, as people learnt Greek grammar without learning comparative

τέρως): though according to rule the comp. adv. would be περισσότερον.

* One may illustrate by an example in another language. Cicero declined to pronounce whether "Pompey in his third consulship" should be described as *Consul Tertium* or *Tertio*. Down to his time, a third consulship was all but unknown except in the unique case of Marius: but in the reign of Augustus, people were forced to decide—in favour of *tertium*, as every one knows who has seen the Pantheon or a picture of it.

† Ἐβέβλητο in Luke xvi. 20, συνετέθειντο in John ix. 22, are the most certain cases of an augmented plupf. in the N. T., these being forms to which there is no euphonic objection. It may have counted for something, that in the oldest Greek the Z augment could always be omitted.

‡ Ἴσμεν never occurs in the N. T. at all; ἴστε as an imper. in the probable texts of Eph. v. 5, James i. 19; but as an indic. in Heb. xii. 17 only, where it, like ἴσασι in Acts xxvi. 4, may be a conscious classicism.

philology; and double augments were in some cases eliminated, though in others they were introduced, or either retained or omitted as might happen.* We must not forget that we have to do, not with doctrinaire purists correcting the usages of a language by its supposed principles (like the revisers of the American Prayer Book, who in the Lord's Prayer wrote not only "who" for "which," but "those who" for "them that"), but with writers whose familiarity with usage was limited, and who therefore sometimes followed usages that were not the best, and sometimes substituted deduction for usage as their guide.

With respect to the "temporal augment" of verbs beginning with a vowel or diphthong, N. T. usage seems to differ from classical in some details, without any consistent rule or principle. Certain compound verbs have even a short vowel unaugmented —προορώμην seems to be certain both in the LXX. of Psalm xv. (xvi.) 8, and in the quotation of it in Acts ii. 25. Still commoner is the omission of augment in verbs beginning with a diphthong, especially οι: *e.g.* ἐπαισχύνθη in 2 Tim. i. 16 is practically certain; οἰκοδόμησεν in Acts vii. 47 has the authority of BD, followed by Westcott and Hort, who doubt if the latter verb *ever* forms ᾠκοδ. except in two places in the Gospels. Ευ- is oftener augmented into ηυ- than in classical Greek: evidence sometimes (*e.g.* Mark xiv.

* We have (in the best texts) ἀνεσχόμην in Acts xviii. 14, ἀνείχεσθε in 2 Cor. xi. 1, and perhaps 4, instead of the classical ἠνεσχ., ἠνειχ., which the T. R. substitutes. But ἀπεκατεστάθη is certain in Matt. xii. 13=Mark iii. 5=Luke vi. 10. And we get side by side in the same writer ἠνεῴχθησαν and ἀνέῳξεν (John ix. 10, 14), and ἠνεῳγμένη and ἤνοιξεν (Rev. iv. 1, vi. 1 etc.); besides the altogether anomalous ἀνεῳχθῆναι (as it were assimilated to ἀνεῴχθαι) of Luke iii. 21.

FORMATION OF PRETERITE TENSES. 35

55) predominates even for ηὕρισκον. There are scarcely any signs in the N. T. of the tendency, apparent in mediæval and dominant in modern Greek, to put the augment at the very beginning of compound verbs, instead of after the prep. It is no exception that the correct forms are always * ἐπροφήτευον, -τευσα, not προεφ.: the prep. being already incorporated in the subst. προφήτης forms part of the stem of the denominative verb. On the same principle we ought to get ἐδιακόνουν: but in fact we always have διηκ.

Irregularities in reduplication are few. Probably in Luke i. 27, almost certainly in ii. 5, we should read the classical ἐμνηστευμένην, -νῃ, not μεμν. with the T. R. But in Heb. x. 22 we have the exceptional ρεραντισμένοι (as the second ρ is not doubled, editors hesitate to aspirate the first), and in Rev. xix. 13 we should probably read that or a similar form.†

There was naturally a nearer approach made to symmetry and uniformity in the inflexion of particular tenses than in the formation of the stem of each tense. In the larger class of Greek verbs, indeed, the inflexion of each tense was regular enough in the classical language; but there were three tenses, the two aorists and the perf., between which there either was no distinction of sense, or the distinction was tending to disappear. The consequence is, that we find three points in which 2nd aorists and perfects are assimilated to 1st aorists. The vowels o and ε that introduce the longer 2nd

---

* Except perhaps Jude 14: even there B has επροφ., ℵ επροεφ. The latter form is actually quoted from a Byzantine writer: but here it is unlikely that the scribe deliberately intended the double augment. He had it in one place in his copy, in the other in his head: unluckily we cannot tell which was which.

† We are reminded of the Homeric ῥερυπωμένα.

aor. terminations are changed into α—almost* constantly in the indic. of πεσεῖν, where indeed ἔπεσα (Acts xxii. 7, Rev. xix. 10), makes a fairly regular 1st aor., but very frequently also in forms like ἐλθάτω (Matt. vi. 10), εἵλατο (2 Thess. ii. 13), εὑράμενος (Heb. ix. 12); not to speak of εἶπα (Acts xxvi. 15) which existed in classical times and, in some persons, was the usual Attic form—in the N. T. εἶπαν is, by MS. evidence, much commoner than εἶπον, but not to the exclusion of the latter.†

The 3rd person pl. of the perf. is several times made to end in -αν, like that of the 1st aor.—Luke ix. 36, John xvii. 6, 7, Acts xvi. 36, Rom. xvi. 7, Col. ii. 1, James v. 4, Rev. xix. 3, xxi. 6. (The true reading is hardly doubtful in any of these places: even the T. R. retains the form in -καν in John xvii. 7, Rev. xix. 3. Perhaps this is significant: in both places we get perfects and aorists approximating to each other in sense or form: and the approximation may have had its influence on the writers, as well as on the scribes who here only tolerated the exceptional forms.)

Again, the 3rd person pl. of both the impf. and the 2nd aor. takes the termination -οσαν often in the LXX., and sometimes (John xv. 22, 24, 2 Thess. iii.

---

* The passage where the MS. evidence is least decidedly in favour of the α form is the virtually identical one in Luke xxiii. 30, Rev. vi. 16. Evidence is also doubtful in the LXX. of Hos. x. 8, whence the words are derived. Tischendorf reads πέσατε in St. Luke but πέσετε in Rev., Westcott and Hort -ατε in both.

† In colloquial modern Greek, we not only have such aorists as ἔλαβα, but α is used as an alternative for ε in at least the 2nd person sing. and pl. of the impf. [Geldart's. *Guide to Modern Greek*, p. 272 n.]

6, v. l., besides the quotation in Rom. iii. 13) in the N. T. also. (This, however, may be supposed rather to have originated in differentiation from the 1st person sing. than in assimilation to the 1st aor. form.) This and the last are called Alexandrian forms with somewhat better right than others characteristic of late Greek: they are not exclusively Hellenistic nor colloquial, but occur in Lycophron and other continuators of classical literature who wrote at Alexandria.

But there are cases of assimilation in the opposite direction to at least the first and last of these three. There is strong authority for the termination -κες instead of -κας in perfects or aorists resembling them, especially in several passages of St. John's Gospel and Revelation: in Rev. ii. 3, 4, 5, the evidence for κεκοπίακες and ἀφῆκες, perhaps for πέπτωκες, seems to preponderate. (See Westcott and Hort's "Notes on Orthography," *New Testament in Greek*, vol. ii. p. 166.) And the 3rd pl. impf. of verbs in -μι, which regularly ends in -σαν preceded by the stem vowel, is assimilated to that of contracted verbs—most certainly in the Acts: see iii. 2, iv. 35 for ἐτίθουν, iv. 33 and xxvii. 1 for (ἀπ- and παρ-) ἐδίδουν. The latter forms are quite classical, perhaps commoner than those in -σαν: but the former is late, though justified by analogies in the Attic inflection of the sing.

It is doubtful how far assimilation is carried in other inflexions of verbs in -μι. In Acts xiv. 17 ἐμπιπλῶν is (as far as the termination goes*) without variant: but, of other forms implying a pres. in

---

* Some MSS. (but not here, as often, the best) retain ν in the first syllable: and some insert μ in the second.

-άω, Westcott and Hort admit none into their text, and regard none as possibly right except συνιστᾶν in 2 Cor. iii. 1. There is little doubt that ἱστάνω is the form of the pres. generally used. Ἵημι being a more "irregular verb," assimilations to "regular" ones are more frequent. Ἀφίουσιν in Rev. xi. 9 might be a mere blunder, or be written -οῦσιν as a contracted form; cf. ἀφεῖς in ii. 20: but it is supported by ἀφίομεν in Luke xi. 4, συνίουσιν in Matt. xiii. 13, besides more doubtful cases: and there is no question about the still more anomalous ἤφιεν in Mark i. 34, xi. 16. The same principle appears in the assimilation, though the vowel-change is the converse one, of ἐξέδοτο to ἐξέδετο in Matt. xxi. 33 = Mark xii. 1 = Luke xx. 9;* so ἐξεκρέμετο in Luke xix. 48. Ἀφέωνται, which certainly occurs in St. Luke (v. 20, 23, vii. 47-8) and John (xx. 23, 1 Ep. ii. 12), though critical texts reject it elsewhere, is a little less strange: we get ἀνέωνται in Herodotus, and other analogous forms. We may mention here the preference of α for η in the 1st aor. of verbs in -αίνω: in Luke i. 79, we have even [ἐπι]φᾶναι, which justifies φάνῃ, not φανῇ, as the accentuation in Rev. viii. 12, xviii. 23.

Of verbs confessedly irregular, the most important N. T. variations from the usual inflexion are in certain parts of the verb εἶναι. In the impf. ἤμην is usual, and the pl. ἤμεθα seems to occur (Matt. xxiii. 30 bis, Acts xxvii. 37, perhaps Gal. iv. 3, Eph. ii. 3). About

* Perhaps the fact that this irregular form, like ἀπεκατεστάθη (p. 34 n.), runs through all three Gospels is to be ranked as evidence (though one such case, or even two, is far short of proof) of a written Greek document used by the authors of all. Of the two words cited, ἐξέδετο proves most, as there is less evidence of its frequent use.

equally frequent is ᾖς for the 2nd sing. (Matt. xxv. 21, 23, John xi. 21, 32, xxi. 18, Rev. iii. 15). Less common, and with less ground in analogy, is the 3rd imper. ἤτω (1 Cor. xvi. 22, James v. 12).

The last of these anomalies that we need notice is the formation of persons other than the 1st, and of participles and infinitives, of contracted verbs. Verbs in -άω regularly make, by a sort of return to first principles, -ᾶσαι in the 2nd sing. med. (Luke xvi. 25, Rom. ii. 17, etc.): cf. φάγεσαι καὶ πίεσαι in Luke xvii. 8: but an opposite tendency appears in the (originally Ionic) δύνῃ of Luke xvi. 2, for δύνασαι. Further, in these verbs there is often an apparent uncertainty between α and ε, perhaps sometimes between ε and ο, as the vowel ending the stem. Ἠρώτουν seems decisively attested in Matt. xv. 23, and has some evidence in Mark iv. 10: similarly there is a good deal of authority for κοπιοῦσιν in Matt. vi. 28, for νικοῦντι in Rev. ii. 7, 17, and νικοῦντας ibid. xv. 2. One hardly knows how to write the N. T. form of what in classical Greek (but in a different sense) is ἐμβριμᾶσθαι: both in Mark xiv. 5 and John xi. 38 Tischendorf adopts, and Westcott and Hort admit as possible, the forms ἐνεβριμοῦντο and ἐμβριμούμενος. The other N. T. instances of the word are aorists, which might come equally well from -ῶμαι, -ᾶσθαι, or from -οῦμαι, -οῦσθαι.

Conversely, certain verbs that normally have an ε stem are conjugated with α. This appears to be the case with ἐλεᾶν for -εῖν in the LXX. on the one hand, and in SS. Clement and Polycarp on the other: ἐλεᾶτε is well attested in Jude 23 (and 22, if we read the verb at all), and ἐλεῶντος overwhelmingly in Rom. ix. 16: but ibid. 18 the evidence preponderates for ἐλεεῖ. Here again in the great majority of N. T. passages we have forms that would suit with either pres., the aor. imp. ἐλέησον being very frequent. There is no doubt about ἐλλόγα in Philem. 18; but there is little evidence for ἐλλογᾶται (more for the anomalous ἐλλογᾶτο) in Rom. v. 13.

There is, at least in one or two cases, similar uncertainty between the forms ἐξουδενέω (or ἐξουθενέω) and -νόω.

It is judged that verbs in -όω always make the inf. in -οῖν not -οῦν, except πληροῦν in Luke ix. 31. Certain other forms from stems in o raise syntactical questions, for which see below (p. 107-8). But we may notice here the διδῶ which in Rev. iii. 9 seems to stand for δίδωμι, and the (not unnatural) formation ἀποδιδοῦν which is not improbable in xxii. 2. In all these points, it is hard to draw the line between questions of inflexion and questions of orthography —the latter of which we do not think it needful to discuss. And in nearly all, the question is complicated with that of uncertainties of reading. For a full discussion of these, we must refer to Westcott and Hort's Appendix II. We can only say, as a summary of the conclusions there arrived at, what were the general habits of the chief groups of MSS. in reproducing or disguising what we may regard as the spelling of the N. T. writers.* Apparently, those MSS. which transmit the text with least modification transmit the spelling with least modification too; though here we have to allow a good deal for

* We must remember, when we use this phrase, that in the case of St. Paul at least, the most that we can arrive at is the practice, not of the Apostle, but of his various amanuenses.

VARIATIONS OF SPELLING. 41

individualisms—*e.g.* Cod. B is a great deal too fond of the diphthong ει in place of the simple ι, while ℵ has the reverse tendency. But spellings (or grammatical forms) diverging from the classical type were introduced (as substantive various readings were) very freely by the second-century transcribers or editors with whom the so-called "Western text" arose. On the other hand, mediæval scribes (at least those of Constantinople: those of Southern Italy had not the requisite scholarship) made a conscience of suppressing such forms; as one can see by comparing the letters inked over by the "third hand" of B (in the 10th century?) with the original. It is very frequent to find the ν ἐφελκυστικόν before consonants elaborately scratched out by the διορθωτής in cursive MSS., which inserted it most frequently when they were reproducing an ancient text.*

* The twelfth century Cod. Ev. 604, which has a very ancient and interesting element in its text very unequally distributed, has the ν (erased or otherwise) 102 times in the first 12 cc. of St. Luke, and only 15 times in the last 12: the difference in the proportion of substantive "pre-Syrian" readings being even larger.

III. Particles, and Composition of Verbs.

In the late stages of a language it is common for words to have their distinctive force lost or weakened by frequent use, so that it is felt necessary, if that force is to be recalled, to emphasise it by an accumulation of synonymous words. We are familiar with this phenomenon in the Romance languages compared with Latin: when *e.g.*, *ipse* came to mean little more than "he," [*se*]*met* or [*se*]*ipsum* did not seem clearly or emphatically to express "himself," and people said [*se*]*metipsissimum*, whence *medesimo* and *même*. In the same way, some words in modern Greek have had their senses weakened—*e.g.* περισσότερος has come to mean simply "more" (it is hardly so vague anywhere in the N. T., but see Dan. iv. 33 Theod.):* and so some words (particles especially) have to be combined, to give them any distinctive meaning.

We get beginnings, but not more than beginnings, of this tendency in the Greek of the N. T., in words like παρεκτός, ὑπερεκπερισσοῦ, κατενώπιον, κατέναντι, ἀπέναντι, ἐπάνω †—words, for the most part, peculiar to biblical Greek. They are in fact less like anything in Attic than such Homeric forms as παρέξ ὑπέκ, κ.τ.λ.

---

* "Theodotion" must be accepted as a conventional name for the received Greek text of Daniel, though doubt has been thrown on its being really his : just as the Chigi text is conventionally cited as "LXX."

† Perhaps ἐπάνω always means more than the simple ἐπί. Comparing Rev. vi. 8 with ibid. 2, 4, 5, we may think that, while the riders in human form sat "on" their horses and managed them, the last demon or spectre only appeared "over" or "atop of" his horse.

NON-SIGNIFICANT COMPOUND FORMS. 43

With these compounded or emphasised particles we may compare the cases where verbs are compounded with two prepositions instead of one, or even where a compound verb is used instead of a simple, without anything being contributed by the composition or re-composition, (here again we have Homeric parallels) except some measure of emphasis. This is the case with ἀπεκδέχεσθαι, still more with ἀπεκδύεσθαι, and more or less with ἀποκαταλλάσσειν, διακατελέγχεσθαι, διαπαρατριβή (the true text in 1 Tim. vi. 5), ἐξανιστάναι,* ἐπιδιορθοῖν, ἐπικατάρατος, ἐπισυναγωγή,† κατεπιστῆναι, προσαναβαίνειν, προσανατίθεσθαι, συναντιλαμβάνεσθαι, συνπεριλαμβάνειν, ὑπερεκπερισσοῦ. So again with ἀνατάττεσθαι, ἀποδεκατοῖν or -τεύειν, ἀποθλίβειν, διαγνωρίζειν, διαγογγύζειν, διακαθαρίζειν, ‡ διεγείρειν, διερμηνεύειν, ἐκδιώκειν (probably), ἐκζητεῖν, ἐκθαμβεῖσθαι, ἐκθαυμάζειν, ἐκκεντεῖν, ἐκμυκτηριάζειν, ἐκπειράζειν, ἐκπορνεύειν, ἐνδυναμοῦσθαι, ἐξολεθρεύειν, ἐξομολογεῖσθαι, ἐπιπόθησις and cognate words, ἐπιστηρίζειν, ἐπιχορηγεῖν, καταγγέλλειν, καταγράφειν (the best attested text of [John] viii. 6, if not 8), καταλιθάζειν, κατασύρειν, καταφιλεῖν (probably), κατευλογεῖν, κατηχεῖν, παραπικραίνειν (-ασμός), παρομοιάζειν, περιάπτειν, περικάθαρμα, προσοχθίζειν, συμψηφίζειν, συνευδοκεῖν, συνθλᾶν,

* The use in Acts xv. 5 is the only N. T. one that can be called classical. But ἐξανάστασις is found in Polyb. V. iv. 4, of Hannibal's men "getting up out of" the soft snow that lay over the frozen mass.

† The verb ἐπισυνάγειν is late but not exclusively Biblical. The subst. is formed from it, because the simple συναγωγή had a special meaning fixed in usage. In 2 Thess. ii. 1 the ἐπί though redundant is not meaningless: but the occurrence of the word there fixes the sense in Heb. x. 25, and forbids us to think of an "additional synagogue" or meeting of Christian Jews, after that in which they shared with unbelieving ones.

‡ Διακαθαίρειν is classical.

συνθρύπτειν, συνκοινωνός, συνλυπεῖσθαι, συνμιμητής, συνοικοδομεῖν, συνπνίγειν, συσπαράττειν, ὑπακοή.* Most of these words are late, some exclusively biblical: and when the words are used in classical authors, it is in other senses—generally senses in which the prep. has more distinctive force.†

Still no doubt the faculty for forming compounds of the classical type still survives. Words like κατακαυχᾶσθαι, προαιτιᾶσθαι (St. Paul in particular has many such compounds of πρό), συνκακοπαθεῖν, συνκακουχεῖσθαι, attest this. So do compound words for distinctive Christian ideas, such as ἀναγεννᾶν, ἀναζῆν, συνσταυροῦσθαι: so do even double compounds like ἀντιπαρελθεῖν, παρείσακτος, προενάρχεσθαι, προεπαγγέλλειν and προκαταγγέλλειν, συνκαταψηφίζειν, συναναπαύεσθαι: but the greater proportion of words like these, compared with those used in earlier Greek, is still significant. So is the growth of compounds and double compounds in which the prepositional elements, if not without meaning, have only an indirect one as contributing to the general notion of the verb, e.g., συναπάγεσθαι.

* Perhaps this word (and παρακοή, correlative to παρακούειν in its biblical, non-classical sense) should rather be reckoned among words formed on classical lines to express Christian thoughts.

† E.g. in St. Luke i. 1 ἀνατάξασθαι is simply "to set in order." In Plut. de Sollert. Anim. c. 12, the only other passage cited for the word, it is used of a performing elephant "going through" his exercises "over again."

CHAPTER III.

CHARACTERISTICS OF NEW TESTAMENT GREEK IN THE SYNTACTICAL USE OF ARTICLES AND PRONOUNS.

IN general, the rules for the use of the art. in N. T. Greek are just the same as in classical; what difference there is comes from the growing laxity of a decaying language, not from any influence peculiarly Hellenistic. For in biblical Hebrew * the use of the art. is as nearly identical with the Greek as can be expected in the case of languages of such different structure: and in consequence the LXX. had not tended to make Hellenistic usage in this point diverge from classical. It had at most made it relatively more frequent for an adj. or attributive clause to stand after the subst. with a second art., instead of between the art. and subst. We can scarcely say that it is an irregularity that, as indecl. pr. nn. are so much more frequent than in pure Greek, the art. is often used with them to supply the want of inflexion, where the context does not call for it, *e.g.*, in the series of accusatives in

* In Aramaic there is a kind of postpositive art., resembling the Greek much less. If this has any influence on the language of the N. T., it is (except perhaps in the Apocalypse —see p. 51-2) confined to the modification of certain words Grecised and used almost or quite as pr. nn.—*e.g.*, Σατανᾶς (so always, probably even in 2 Cor. xii. 7, where T. R. has Σατᾶν, μαμωνᾶς.

Matt. i. 2-16. (Τὸν Βαραββᾶν in Luke xxiii. 18, John xviii. 40, is used with dramatic fitness; it is the first time the *readers* have heard of Barabbas, but the *speakers* and their hearer know all about him.)

There are however instances where the position, or the use or omission, of the art. cannot be justified according to strict grammatical rule; or only by supposing a far-fetched and improbable refinement of sense to be intended. *E.g.* in John vi. 32 the sense—the only one giving a reason for the actual order of clauses—appears to be τὸν ἐκ τοῦ οὐρανοῦ ἄρτον. Still more decidedly in xii. 9, 12, it seems impossible that ὁ ὄχλος πολύς can mean anything different from ὁ πολὺς ὄχλος: to say (with Buttmann) that ὄχλος πολύς ranks as one word seems arbitrary, and would prove too much. Ibid. viii. 44 we should, in better Greek, have had for the first clause ἐκ πατρὸς τοῦ δ., if the sense be, as commonly understood, " Ye are [born] of the devil as father." And in the last clause, if ὁ πατὴρ αὐτοῦ be a predicate, co-ordinate with ψεύστης, it should like it have been anarthrous. But there is no doubt that, from a purely grammatical point of view,* the easiest translation of the verse would be " Ye are *of the father of the* devil . . . he" (the devil at least as probably as his father) "was a murderer . . . because *his*

* The verse was probably thus understood by the author of the *Acta Thomæ* (c. 32 in Tisch. *Acta Apost. Apocrypha*). The arguments are incommensurable with each other, in favour of this interpretation, that it was adopted by a Greek-speaking Christian of the second century, and against it, that any one who adopted it did so as harmonising with the strange superstitions and heresies of that work. Origen *in loc.* considers the constr. ambiguous: he does not speak of the startling interpretation as though it were exclusively Gnostic.

father also is a liar." But as grammatical considerations are not the only ones to be taken into account on a point of exegesis, so it is important to know how much laxity St. John allows himself in the matter, since the requirements of grammatical rule would tell for more in the case of a more accurate writer.

In Luke i. 5, the best attested text is Ἡρῴδου βασιλέως τῆς Ἰουδαίας. The insertion of τοῦ before βασ. in the received text (even in its oldest form, in Cod. A) no doubt comes from a sound instinct as to what was elegant Greek: but one could hardly say that the omission of the art. is an error.* If it be, it arises from assimilation to the prevailing usage of the LXX., and so indirectly from Hebrew idiom, which (like English) naturally speaks of " A. king of B." (see *e.g.* Gen. xiv. 1, 2, 9, 18). Similarly the art. should be omitted (here the insertion is less universal in the later text) in Mark ii. 26 before ἀρχιερέως. It is a mistake to stake the accuracy of the Gospel narrative on a refinement such as has been raised here, that the event took place " in the days of Abiathar, the famous high priest," but not " in the days of Abiathar's being high priest," since his father still held the office.

Still more is it a mistake to build theological inferences on the use or non-use of the art. with divine names or titles, or other theological terms. No doubt, we ought to notice whether it is used or not. Where, as in Rom. iii. 30, v. 7, two words are balanced

* Certainly Ἡρῴδου βασιλέως Ἰουδαίας (without τῆς) would not be bad Greek. But of all pr. nn., names of *countries* in *-ia* are those that most constantly have the art. And this is not arbitrary: they are strictly fem. adjectives, " the [country] of Judah " or the like.

against each other, one with the art. and one without, we may fairly presume that there is a reason for the difference: and even when the omission or insertion is less pointed than this, we must not hastily assume it to be accidental. But neither must we be hypercritical in insisting that it shall be significant; and we have the less right, not the more, to be so, in proportion to the importance of the significance, if admitted.

To come to instances: in classical writers the "God" of so-called natural religion, the providential or retributive Ruler of the world, is as a rule spoken of as ὁ Θεός. Θεός by itself can bear the same sense, but is equally likely to mean "a god" known to mythology (note the absence of the art. in the inscription in Acts xvii. 23, which St. Paul takes in a monotheist sense, but which we may be sure was not so intended). Ὁ θεός, of course, can only bear a mythological sense if the god has been named, or can be identified from the context. In Jewish and Christian writers, on the other hand, Θεός is a name belonging to One only, and so is used like a pr. n., with or without the art. according to its place in the sentence: and beyond one or two broad rules, it seems that there is hardly any principle involved in the retention or omission. In John i. 1 *fin.* ὁ Θεὸς ἦν ὁ Λόγος would have been much more a solecism than a heresy: Θεός is without the art., not because St. John means to teach Arianism (the Word was a divine being), nor because he pointedly does not mean to teach Sabellianism* ("God" and "the Word" were

---

* It should be remembered that the great majority o Catholic Christians have known this text in the form *Deus erat Verbum*.

one and the same: cf. 1 Ep. iii. 4, where it *is* meant that ἁμαρτία and ἀνομία are equivalent and coextensive), but simply because ὁ Λόγος is subject and Θεός predicate, though the latter, as more emphatic, stands first. Similarly, it is grammatical not theological considerations that determine whether Πνεῦμα (with or without the epithet ἅγιον) shall take the art. Perhaps in a place like Acts xix. 2 we might render "Did ye receive any holy inspiration?" and we notice that in viii. 17, 19 (of the parallelism to which the author was probably conscious), the words are similarly anarthrous; so too John xx. 22. But when we see that in Acts viii. 18, xix. 6, the subst. has the art., in the latter repeated with the epithet also—that it is so used in a similar context in x. 44-7, and in Gal. iii. 2—we perceive that, whether it be possible or no to draw a line between places where the word designates the Person of the Paraclete and where it means only the divine gift to the human spirit, at any rate the line cannot be drawn mechanically, by the mere presence or absence of the article. Perhaps there is more significance in its presence or absence with the names Κύριος and Χριστός; its absence showing, in contexts where the art. would be grammatically admissible, that the words are used virtually as pr. nn.—while its presence of course is no proof that they are not. And since the anarthrous Κύριος is, as a rule, the representative of the Tetragrammaton, of course important theological issues are raised, when the term is used of Christ, or when Old Testament passages containing it are applied to Him. But here again exegesis is a higher thing than grammar. Grammar may be a valuable servant to theology: but the earth is disquieted for a handmaid that is heir to her mistress.—It will be understood, that in Tit. ii. 13, 2 Peter i. 1, we regard Θεοῦ and σωτῆρος as indicating two Persons, though only the former word has the art. The gen. ἡμῶν, which is expressed in St. Paul and supplied in St. Peter, makes σωτῆρος sufficiently definite without it: but it may be allowed that St. Peter would, if he had used the art. with accuracy up to the standard of the First Epistle, either have omitted the art. with both nouns or have supplied it with both. How little right we have to assume that the repetition or non-repetition of the art. with co-ordinate nouns implies a difference in their relations is shown by a comparison of Matt. xxi. 12 with what is certainly the true text of Mark xi. 15, or Acts xv. 6 with that of xvi. 4.

Equally wrong is the attempt to argue from the use or non-use of the art. with νόμος in St. Paul's Epistles whether he means by the word the Mosaic Law or the Divine Law in general. Careful study of such passages as Rom. ii. 23-27 or vii. 7-25, will show that in almost every case where the word occurs, a definite reason can be assigned for its having or not having the art.; but that these reasons are, in the first instance, purely such as arise from the place of the word in the structure of the sentence. It is only indirectly, and in some passages, that the fact of the word holding different places in the sentence shows that its sense is not quite the same.* It is the more

---

* We may give in illustration a gloss on the former of the passages referred to. "Thou who boastest of living under a law,'—as we should say, "of enjoying a revelation," or as

possible to trace a grammatical reason, and to recognise that we need not look for a theological, in St. Paul's practice in this respect, if we first have recognised that the cases in which the art. can be omitted and inserted in Greek are not exactly the same in which it is desirable to omit or insert it in a fluent English translation.

The one New Testament usage of the art. which may fairly be called, not merely lax but systematically incorrect, is one confined to the Apocalypse. In vi. 8, viii. 11, xii. 9, xx. 2, pr. nn. stand as predicates, and ought not, according to correct Greek usage, to have the art. as they have. (The art. in the first passage, and the former one in the last, are not textually certain; but in the first at least the omission is probably due to the instinct of Greek transcribers, and the insertion to their fidelity). In xix. 13 the art. is more defensible: "*The* Word of God" is so absolutely and necessarily One, that the art. forms actually part of His name: it would not adequately designate Him without it. Similarly we might defend ὁ διάβολος in xx. 2—it is equivalent to a pr. n. with the art., but not (John vi. 70) without it.

Moslems talk of " people of a book,"—" dost thou, by breaking *the* law" under which thou livest, "dishonour God? Circumcision is profitable, if thy life be according to law: but if thou be a law-breaker, thy circumcision. . . . If therefore the uncircumcision keep the righteous ordinances of the law"—that law which thou knowest, whereof thou boastest— "shall not . . . and [shall not] the natural uncircumcision, accomplishing *the* law, judge thee, who usest," St. Paul might have said, "*the* writings and *the* ceremonial seal [of *the* law] to break the law?" but what he does in fact say is equivalent to "usest Scripture and circumcision for law-breaking "— only makest thyself the more a transgressor, because thou hast these things to transgress.

But ὁ Σατανᾶς, taking it as actually a pr. n., cannot be right: perhaps however St. John remembers that in the Hebrew Scriptures the word is still on the same footing as Διάβολος—that it is only with the art. that it is equivalent to a pr. n.

The primitive* pronominal use of the art. has come a step nearer to extinction in the N. T. than in Attic. Not only is it confined to the phrases with the particles μέν and δέ—not, it is true, to the particular case where these are opposed to each other; for we have both οἱ μέν answered by ἄλλοι [δέ] in John vii. 12 (if not in Matt. xvi. 14), and οἱ δέ, ὁ δέ, ἡ δέ, more rarely, οἱ μέν, in plain narrative in Matt. ii. 5, 9, Luke i. 29, Acts i. 6, etc.:—but it is apparently, with one exception, only used in the nom. masc. and fem. sing. and pl.,—in the forms, in fact, that begin with the aspirate, not with τ. In Eph. iv. 11 we have τοὺς μὲν . . . τοὺς δὲ . . . τοὺς δέ . . . but in Mark xii. 5 we should read οὕς, and so everywhere where neuters or oblique cases occur in phrases of this type. And even in the nom. it is only in the masc. sing. that we can tell (since the accents of our modern text do not represent a primitive tradition) whether the pron. is of the form identical with the art. or with the rel. The latter, after becoming almost extinct in the earlier Attic (καὶ ὅς was rare, ἢ δ' ὅς apparently only colloquial), becomes frequent from Demosthenes onwards with μέν and δέ in antithetical clauses. Ὃς δὲ ἀπεκρίθη αὐτοῖς, which is strongly attested in John v. 11, would

* Of course the poetical archaism of Aratus, quoted in Acts xvii. 28, is no instance of N. T. nor even of real Alexandrian idiom.

hardly have been admitted in Attic of any period: but if ἢ δ' ὅς or καὶ ὅς . . . ἔφη was Greek, a writer like St. John felt that there was no reason why this should not be. Ὃς δὲ οὐκ ἔλαβεν in Mark xv. 23 is still better attested, and still further from Attic usage.

"The personal pronouns are used much more frequently in the N. T. than in ordinary Greek" (Winer). As regards the nom., the same rule may fairly be said to be observed as in the classical language—that a pron. as subject to a finite verb is not expressed except when emphatic,* though Matt. viii. 7, x. 16, etc., may lead us to think a very slight degree of emphasis suffices. But in the oblique cases it is usual to have pronouns expressed which in classical Greek would probably have been left to be understood, and not unusual to have them repeated when in classical Greek one expression would certainly have been enough.

It is not certain to which element of the N. T. language, the modern or the Hebraising, this frequency of pronouns is to be ascribed. In Hebrew their oblique cases are expressed by suffixes, which can be inserted or repeated with less cumbrousness than independent words; on the other hand, the frequency of pronouns is observable in modern Greek generally, and it hardly seems as though so fundamental a matter of idiom as this could arise only

* In the σὺ λέγεις, σὺ εἶπας of the last chapters of the Gospels, there is no doubt that the σὺ is emphatic, though it may be doubtful what the point of the emphasis is—whether "You say that, not I: you are responsible for putting it that way," which is supported by Luke xxii. 70; or taking the words as interrogative, "Is that question your own?" cf. John xviii. 34.

from the influence of biblical language upon popular. Moreover, the forms multiplied or repeated are almost exclusively the unemphatic enclitic ones;* these, like the Hebrew suffixes, were in their own nature easier to multiply, though it may be true that their likeness to suffixes encouraged their use in reproducing sentences of Hebraic type.

Certainly it is in the most Hebraising books—the Apocalypse, and after this the Synoptic Gospels—that this redundant use of pronouns is most frequent: see Rev. i. 14-16, ii. 13, etc., Matt. i. 19, iii. 4, vi. 3, 4, etc. The only *convincing* instances that it is possible to give are cases where the pron. is repeated—even in Matt. i. 19 it would be rash to say that a more classical writer would have omitted one or the other αὐτήν. But in sentences of the common type ἐν τῷ σπείρειν αὐτὸν (Matt. xiii. 4), we see a characteristically Hellenistic use of the pron. as well as of the prep., the whole constr. being equivalent to a common Hebrew one.

Not less characteristically Hellenistic is the use of the enclitic gen. of the personal pronouns, to the almost complete exclusion of the adjectival possessives. The latter are *never* used unless emphatic: when used, they always have the art. (Matt. xviii. 20, Mark viii. 38, etc.), except where they stand as predicates (Matt. xx. 23 = Mark x. 40, John xiii. 35, xiv. 24, xv. 8, xvi. 15, xvii. 10, 2 Cor. viii. 23; Luke xv. 31, John xvii. 6, 9, 10, Luke vi. 20; John iv. 34, Phil. iii. 9 really come under this principle,

* Modern Greek has an enclitic pron. of the 3rd person, τον, του, etc.: apparently rather apocopated from αὐτόν, αὐτοῦ, etc., than a revival of the pronominal use of the art.

USE OF POSSESSIVE GENITIVE. 55

though the predication is less direct). St. Paul sometimes writes ὁ ὑμῶν instead of ὁ ὑμέτερος (Rom. xvi. 19, 1 Cor. vii. 35, ix. 12, xvi. 18, 2 Cor. i. 6, vii. 7, 15, viii. 14, xii. 19, xiii. 9, Phil. i. 19, 25, ii. 30, Col. i. 8, 1 Thess. iii. 7): but this usage is confined to his writings, and in them to the pron. of the 2nd person pl. (Τὸ ἐκείνων περίσσευμα in 2 Cor. viii. 14 of course is no exception, as there is no possessive pron. correlative to ἐκεῖνος.)

The gen. of the pronouns of the 1st and 2nd persons sing., when used possessively, is always of the enclitic form, except where emphasised in contradistinction to another pron. (Rom. i. 12, xvi. 13), and in the one case (according to the probable text) of Matt. xvi. 23, where also the pron. is emphatic: and it generally, but not always,* holds the position of a suffix after the subst. of the thing possessed. In cases where this normal order is departed from, there seems always to be a definite reason. The pron. stands first: (1) when it forms a predicate (Luke xxii. 53, Eph. ii. 10) or is otherwise emphatic (Luke xii. 30, Phil. iii. 20); (2) when the relation indicated by the gen. is a *natural* and *necessary* one—*e.g.*, that of the body or soul, or parts of the body or qualities of mind, to the person to whom we ascribe them. Thus we get μυρίσαι μου τὸ

---

* There appear to be in the whole N. T. 389 cases where μου stands after the governing subst., 41 where it is before it. No difference, other than the accidental one of more or fewer cases arising for the principle of the text to be applied, can be traced in different authors, though accidental differences are large. *E.g.* in Heb. we never (except in quotations and the *f. l.* in x. 34) get the possessive μου at all: in the Catholic Epistles never before its case, and in the Apoc. only once. But we have σου before its case three times in 3 John (2, 3, 6), and eight times in Apoc.

σῶμα (Mark xiv. 8, *si vera l.*), εὐοδοῦταί σου ἡ ψυχή (3 John 2), ἔβρεξέν μου τοὺς πόδας (Luke vii. 44, 45, perhaps 46), βοήθει μου τῇ ἀπιστίᾳ (Mark ix. 24), μαρτυρούντων σου τῇ ἀληθείᾳ (3 John 3); see also John vi. 54-6. And the principle, as above stated, explains sentences like ἀκούων μου τοὺς λόγους (Matt. vii. 24, 26), ἵνα μου ὑπὸ τὴν στέγην εἰσέλθῃς (viii. 8, cf. Luke xii. 18); but (ibid.) ὁ παῖς μου, for it is not so much a matter of course that he should have a servant as a house. Yet we have αὐτός μου ἀδελφός (xii. 50), and ἐλέησόν μου τὸν υἱόν (xvii. 15), the relationship being closer: so οὐ δύναταί μου εἶναι μαθητής (Luke xiv. 26, 27), and even χρονίζει μου ὁ κύριος (Matt. xxiv. 48, true text). These instances show, however, that it is rather arbitrary where the line is drawn as to which order is more appropriate. In almost any of these cases, the pron. could have come after the subst.; perhaps the case where it is hardest to account for its coming before it is γεύσεταί μου τοῦ δείπνου (Luke xiv. 24) Even there we may say that the order brings out the sense, "They shall not be *my* guests, not be received to *my* table," instead of "They shall not enjoy the good supper that I had prepared."

Even if we are right in considering these uses of the gen. and acc. of the personal pronouns as being commended to the N. T. writers by their analogy to the Semitic use of pronominal suffixes, still there is in them no transgression of the rules of Greek grammar; but at most a deviation from the elegances of Greek style, perhaps only a preference for the simpler or more Hebraic among alternative Greek idioms. We come somewhat nearer to actual violation of the rules of classical grammar, when we have sentences beginning with a participial clause, having a subst. or pron. in it, and then in the principal sentence have a pron. which is a mere repetition of this. If they are in the same case and constr., the second pronoun is redundant, not only in the sense that it might be omitted without loss in clearness and with gain in elegance, but in the sense of having no proper place in the sentence: and if the foregoing clause be a gen. abs., this is itself an irregular extension of the use of that constr., which is proper only when there is no relation in the sentence calling for another case.

We have *e.g.*, a quite regular sentence in Matt. ix. 27, καὶ παράγοντι ἐκεῖθεν τῷ Ἰησοῦ ἠκολούθησαν δύο τυφλοί; and so again in the next ver., ἐλθόντι δὲ εἰς τὴν οἰκίαν προσῆλθαν αὐτῷ οἱ τυφλοί. Again, it is equally regular, when in ver. 32 we have a gen. abs. introducing the next incident, αὐτῶν δὲ ἐξερχομένων ἰδοὺ προσήνεγκαν αὐτῷ κωφὸν δαιμονιζόμενον. But in v. 1 we have (according to the more probable text) a sentence constructed on the latter type where grammatical rule calls for the former, καθίσαντος αὐτοῦ προσῆλθαν αὐτῷ* οἱ μαθηταὶ αὐτοῦ: so viii. 1,* 5,* 28,* xxi. 23,* xxiv. 3, xxvi. 6, 7, and nearly so xvii. 22. One may see a little more reason for the use of the two cases in i. 18, 20, xxii. 41: and in general, the gen. abs. may be defended where the second mention of its subject does not come till far on in the sentence, or where (as in Mark v. 21) its case is not constructed in relation to the main sentence, but depends upon a

---

* In the first passage there is high but limited authority for omitting the pron., and in the next four there is some, sometimes much, for assimilating the constr. to that of viii. 23.

prep. But what can be said of a constr. like that which occurs as a variant in some of these places, and without variation in Matt. viii. 23 ?—ἐμβάντι αὐτῷ εἰς πλοῖον ἠκολούθησαν αὐτῷ οἱ μαθηταὶ αὐτοῦ. Plainly here the second αὐτῷ is in the strictest sense redundant: and the use of the first in the dat. shows that we are not hypercritical, in saying that that case would have been more correct than the gen. abs. in sentences like that cited from v. 1.

This irregularity, in one form or the other, is somewhat more frequent in Matt. than elsewhere; chiefly because, as in the instances cited, St. Matthew's favourite formula προσῆλθεν or προσελθὼν αὐτῷ lends itself so easily to it. But it is in fact common to all the historical books, except St. John's Gospel: he does not misuse the gen. abs., because he makes rare use of it, as of other idiomatic Greek constructions. In St. Luke's Gospel the irregularity is rare, for a similar reason: with him the gen. abs. is almost superseded by the Hebraistic ἐν τῷ c. infin. But even there xxii. 53, xxiv. 41—perhaps xxiv. 5 and one or two more—are instances though not harsh ones: xx. 1 has not the redundant pron. in the second clause, but has the irregular gen. abs. in the first. And in Acts there are several cases as decided as any in Matt. or Mark—iv. 1, x. 19,* xvi. 16, xix. 30, xxi. 17, xxv. 7: while xxii. 17 is a compound instance, and perhaps the harshest in the whole New Testament, except Mark vi. 22. In the last cited passage, no one can doubt that any correct Greek

---

* Here, as in Matt. v. 1, B is "subsingular" in omitting the pron. In several of the other passages there are variants, but not of much authority.

author would have written γενομένης ἡμέρας εὐκ., ὅτε
... Γαλιλαίας, εἰσελθοῦσα ἡ θυγάτηρ ... καὶ ὀρχησαμένη, ἤρεσεν κ.τ.λ. 2 Cor. iv. 18 is perhaps the only example of this irregularity in St. Paul: there the pron. is ἡμεῖς, not αὐτός, but the gen. abs. is redundant in just the same way.

Another redundant use of the oblique cases of αὐτός is in relative sentences; which may perhaps be thought to have furnished the type to which Matt. viii. 23 is conformed. In Hebrew, the relative is an indecl. particle—in late Hebrew hardly more than an inseparable prefix—so that, to define its constr., it is necessary to insert a pron. or pronominal adv. at the proper place in the sentence: just as in modern Greek or in vulgar modern English we get πρᾶγμα ὁποῦ δὲν τὸ νοστιμεύομαι,* " a thing which I don't like it." The reproduction of this constr., not unknown in Hellenistic Greek generally,† is carried very far in the Apoc.: see iii. 8, vii. 2, 9, xii. 6, 14, xiii. 12, xvii. 9, xx. 8. Mark xiii. 19, θλίψις οἷα οὐ γέγονεν τοιαύτη, is similar to Rev. xvi. 18, οἷος οὐκ ἐγένετο ... τηλικοῦτος σεισμὸς οὕτω μέγας: but while in the latter the last clause is no doubt redundant as it stands (even apart from the fact that οὕτω μέγας is scarcely more than a mere equivalent to τηλικοῦτος), even there, and much more in Mark l. c., the demonstr. may be held to be rather transposed than to be

* Sophocles' *Romaic Grammar*, § 164. 1. He says the constr. can be used, even if the rel. is inflected.
† There is only one unmistakable instance in the N. T. outside the Apoc., Mark i. 7 = Luke iii. 16. In all other cases, either the pron. has another constr. to legitimate it, or there is authority for its omission. But there is little doubt that it should stand in Mark vii. 25, and there if retained it is certainly redundant.

exactly redundant. Σεισμὸς ἐγένετο μέγας, τηλικοῦτος οἷος οὐκ ἐγένετο κ.τ.λ. would be quite grammatical Greek: and (waiving the question of the peculiar constr. of the first words in St. Mark), ἔσται θλίψις τοιαύτη οἵα οὐ γέγονεν would be not only grammatical but easy—perhaps more elegant than if οἵα stood alone.

We have thus far spoken of αὐτός when used as a personal pron., as it confessedly is in all Greek, in its oblique cases. But we have to consider the question, Is the word used in the New Testament as a mere personal pron. in the nom. also? It is no proof to the contrary, that it "never occurs without a certain degree of emphasis" (Winer); for this is true of the nom. of all personal pronouns: the question we have to consider is, whether it is not used where the only thing to be emphasised is the mention of the person.

Now where αὐτός is used of the principal agent, as distinguished from other persons (Mark ii. 25, αὐτὸς καὶ οἱ μετ' αὐτοῦ, etc.), of course the use is strictly classical. It is not incorrect even in sentences like Matt. i. 21, where αὐτὸς γὰρ σώσει means more than σώσει γάρ,* or Mark iv. 38, where αὐτός means, "He, the principal person of the story," as distinguished from the disciples named in ver. 34, who have been spoken of since by pronouns and 3rd persons of verbs: though the use in sentences like one or other of these is relatively more frequent than in classical Greek. In Matt. iii. 11, xi. 14, xii. 50, and elsewhere, ἐκεῖνος,

---

* Best translated with the R. V., "it is He that shall save." Even if there be a reference to the etymology of the Name recorded in Num. xiii. 16, anything that suggested that reference would be a gloss rather than a translation.

or sometimes οὗτος, would be more natural or more elegant, though we might not say that αὐτός is impossible. The same might be said of some passages in St. Paul and John, Eph. ii. 14, Col. i. 17, John Ep. I. iii. 24, iv. 13, 15, being the most marked. But the most certainly unhellenic use of the word is one confined to the Apocalypse (xiv. 10, xix. 15—not only iii. 20, but xiv. 17, and prob. xvii. 11 are different) and St. Luke's Gospel; which in this as in other points is more Hebraistic than the others in the method of introducing narratives, though sometimes more classical in their substance. Καὶ αὐτός in Luke i. 22, ii. 28, v. 1, 17, viii. 1, 22, xvii. 11, xix. 2, καὶ αὐτή in ii. 37, καὶ αὐτοί in xiv. 1, xxiv. 14 are plainly as Hebraistic as the καὶ ἐγένετο ἐν τῷ . . . or καὶ ἰδού that usually precede them: and these are only the clearest cases, shading off through passages like iv. 15, v. 14, xv. 14, into others like v. 16, vi. 20, etc., where αὐτός often stands without καί, and in any case does not go beyond the usage of the other Gospels.

With regard to the use of the accented or the enclitic forms of the oblique cases of the personal pronouns, it is only in the case of the 1st person (ἐμέ, ἐμοῦ, ἐμοί as distinct from με κ.τ.λ.) that we have direct evidence. In modern Greek, the rule is stated as absolute (Soph., *Rom. Gr.*, § 160-2) that enclitic pronouns are not used after prepositions: and modern usage is the more worth attending to, because here we have facts, not the theories of grammarians transmitted by scribes or printers. But in the N. T. there is one frequent exception to this rule, in the combination πρός με, which we find often, even when the pron. has no small emphasis. In John

vi. 44, 45, the reading varies between πρός με and πρὸς ἐμέ: in ver. 35-7 we get the two side by side, and are not surprised at the unemphatic form being used when the emphatic precedes it. But in ver. 65, and in v. 40, vii. 37, we have πρός με standing by itself: so Matt. iii. 14, xi. 28, xix. 14 (=Mark x. 14=Luke xviii. 16), xxv. 36, Mark ix. 19, Luke i. 43? vi. 47, xi. 6, xiv. 26, Acts xi. 11, xxii. 10, 21, xxvi. 14 (xxii. 8, xxiii. 22, xxiv. 19 T. R.). Not all of these are emphatic, but many are: one fails to trace any principle that should tell us whether to write or pronounce πρός σε or πρὸς σέ.

With regard to reflexive pronouns, there is less doubt what the N. T. usage is, than how far it differs from that of classical Greek. Those belonging to the 1st and 2nd persons, ἐμαυτοῦ and σεαυτοῦ (never contracted into σαυτοῦ as in Attic poetry) are certainly in use, but in the sing. only: for their so-called plurals ἡμῶν αὐτῶν etc. never occur in the N.T. (In 2 Thess. i. 4, read αὐτοὺς ἡμᾶς: in 1 Cor. vii. 35 the words ὑμῶν αὐτῶν no doubt occur, but the sense is the same as with the other order, emphatic, not reflexive.) Ἑαυτοῦ on the other hand is freely used both in the sing. and pl.: and its pl. is found in the various senses: (1) "themselves," the primary one; (2) "one another," between which and the first it is not always easy to draw a line; (3) "ourselves" or "yourselves"—ἑαυτῶν supplying the place of the pl. to ἐμαυτοῦ and σεαυτοῦ, as well as ἑαυτοῦ.

For all these usages there is plenty of classical precedent: and so far the N. T. language shows no signs of degeneracy—it is hardly one, that ἡμῶν αὐτῶν etc., are disused, for ἑαυτῶν is [much more manageable.* But in modern Greek ἑαυτοῦ is used also in the sing. in reference to all three persons.† This modern usage, accordingly, has found its way into the later texts of the N. T.: but the best critics are now agreed, that it has originally no place there: we should read σεαυτοῦ, σεαυτόν, even in John xviii. 34, and in the various places where Levit. xix. 18 is quoted.

In classical Attic, however, not only ἑαυτῶν etc., are used for all persons, but αὑτοῦ etc., are so used in the sing. There also, however, more accurate textual criticism tends to show that ἑαυτοῦ, etc., are not: we learn, not that the use of this word for all persons is not peculiar to the decline of the language,‡ but to ask whether, when the sense is reflexive, we are to suppose that the emphatic pron. αὐτός, used in its oblique cases, was sufficient by itself, or whether we must suppose that the contracted form αὑτοῦ for ἑαυτοῦ had received an extension of use which the uncontracted form had not. Of evidence more trustworthy than the usage of the comparatively late MSS. that mark the breathings, we have the modification by elision of a preceding word only in Æsch. *Theb.* 194, *Cho.* 221: in the former place the primary MS. reads αὐτοὶ δ' ὑφ' αὑτῶν, but in the latter αὐτὸς κατ' αὑτοῦ.

* See *e.g.*, 2 Cor. xiii. 5; where, if one clause had stood alone, αὐτοὶ ὑμᾶς αὐτοὺς πειράζετε might have been more forcible; but to have put ὑμᾶς αὐτούς thrice, as ἑαυτούς stands, would have been insufferably cumbrous.

† When it is desired to express emphatically which person is meant, it is done by the cumbrous use of a gen., τοῦ ἑαυτοῦ μου, etc., something like the modern English " myself " and " yourself," to which vulgar usage seeks to assimilate the really older and more grammatical " him self."

‡ As *e.g.*, in Epict. *Diss.* I. vi. 35 we get αὐτῷ ταῦτά σε δεῖ κατασκευάζειν

Such decisive evidence is nowhere forthcoming in the N. T., in the passages (not very numerous) where αὐτόν, -οῦ etc. have a directly reflexive rather than either a personal or an emphatic sense. The smooth breathing is certain in Matt. iii. 16, Luke vi. 3, 4, Rev. ix. 11 : but the question is, are reflexive pronouns really called for here? We get (as in English) the simple pers. pron. often used after prepositions where logically we should have the refl.—*e.g.*, Matt. v. 29, 30, vi. 2, xviii. 16 : we even get ὑμῖν, not ἑαυτοῖς, in vi. 19, 20, where the pron. does not depend on a prep. : and in Matt. xxv. 1, 3, 4, 7, αὐτῶν and ἑαυτῶν are interchanged, no MSS. or editors adhering consistently to either form. In none of the three cases cited with elisions is the reflexive sense as undeniable as in αὐτὸς περὶ αὐτοῦ in John ix. 21, (T.R.) still less as much so as in John ii. 24, xix. 17,* Acts xiv. 17, Rev. viii. 6, xviii. 7, and the like. Even in places like these most recent critical editors think it best always to write αὑτοῦ, etc. : Westcott and Hort feel (and ordinary readers, brought up on ordinary grammatical traditions, will feel with them) that this sometimes makes a passage read very harshly, *e.g.*, in nearly all the places last cited. They therefore admit αὑτοῦ into their text nearly twenty times : see their Appendix, ii., 1., pp. 144-5.

If there be any practicable way of setting the question at rest, the most hopeful would be, first to ascertain whether classical usage allows the simple αὐτόν, -τοῦ κ.τ.λ. to bear (in any person) a reflexive sense : if so, it is probable that αὐτόν is sometimes so

* St. John, it is to be noted, is more careful to use full reflexive forms, even after prepositions, *e.g.*, v. 42, ἐν ἑαυτοῖς.

USE OF DEMONSTRATIVE PRONOUNS. 65

used (but in the 3rd person only) in the N. T., and that ἑαυτοῦ is *not* there contracted into αὑτοῦ.

There is hardly anything to be called irregular in the N. T. use of demonstr. pronouns: yet one or two deviations from classical usage may be noted. Ὅδε is all but obsolete—it has at any rate ceased to be used in its primary vivid sense, "this [person or thing] now here present." See John xviii. 21, where οὗτοι bears this sense, Acts iv. 10, 11, where οὗτος is used of two persons and a thing, and ὅδε to designate the lame man would have contributed much to clearness; and on the other hand Luke x. 39, the only place where ὅδε is used with a personal reference (for in xvi. 25 read ὧδε, a not uncommon N. T. word), and where ταύτῃ would be more appropriate. Besides this passage, the N. T. uses of the word are two only: once virtually indefinite, Jas. iv. 13, a sense hardly known to classical Greek, but of which we see the beginnings in Aristotle;* and occasionally in reference to a speech or letter about to be recited; Acts xxi. 11 (and xv. 23, T. R.), and in Apoc. ii., iii., before each of the Epp. to the Seven Churches. (In 2 Cor. xii. 19, of course we should read read τὰ δέ as two words.)

Οὗτος and ἐκεῖνος are used much as in earlier Greek, except in the greater relative frequency of what may be called their epexegetical use—where they

* Plut. *Symp.* I. vi. 1 is quoted as a parallel. There Plutarch says, as a proof of Alexander's intemperance, that in his official journal συνεχέστατα γέγραπται καὶ πλειστάκις, ὅτι τήνδε τὴν ἡμέραν ἐκ τοῦ πότου ἐκάθευδεν. But there the words introduced by ὅτι are, no doubt, given as a *verbatim* extract from the journal. Still, though not a parallel to the one in St. James, this passage is a sort of illustration of the way that that use arose.

5

stand in app. to a foregoing noun, or more frequently to a participial or equivalent cause, accentuating and calling attention to the thing designated by that word or clause as the subject, or less often the object, of the sentence. We have real instances of this construction in classical writers, beginning with Xen. *Ages.* iv. 4, οἱ προῖκα εὖ πεπονθότες, οὗτοι ἀεὶ ἡδέως ὑπηρετοῦσι τῷ εὐεργέτῃ, Id. *Symp.* viii. 33, and we have approximations to it still earlier: but it is never so common in pure Greek as in the N. T. To show its frequency there, we can only refer to the passages marked * * (or in some oblique cases * * *) in Bruder's Concordance, *s.vv.* οὗτος and ἐκεῖνος; instead of enumerating these, we can only call attention to John xii. 48, Rom. vii. 10 (prob.), where the preceding word is a subst.; Matt xiii. 38, (John xvi. 13), where it is a subst. different in gender and number from the pron.; John xiv. 26, Acts ii. 22-3, vii. 35, where it is a group of substantives already in app., and relative clauses; Acts iv. 10, 1 Cor. vii. 20, where it is a subst. depending on a prep., which is repeated with the pron.; Rom. ix. 6, Gal. iii. 7, where there is no ptcp., and it is hardly necessary to supply one; and 1 Cor. viii. 3, 2 Thess. iii. 14, James iii. 2, where εἴ τις c. indic. takes the place of the ptcp. with art. This last is hardly distinguishable from conditional sentences like John ix. 31, or relative ones like Matt. v. 19, where οὗτος is no longer epexegetical, but stands naturally in the apodosis. Αὐτὸ τοῦτο (τοῦτο αὐτὸ in 2 Cor. ii. 3) is peculiar to St. Paul, except for 2 Peter i. 5.

The most marked irregularity in the use of the rel. pron., the use of a personal or demonstr. pron.

RELATIVES AND INTERROGATIVES. 67

in a kind of remote apposition with it, has already been noticed (p. 59). But, besides this comparatively rare Hebraism, there are other signs in the use of the rel. of the late stage of the language, signs less conspicuous, but more significant of internal change. In English, the originally interrogative pronouns "who" and "which" have encroached largely on the use of the primitive relative "that"—which as in Greek was identical in form, though not in accent, with the demonstr. pron. that became a definite art. In Greek, we are able to trace the process by which the boundary between rel. and interrog. sentences is liable to be obliterated. In 1 Tim. i. 7 we have the two used side by side, and see that the use of one or other makes hardly any difference to the sense :* the sentence may be conceived as either relative or (in a wide sense of the term) interrogative, in such phrases as "I know who . . . ," "He told him who it was," and the like. Now in Greek there existed a pron. combining in form the rel. and the interrog., and having among its uses that of serving for cases like those that lie on the borders of the two senses: but this word ὅστις, though not uncommon in the N. T. in other usages, is, curiously enough, never, or only once, there employed in this. But it, as well as the separate ὅς and τίς, each usurp some functions for which one of the others might be thought more proper,

For it appears on the whole to be proved, that in late Greek ὅστις, at least its neut. ὅτι, is occasionally though rarely used in direct questions: and hence

* Even if διαβεβαιοῦνται be a deliberative subj. (see p. 107 n.), the difference, though real, is slight.

there is no necessity, hardly any probability, for denying that it is so used in the N. T. No passage indeed in which it is so used is quite free from question as to reading or sense. If we read ὅτι in Matt. vii. 14, it seems certainly easiest to translate it "Because." In Mark ix. 11, on the contrary "Why . . . ?" is the natural and obvious sense: it is only if we have an *a priori* scruple against admitting it, that we shall reflect that it makes a sort of sense to translate, "They questioned Him, saying, 'The scribes say . . . ;'"—the statement of fact, that the scribes said so, *suggesting* the question "What do they mean by it?" or "In what sense is it true?" But when we see that the passage does not stand alone, that in ver. 28 it is even more difficult to explain the word as otherwise than interrog., that moreover in 1 Paral. xvii. 6 ὅτι stands for "Why" in the LXX., or at least can only be taken otherwise by another far-fetched explanation—we can hardly fail to admit the use as established: the only question that remains is as to the limits of its rarity. In Mark ii. 16 there is hardly any doubt that ὅτι without τί is the true reading; but the categorical or the interrogative sentence will make almost equally good sense. In John viii. 25, the question is a very difficult one, but it is one of exegesis not of grammar: as grammarians we can only report, that the words can be taken as interrogative, if exegetically that view seems best.

Are we to say that in Matt. xxvi. 50, the simple ὅ is used interrogatively? If not, we have to suppose a rather harsh ellipsis: but no such use of ὅς is quoted from Greek of any period. Ὁποῖος and such words, like ὅστις, are regularly used in indirect questions; even ὅς is occasionally found (and that as early as in Plat. *Rep.* viii. p. 559a) in a sentence where ὅστις or even τίς might have been expected: but the step from vague instances like these to the use in a direct question seems a hard one to take. If defensible at all, it must be explained from the influence of Latin, in which the relative pron. is always in form nearly akin to the interrogative, and may itself in certain cases (of which this is not one) be used interrogatively.

Ὅστις is, in the N. T., as a rule confined to two of its relative usages—the indefinite one, almost exactly expressed by the Latin *quicumque* or the English "whosoever," and a less strictly definable one, corresponding to the Latin *qui* with the subj., and capable of various more or less adequate translations in English according to the context or the exact shade of meaning—"which,"* "such as," "such that," or "seeing that he. . . ." Only in Acts ix. 6 (true text) ὅτι is used in an indirect question, in the wide grammatical sense of the term.

Of the cases where τίς is used and ὅστις might have been, the most defensible cases, those where the usurpation of the functions of the rel. is least, are those where it follows ἔχειν or rather οὐκ ἔχειν—Matt. xv. 32 = Mark viii. 1, 2; cf. vi. 36. These are not more harsh than *e.g.*, Mark ix. 6, οὐ γὰρ ᾔδει τί λαλήσῃ: and in fact this phrase has unquestionable classical precedents, Soph. *Œ. C.* 317; Xen. *Hell.* I.

---

* In the archaic use of "which," according to which it is not exclusively neut., it differs from "who" almost exactly as ὅστις from ὅς.

vi. 5, etc. The same might be said of Mark xiii. 11, μὴ προμεριμνᾶτε τί λαλήσητε: and this helps us far on the way towards Matt. x. 19, where almost the same words are followed by δοθήσεται γὰρ ὑμῖν ἐν ἐκείνῃ τῇ ὥρᾳ τί λαλήσητε. Or this might be compared with Acts ix. 6, where we might have had—the T. R. actually has—λαληθήσεταί σοι τί σε δεῖ ποιεῖν. But, if δοθήσεται . . . τί λαλήσητε be admitted, it is hard to object to ἑτοίμασον τί δειπνήσω (Luke xvii. 8). A further step is taken towards a purely rel. sense in Mark xiv. 36, οὐ τί ἐγὼ θέλω, ἀλλὰ τί σύ, and perhaps in Acts xiii. 25, τί (v. l. τίνα) ἐμὲ ὑπονοεῖτε εἶναι οὐκ εἰμὶ ἐγώ. In the latter place indeed it is perhaps better to punctuate and translate as the A. V.—the gloss ὁ $\overline{XC}$. after ἐγώ, old enough to have crept into the text, shows that this punctuation was a natural one: and in the other it may be argued that the use of the interrog. suggests a modification of the sense, "the question is not what I will, but what Thou." But one cannot deny that the transition of meaning is almost made; and one can only question how far it goes further than is possible in pure Greek: see Soph. *El.* 316, ἱστόρει τί σοι φίλον. There are several other passages in Sophocles where, as in Acts l. c., many editors punctuate so as to require the same sense of τίς or τί: but there is no other certain instance till quite late writers, and on the whole it seems best to regard the use as a late development of a tendency native to pure Greek.

A slighter extension of the use of τίς comes from the complete disuse in the N. T. of πότερος; for which we get the periphrasis τίς ἐκ τῶν δύο (Matt. xxi. 31). The adverbial πότερον occurs once (John

vii. 17) in an indirect question—a survival paralleled in its limits by that of the etymologically identical " whether " in English.

The various uses of the indef. pron., the unaccented τις, contain no deviation from classical usage. But there are one or two words, not strictly pronouns, which may be noted here as having unclassical quasi-pronominal uses. Εἷς approaches, as in late Hebrew and Aramaic, the sense of a mere indef. art. in a few passages of the Gospels and Apoc.—Matt. viii. 19, ix. 18 (?), xxvi. 69; Rev. viii. 13, xviii. 21, xix. 17. In Matt. xviii. 24, John vi. 9 (?) the word no doubt has a distinctive meaning: but in Matt. xix. 16 = Mark x. 17, it seems to be merely = τις. Intermediate are cases like Matt. xvi. 14 = Mark vi. 15, Matt. xviii. 28; or again Mark ix. 17, Luke v. 12, 17, etc., where εἷς is followed by a gen. or the prep. ἐξ, and thus, though there is no emphatic insistence on singularity (as there is *e.g.*, in Matt. x. 29, xviii. 6, 10, 12), there is a certain amount of antithesis between the individual and the class out of which he is selected. If we cannot say that the use of εἷς c. gen. in Matt. xxvi. 14, etc., is unclassical, we may say it is found more frequently and used more freely than in classical Greek.

In antithetical sentences such as Matt. xx. 21, xxiv. 40, xxvii. 48, it can hardly be said that the use of εἷς is unclassical, for the sense is not so much " the one . . . the other " as " one . . . and one " of the two (or in Matt. xvii. 4, and parallels the three) already mentioned or referred to.* But there appear to be no exact classical precedents for the opposition

* It is otherwise in Mark iv. 8, 20, if we there read ἕν.

of εἷς and ἕτερος (each sometimes with and sometimes without the art.) which we get in Matt. vi. 24 = Luke xvi. 13; Luke vii. 41, xvii. 34, xviii. 10; Acts xxiii. 6; 1 Cor. iv. 6. This does not however differ in principle from the classical εἷς μὲν ... ὁ δὲ ..., of which we have something like an instance in Gal. iv. 24. More serious is the deviation from Greek usage where the word is used reciprocally, as 1 Thess. v. 11, or distributively in the phrases καθ' εἷς and its modifications (Mark xiv. 19, ps. John viii. 9, Rom. xii. 5), or ἀνὰ εἷς ἕκαστος (Apoc. xxi. 21). The first is said to be an Aramaism: καθ' εἷς, though condemned as bad Greek, seems to be a native Greek growth. But when we compare εἷς κατὰ εἷς of Mark xiv. 19 with δύο δύο vi. 7 (Ecclus. xxxiii. (xxxvi.) 15: Luke x. 1 ἀνὰ δύο or ἀνὰ δύο δύο),* and this with vi. 39, 40, συμπόσια συμπόσια ... πρασιαὶ πρασιαὶ κατὰ ἑκατὸν καὶ κατὰ πεντήκοντα, we seem to feel that there is a foreign as well as a native element in the change of idiom.

Another word, not commonly called a pronoun but used as equivalent to one, is ἴδιος: see Matt. xxii. 5, 1 Cor. vii. 2, for cases where it is coupled with a pronominal gen. with apparently no distinction in sense.

Lastly we may mention under this head the Hebraistic use of οὐ (or more rarely μή) ... πᾶς as

* While speaking of these Hebraistic uses of numerals, we may mention in passing the frequent μία σαββάτων. That here, μία is "used for" an ordinal may be admitted, in view of the πρώτῃ σαββάτου of [Mark] xvi. 9: at least that shows that in Greek, as in English, an ordinal would be the natural way of expressing what is meant. Note also Psalm xxiii. (xxiv.), title, τῆς μιᾶς σαββάτου, xlvii. (xlviii.) δευτέρᾳ σαββάτου, xciii. (xciv.) τετράδι σαββάτου—which is less remote from μία.

equivalent to οὐδείς: see Matt. xxiv. 22 = Mark xiii. 20, Luke i. 37, Acts x. 14, Rom. iii. 20 = Gal. ii. 16, 1 Cor. i. 29, Rev. ix. 4. Distinct from this is, not only the use of οὐ πᾶς without an intervening word, and meaning, "not all," of Matt. vii. 21, 1 Cor. xv. 39, but that of πᾶς οὐ rather frequent in St. John, and perhaps giving a sense slightly modified from οὐδείς. See John iii. (15 ?) 16, vi. 39, xii. 46, 1 Ep. ii. 21, iii. 15, Eph. iv. 29, v. 5, besides the v. l. in the quotation in Rom. ix. 33.

CHAPTER IV.

CHARACTERISTICS OF NEW TESTAMENT GREEK IN THE SYNTACTICAL USE OF NOUNS.

(a) *Substantive.*

IN discussing the use made in the N. T. of the Greek cases of the noun, we must distinguish between such peculiarities of usage as are purely grammatical, and those where there is nothing at all peculiar in the grammar, but where ordinary constructions are used to express, whether more or less adequately, peculiarly or distinctively biblical thoughts. Thus it is a question for the commentator not for the grammarian, what is St. Paul's exact meaning when he speaks of "dying *to* sin," "living *to* God" (Rom. vi. 10, etc.), or again by a person being, or a fact subsisting, "in Christ" (*e.g.*, 2 Cor. v. 17; Gal. iii. 28, v. 6). Doubtless, the way to investigate points like these is much the same as that for studying obscure points of grammar: we must examine and compare the various passages where the phrases occur; we must illustrate them, as far as possible, by passages similar in context and in general purport, but differing in form of expression; and must seek to trace what difference, if any, that difference of form makes in the sense. But when our study is complete we shall know more, not of the force of the dative case or of the prep. ἐν as used in N. T. Greek, but of St. Paul's theological doctrines. It is different, when expositors ask whether ἀκούειν φωνῆς in Acts ix. 7 differs at all in sense from φωνὴν ἀκούειν in xxii. 9; this is a grammatical question to be answered on grammatical grounds:—though the best answer will here also be arrived at by examination of usage, not by deduction from the supposed nature of the gen. or acc. Still more plainly, the grammarian has a right to speak where the writer himself calls attention to a constr. or to a particle: *e.g.*, in passages like Rom. xi. 36, 1 Cor. viii. 6, Eph. iv. 6, we have to consider the grammatical question of the force of the prepositions, before we can settle the exegetical or theological question, what εἰς αὐτόν or ἐν πᾶσιν can mean in these particular contexts:

The Greek language has even to the present day retained the primitive case-inflexions of the noun to an extent very unusual among modern languages:* though the dat. has become almost obsolete. But it has shared the tendency common to all modern languages to become more analytical—to supplement or supersede inflexion by the use of particles: and we see this tendency to some extent at work in the N. T. Any tendency that there was in this direction

* How rapidly such forms may disappear can be seen in the case of the Celtic languages. As known from inscriptions down to at least the first century A.D., they have a full declension of case-endings, closely akin to the Latin and in some respects more primitive: but in the oldest Irish and Welsh literature (of perhaps the fifth and sixth centuries respectively) their terminations have all disappeared, except that in Irish there are traces of the dat. pl. The non-specialist can trace the disintegration in such a book as Prof. Rhys' *Celtic Britain.*

in the popular Greek language of the age would be sure to be reinforced in Hellenistic Greek, by the imitation of Semitic idioms, where case-inflexion hardly exists, and where prepositions (or at least inseparable particles which may be fairly so called) are used very extensively. But apart from this tendency (for instances of which see pp. 137 *sqq.*), there is not very much that is peculiar in the N. T. use of the cases themselves. We have, however, two or three irregular uses of the nom. With the art., it stands very often for the voc.;* as Matt. xi. 26, where ὁ Πατήρ is exactly parallel to Πάτερ in the preceding verse; Mark xiv. 36, Rom. viii. 15, Gal. iv. 6 —all which show that ὁ Πατήρ was the recognised, quasi-liturgical "interpretation" for the γλῶσσα Ἀββᾶ of inspired prayer. Perhaps we may illustrate this usage by the way that the 3rd person is used in German as more contemptuous, and in Italian as more respectful than the 2nd: you talk *to* equals, but *of* superiors and *at* inferiors. Not that the use or omission of the art. corresponds with the tone being reverential or objurgatory. We get ἡ παῖς in Luke viii. 54 (cf. Mark v. 4), τὸ μικρὸν ποίμνιον in xii. 32, where the tone, though kindly, is condescending: the nearest classical parallel is the use of ὁ παῖς in Ar. *Ran.* 40, which seems to have been only colloquial, and apparently always curt. Somewhat different

* It is a mistake to note as unclassical the use of the voc. without ὦ at the beginning of speeches, as with the phrase ἄνδρες ἀδελφοί in Acts i. 16 *et passim*, or Ἄνδρες Ἀθηναῖοι, Ἐφέσιοι, in the more classicalising passages, xvii. 22, xix. 35. This is a transgression of the usage, not of classical orators but of late rhetoricians and grammarians: according to the best MS. evidence, Demosthenes habitually, at least in some speeches, said ἄνδρες Ἀθηναῖοι without ὦ.

is the use of the nom. without the art. in Luke xii. 20, 1 Cor. xv. 36 : there one may say we have simply cases of non-use of the distinctive vocative inflexion. Moreover, though ἄφρων appears to be decidedly the true text in both passages, we must remember that confusion between o and ω was one of the earliest forms of error or irregularity to appear in Greek spelling, so that even the best MSS. are less absolutely to be trusted on this point than on others.

A more serious irregularity is found in the usage of the Apoc., where, of two nouns in appos., the second is regularly put in the nom., whatever be the case of the former—i. 5, ii. 20, etc. In such a crude form as this, the usage is confined to this one book, and might be reckoned rather as one of its peculiar anomalies of language than as representing a tendency of Hellenistic Greek generally. But when we look at Mark xii. 38-40 in the light of these passages, it is hard to avoid thinking that we have a parallel case : the force of the sentence is weakened, if we put a pause before οἱ κατέσθοντες, or do away with that after προσευχόμενοι : see also Luke xx. 27, and even Acts x. 37. 2 Cor. xi. 28 ; James iii. 8 are not parallel cases—there is there a real break in the sentence : but in Phil. iii. 18, 19 it is hard to make οἱ τὰ ἐπίγεια φρονοῦντες stand as quite regular : the art., if nothing else, prevents our connecting it closely with περιπατοῦσιν. Yet even this may be considered rather an inadvertence than an unclassical idiom : after the two clauses beginning with ὧν, the gen. is properly dropped, but the author forgets that he ought strictly to have reverted to the acc. not the nom.—that is, when he had once introduced the acc. τοὺς ἐχθρούς, which comes in by a somewhat irregular attraction, with which cf. Philem. 10, 1 John ii. 25. Acts iv. 5, (true text) is in some sort parallel to Phil. l. c. though it is a case, not of apposition, but of nouns co-ordinated by a conj. when in different cases. The last irregular use of the nom. that we have to mention is in certain notes of time in two or three places in the Synoptic Gospels—Matt. xv. 32 = Mark viii. 2 (true text), Luke ix. 28. In the last place, the only irregularity is the sing. ἐγένετο, which prob. really is not a solecistic ἐγένετο ἡμέραι, but a case of the Lucan ἐγένετο δὲ . . . καί . . . Probably in all three cases there is a sort of break or parenthesis: "They continue with me—it is now three days:" "it came to pass—it was eight days after." Buttmann compares the parenthetic use of . . . ὄνομα αὐτῷ in John i. 6, iii. 1. We may also note the use of ἄγει without a subj. in Luke xxiv. 21, as a proof that notes of time were especially liable to lose sight of strict grammatical constr.

The N. T. use of the acc. and dat. may be regarded as identical in principle with the classical, though we note a few variations in detail. In 1 Cor. vii. 31 we get χρῆσθαι c. acc.: this is unique, and is perhaps made somewhat easier by the fact that καταχρῆσθαι is so used,—only, it is true, by later writers than St. Paul, so far as we now know; but it may have been usual, at least colloquially, in his time. The use of the acc. in Rom. viii. 3, 2 Cor. vi. 13 is really an extension of the cognate acc. and may be called idiomatic Greek, if not quite regular: see also Acts xxvi. 3. Acts xiii. 32 is also an instance of the cognate acc. in a wide sense. We cannot say that there εὐαγγελίζεσθαι has a double acc., for the good news announced is, not "the promise" but "that God hath fulfilled the promise." Τὴν ἐπαγγ. stands first for emphasis, and ταύτην occupies the place in the constr. belonging to it. (Acts x. 36 would be just a similar case, if we retain ὅν after τὸν λόγον). It is certain that εὐαγγελίζεσθαι, which in the N. T. receives such a novel force as to be felt like a new word, is used with an acc. both of the person addressed (Luke iii. 18, Acts viii. 25, 40, xiii. 32, xiv. 15, 21, xvi. 10, Gal. i. 9, 1 Peter i. 12), and of the message (Luke viii. 1, Acts v. 42, viii. 4, 12, x. 36, xi. 20, xv. 35, Rom. x. 15 (fr. LXX.), Gal. i. 23): but where the two are combined, the person is always expressed by the dat. (Luke i. 19, ii. 10, iv. 43, Acts viii. 35, xvii. 18, 1 Cor. xv. 1, 2 Cor. xi. 7, Eph. ii. 17, 1 Thess. iii. 6), which is found also, without the acc. of the message, in Luke iv. 18 (from LXX.), Rom. i. 15, Gal. i. 8, iv. 13, and which was the classical constr. or by ἐν c. dat. (Gal. i. 16, Eph. iii. 8). The act. form εὐαγγελίζω is confined to the Apoc. (x. 7, where it has, in the true text, an acc. of the person, and xiv. 6, where it is constructed with ἐπὶ c. acc.): but the pass. use of εὐαγγελίζεσθαι implies it—the subject of the pass. verb being the person addressed in Matt. xi. 5 = Luke viii. 22, Heb. iv. 2, 6, but the message in Luke xvi. 16, Gal. i. 11, 1 Peter i. 25; while in 1 Peter iv. 6 it is impersonal. Somewhat similar is the case of μαθητεύω: the verb is quite classical, but always intr.; but in the N. T., taking a new evangelical sense, it comes to be used (even in Matt. xxvii 57, true text) transitively as a causative, or in the passive.

Διδάσκειν has usually its classical constr., with either or both of the two accusatives, of the person and of the thing. Once in the Apoc. only (ii. 14) it has the constr. which *a priori* would seem natural, with a dat. of the person. In Acts xxvii. 22 it seems hardly right to say that παραινεῖν takes an acc.—ὑμᾶς is rather subject to εὐθυμεῖν than object to παραινῶ: still no doubt in classical Greek the dat. is usual, even when an inf. follows.

Προσκυνεῖν in classical Greek is always treated as a transitive verb, and followed as such by the acc.; but in later Greek it gets the constr. c. dat. which its sense and form make *a priori* natural. In the N. T. the dat. is decidedly the commoner, though of course the reading often varies between the two. In John iv. 23 we have both constructions, with hardly any doubt as to the text, and with apparently no difference of sense: so Rev. xiii. 4,* 8. In Acts vii. 21, xiii. 22, 47 we have εἰς c. acc. where in pure Greek we should have a simple proleptic or predicative acc. The constr. is just correlative to that of εἶναι or γίνεσθαι εἰς (see p. 143), the two being actually coupled in the passage last cited: we notice that all the instances are founded on O. T. passages, if not actual quotations. Similar in principle is λογίζεσθαι εἰς in Rom. ii. 26, ix. 8: εἰς οὐθὲν λογισθῆναι in Acts xix. 27 is meant to be, and probably is, within the limits of classical usage. In Matt. xxvii. 10, ἔδωκαν εἰς must be understood as similar to βαλεῖν εἰς in ver. 6: it is impossible to get out of the prep. the sense of giving one thing

* *Probably* we have not the two cases combined in the former verse, taken alone.

for another, in the sense of exchange; but the Evangelist may have taken it of putting the money *into* the field, as we speak of investing *in* land, or sinking money in it.

There is hardly a sign in the N. T. of any tendency to disuse of the dative case: on the contrary, the simple dat. is used with more freedom and laxity, if not more frequently, than in classical Greek. Besides the Hebraistic ἀστεῖος τῷ Θεῷ of Acts vii. 20, we get it used very vaguely, where one can only gloss it "in relation to"—*e.g.* Rom. vi. 20, ἐλεύθεροι τῇ δικαιοσύνῃ, which would hardly have been intelligible but for ἐδουλώθητε τῇ δικ. in ver. 18: 2 Cor. x. 4 δυνατὰ τῷ Θεῷ (different, of course, in sense even more than in constr. from Matt. xix. 26 and parallels): James ii. 5 (true text) τοὺς πτωχοὺς τῷ κόσμῳ. Under this head fall also sentences such as Rom. vi. 10, already referred to as needing theological rather than grammatical study for their adequate exposition.

It is questionable how far the dat. acquires, in N. T. Greek, the sense of motion to a place, which it rarely has in classical, though the modern use of the prep. *to* obscures the distinction. It seems needless to avoid so understanding ἔρχομαί σοι in Rev. ii. 5, 16, for however incorrect the use may be, such an error would be more in the manner of that book than a refinement like the ethical dat. or *dativus incommodi*. And if this be taken locally, it helps us with the still harder dat. ταῖς προσευχαῖς in viii. 4; which indeed could hardly have been written, but for the ἵνα δώσει ταῖς πρ. in the preceding verse, but when coupled with that is intelligible in Hellenistic Greek as in English: "there was given him much incense, that he should put it *to* the prayers ... and the smoke of the incense went up *to* the prayers." But in Acts ii. 33, v. 31 it seems better to take τῇ δεξιᾷ as instrumental, or if it has any local sense, to render it rather "exalted *at* the right hand" than "*to*." In Acts xxi. 16, the first dat. that occurs is the quite regular one ᾧ after παρά, and the others owe their case to the attraction of this: the constr. is not ἄγοντες Μνάσωνι, whether the sense be ἄγοντες Μνάσωνα or ἄγοντες [ἡμᾶς] παρὰ Μνάσωνα. In Mark xiv. 53, if συνέρχονται αὐτῷ be right, it can be translated "the chief priests ... come [into the judgment hall] *with* him" [Caiaphas]: but if the pron. be retained, it no doubt would be more natural to understand it "come together *to* him" [*i.e.* prob. to Jesus]. The reading here however is too uncertain to prove anything: and in John xi. 33 τοὺς συνελθόντας αὐτῇ is certainly "that came *with* her"—see ver. 31.

One can hardly say whether, in Mark x. 33 (=Matt. xx. 18 *si vera l.*), κατακρινοῦσιν αὐτὸν θανάτῳ, the dat. is one of destination (and so comparable to the more or less local datives we have been considering), or is, in a wide sense, instrumental. The former view is supported, not only by the fact that modern languages have an analogous idiom, but by the v. l. εἰς θάνατον of Cod. ℵ in Matt., adopted by Tischendorf (in Mark, Cod. D has -του): the other, by ψήφῳ θανάτου κατακεκριμένον in Eur. *Andr.* 496. The phrase καταδικάζεσθαι θανάτῳ, implying a constr. of καταδικάζειν like that of κατακρίνειν here, is late but not biblical: and the supposed phrase is in fact hardly found in the act.

Still more peculiar is the dat. τοῖς δόγμασιν in Col. ii. 14. The constr. must be virtually the same as that of ἐν δόγμασιν in the parallel passage, Eph. ii. 15; and grammatically the easiest course is to take the dat., with or without ἐν, as instrumental, in connexion with καταργήσας and ἐξαλείψας respectively in the two places. But here again higher exegetical considerations come in: and the A. V. is probably substantially right.

We must notice one distinct use of the dat. of manner—when the dat. of an abstract verbal noun is used as a representative of the Hebrew "absolute infinitive," and joined with a finite part of the cognate verb, to emphasise the statement of its action. So Luke xxii. 15 ἐπιθυμίᾳ ἐπεθύμησα, John iii. 29 χαρᾷ χαίρει, Acts (iv. 17, T. R.), v. 28, xxiii. 14, James v. 17; besides Matt. xiii. 14 etc., xv. 4, which are quotations (in the latter, note that the subst. and verb are not *formally* cognate: in the LXX. of Ex. xxi. 15 θανάτῳ θανατούσθω, they are). Commoner in the LXX., but rarer in the N. T., is an equivalent use of the ptcp.: see p. 130.

The gen. in its commonest use, where it is dependent on another subst., is in the N. T. almost always put after the governing word—not before it, as generally in Latin and always (if the inflected gen. is used at all) in English. We have it much less often than in Attic placed like an attribute between the art. and the governing subst. Thus we may think that, in a sentence like Matt. ix. 14=Mark ii. 18=Luke v. 33, a classical writer would have preferred οἱ [τοῦ] Ἰωάνου μαθηταί: certainly it would not be safe to say of such a writer, as we may of St. Paul, that ἀπὸ $\overline{\text{KY}}$ $\overline{\text{ΠNC}}$ in 2 Cor. iii. 18 *cannot* mean "from the Spirit of the Lord." Or to take a less imaginary case: where St. Luke is writing Hellenistically (Ev. i. 10) he has πᾶν τὸ πλῆθος ἦν τοῦ λαοῦ (T. R. τοῦ λαοῦ ἦν): so ii. 13, v. 6, vi. 17, viii. 37, xix. 37, xxiii. 27, Acts iv. 32, v. 14, 16, vi 2. But when we come to more Hellenic passages, we have Ἑλλήνων πολὺ πλῆθος in xiv. 1, xvii. 4—cf. xxviii. 3; yet the other order as often—xiv. 4, xxi. 36, xxv. 24.* The fact is, for the governed word to precede the governing is the common order in Greek, but is liable to be modified by the use of the art. and other considerations: while in the Hebrew (what we should consider) the governing word always stands first.

Of other irregularities in the use of this case, the chief is the very wide extension of the independent use of what may be called a partitive gen., or a gen. with or without a prep., depending on τινές or some case of it, which is not expressed. We get such a gen. standing as subject to a verb often—Acts xxi. 16, etc., and for this there is classical precedent, though not with such frequency: but hardly for its carrying a ptcp. as well as a verb, as it does in John vii. 40, where it is subject, and in 2 John 4, where it is object.

An irregularity in that of the gen. abs. has already been noted (p. 57-8). Of other uses of the gen. the most distinctively Hellenistic is the quasi-adjectival gen. of quality. Unmistakable instances of this are found in Luke xvi. 8, 9, xviii. 6, Rev. xiii. 3, and probably James i. 25: nor need we refuse to see the influence of this Hebraistic idiom in theological phrases, such

---

* Where two genitives depend, not one upon another, but in different relations on the same word, one is put before and the other after it. So (Acts v. 32, T. R.,) 2 Cor. v. 1, Phil. ii. 30, 1 Thess. i. 3. This principle perhaps explains what seems the strangeness of order in Rev. vii. 17, ζωῆς πηγὰς ὑδάτων.

as ἀνάστασις ζωῆς, κρίσεως, John v. 29, δικαίωσις ζωῆς, Rom. v. 18, σῶμα τῆς ἁμαρτίας, ib. vi. 6, and even ἐκ τοῦ σώματος τοῦ θανάτου τούτου, ib. vii. 24, though τούτου is probably rather to be taken with θανάτου than σώματος. But in these last passages, though the gen. is one of quality, it would be wrong or impossible to translate it by an adj.: and still more in such places as Col. i. 13, 1 Thess. i. 3, 2 Thess. i. 7, Heb. i. 3, 2 Peter ii. 10—in the last, indeed, μιασμοῦ seems to depend quite regularly on ἐπιθυμίᾳ. Not always clearly distinguishable from this is the use of the gen. for epexegesis— sometimes called the gen. of apposition: of which we have instances in Rom. iv. 11 (best text, but we have apposition as a v. l.), 1 Cor. v. 5: so no doubt John ii. 21, though here as the governing word is also a gen., it is just possible to take it as in apposition. This is hardly to be treated as a Hebraism, but it is carried further in Hellenistic than in pure Greek: there it would hardly go beyond cases like 2 Peter ii. 6. Its relation to the gen. of quality may be illustrated by Luke xxii. 1, where we cannot say that the meaning is not "the feast *characterised by* unleavened bread": but that the classical constr. by apposition (which we get in John vii. 2) did pass in Hellenistic Greek into phrases like this is shown in 2 Macc. vi. 7, τῆς Διονυσίων ἑορτῆς, where the art. and the order exclude apposition. But this constr. also is sometimes pressed beyond its legitimate limits. Here we have points where the instinct of the cultivated man will be sounder than that of the mere "scholar." Biblical Greek, like biblical and even modern English, has been brought under Hebraising influence through translations of the O. T.: but as a rule each language has only assimilated as much Hebraism as was in harmony with its own nature: it is only in such writings as the Apocalypse, and parts of St. Luke's Gospel, that we get anything more. In 1 Cor. xiv. 33, Heb. x. 39, we get what may be called genitives of quality, but these would be quite intelligible—would even appear idiomatic—to a reader accustomed to classical Greek. But in 1 Thess. v. 5 we get genitives just like these coupled with the utterly Hebraistic τέκνα φωτός, τέκνα ἡμέρας—illustrating how easily the passage from the Hebraising use of the gen. to the Hellenic is effected.

As we have already noted of the dat., so the gen. is used very freely to express a wide range of relations, wider perhaps than would be the case in classical Greek, and certainly hard to bring within definite grammatical formulæ. The gen. is, in fact, the case by which the most general relation can be expressed between one noun and another, as the dat. expresses the most general relation between a noun and the action of a verb: and we meet with the gen., as with the dat., in many sentences where the force of the constr. is important, but must be learnt not from considerations of pure grammar, but of wider and higher exegesis. *E.g.* it is easy to say that in John v. 42 τοῦ Θεοῦ is an objective gen., in Rom. viii. 39 a subjective; while in Rom. v. 5 we may ask which it is of the two, and give a definite answer one way or other. But it is less easy to put a grammatical ticket on such a phrase as ἔχετε πίστιν Θεοῦ in Mark xi. 22, or ἐν πίστει . . . . τῇ τοῦ Υἱοῦ τοῦ Θεοῦ, or whatever be the true reading in Gal. ii. 20. Similarly phrases like δικαιοσύνη Θεοῦ (Rom. i. 17, etc.), δικ. πίστεως (iv. 13, etc.), ὑπακοὴν πίστεως (i. 5), πίστις ἀληθείας (2 Thess. ii.

13), ἡ εἰρήνη τοῦ Θεοῦ (Phil. iv. 7, cf. Col. iii. 15, where however the true reading is τοῦ Χριστοῦ), have meanings to be settled by the study of things not of words: grammatically, we can only group them with such genitives of vague relation as we have in Matt. i. 11, 12, x. 5, Luke vi. 12 (where the relation, though sacred, is definite and obvious), Rom. xv. 8 (τῶν πατέρων), etc.

Perhaps of usages that come under strictly grammatical rule, but as to which the rules are not quite the same as in classical Greek, the most important is that with verbs of feeling or consciousness. Speaking generally, the tendency is to assimilate the constr. of these to that of ordinary trans. verbs, and so to restrict the use of the gen.: on the other hand, there are words of sense more or less akin to these, where something of a partitive sense comes in, so that the gen. is used freely. Αἰσθάνεσθαι occurs only once in the N. T. (Luke ix. 45), and then c. acc. Γεύεσθαι in Heb. vi. 4, 5 has the gen. where it is merely a verb of sense, the acc. where it is used of the recognition of a fact—καλόν being (as its position shows) a predicate, Ἀκούειν (disregarding cases where it is used absol., or introducing an *oratio obliqua*, a περί c. gen., or the like) has regularly a gen. of the speaker or an acc. of the thing heard. The two are rarely combined—Acts i. 4 is the only unquestionable case: in Matt. vii. 24, 26 μου may be regarded as merely possessive, as σου in Philem. 5 must be. More commonly, when it is desired to express both *what* is heard and *from whom*, the latter is expressed by a prep., usually παρά (John viii. 38, 40, Acts x. 22, xxviii. 22, 2 Tim. i. 13, ii. 2; cf. also John i. 40, vi. 45, vii. 51, where the acc. is absent —in 2 Tim. i. 13 it is attracted), but sometimes

ἀπό (1 John i. 5; also without an acc., Acts ix. 13).
All this agrees well enough with classical usage,
though the simple gen. is relatively rarer, in comparison with the use of a prep., or of a ptcp. such as
λέγοντος or the like, making an approximation to a
gen. abs.: in St. Mark alone the gen. of the person is
commoner than the acc. of the thing. But we also
get the gen. of the thing, less frequently but not very
rarely. In Mark xiv. 64 τῆς βλασφημίας is overwhelmingly attested, unlikely as it is *a priori* that we
should have not only a meaningless variation from the
parallel Matt. xxvi. 65 (where there is hardly any
authority for the gen.), but a constr. unique in these
two Gospels. We have the *gen. rei*, however, in Luke
vi. 47, xv. 25, xviii. 36 (yet this passage, and perhaps
the preceding, compared with John vii. 32, shows that
the line between person and thing is not always clear),
John vii. 40, xix. 13 (true text), and perhaps a double
gen. in John xii. 47, Acts xxii. 1 (as in Matt. vii. 24, 26,
noted above, it is possible to regard μου as possessive,
but the order gives more reason for taking it with the
verb: see pp. 55-6). Acts vii. 34, Heb. iii. 7, 15,
iv. 7, are hardly N. T. instances: the thrice repeated
passage in Heb. is *verbatim* from the LXX.: the
passage in Acts is not, but perhaps is influenced by a
reminiscence of the LXX. style, in which this constr.
is certainly commoner than in the N. T. Rom. x. 14,
Col. i. 23, are still less clear cases: the gen. in the
latter is almost certainly determined by attraction
(cf. Eph. i. 13), and in the former it almost seems as
though the sense required περὶ οὗ, and the simple gen.
were a condensed or as it were attracted expression of
this. Eph. iv. 21, if regarded as an acc. of the person,

is unique: but the context shows that αὐτόν is regarded as the lesson rather than the Teacher.

But we have postponed hitherto the consideration of one rather Hebraistic phrase, which in sense is in a way intermediate between the cases where the object is a person and a thing—viz. "hearing a voice." We observe that the phrase is almost confined to three books—the Acts, and St. John's Gospel and Apocalypse —with three or four exceptions, mostly quotations from the O. T. Of these isolated cases, Matt. xii. 19 (a quotation, but not from the LXX.) has the acc.: so has 2 Peter i. 18. Heb. iii. 7, 15, iv. 7, as already noted, is from the LXX., and has the gen.: so has xii. 19, where however the gen. is not φωνῆς but a rel. referring to it, and this may possibly not depend on ἀκούσαντες only, but have its case determined by indirect influence from λόγον and even παρῃτήσαντο.

In the books that use the phrase freely, we have the gen. in Acts ix. 7, xi. 7, xxii. 7, John v. 25, 28, x. 3, 16, 27, xviii. 37 (possibly, like xii. 47, a double gen.), Rev. iii. 20, xiv. 13, xvi. 1, xxi. 3; and the acc. in Acts ix. 4, xxii. 9, 14, xxvi. 14, John iii. 8, v. 37, Rev. i. 10, v. 11, vi. 6, 7 (best text), ix. 13, x. 4, xii. 10, xiv. 2, xviii. 4, xix. 1, 6, xxii. 8, 18, and indirectly in iv. 1, xi. 12, and a second time in xiv. 2. In xi. 12 the authorities for the gen. and acc. are nearly evenly balanced.

In view of this evidence, is it possible to draw any distinction of sense between ἀκούειν φωνῆς and φωνήν? So far as there is any distinction between the two constructions with verbs of sense generally, it seems to be that the gen. represents the matter as one affecting the subjective consciousness, and the acc. as a discovery of external fact—compare Soph. *El.* 79 with Id. *Phil.* 445. But the distinction is hardly consistently maintained, even in pure Attic Greek: in the N. T. the two cases seem to be used indifferently as regards the sense. In the special instance before referred to of Acts ix. 7 and xxii. 9, it would be meaningless to say that Saul's companions "were conscious of the voice speaking"—still more, that they "hearkened to the voice"—but that they "did not hear that there was a voice": if we had had the cases reversed in the two passages, it would be possible, though even then far-fetched, to say that they "heard that a voice spake," but did not "hearken to it" in the sense that Saul did.

We have examined this constr. at perhaps disproportionate length, as a sample of the way that evidence of usage can be accumulated, and its value for exegetical purposes estimated. The student may examine for himself how far usage is similar with the rarer compounds εἰσ-, ἐπ-, and παρακούειν, and how it differs more extensively with ὑπακ. Equally impossible does it appear, to trace a distinction in sense between μνημονεύειν c. gen. and c. acc.: see esp. 1 Thess. i. 3, ii. 9. That ἐπιλανθάνεσθαι has a gen. in Heb. vi. 10, xiii. 2, 16, but an acc. in Phil. iii. 13, is less of a mere accident—not that the sense is different, but that the more cultivated writer uses the constr. commoner in literary Greek: such verbs *generally* take the gen. in classical writers, though the acc. is found even in good Attic. Ἀναμιμνήσκεσθαι has always the acc. in the N. T. (even in Mark xiv. 72, true text).

Similar in principle to these verbs of consciousness is the use of ἐνπνέων c. gen. in Acts. ix. 1—though metaphorical, the constr. is the same as that of ὄζειν. Of

CASES USED WITH VERBS OF TOUCH. 91

words of touching or grasping, where the gen. may be regarded as either an object of sense or as partitive, the constr. generally but not always coincides with the classical use. Ἅπτεσθαι has always the gen.—sometimes a double gen., though, as in similar cases already noted, the gen. of the person may be conceived as possessive: so ἔχεσθαι and ἀντέχεσθαι: ἀνέχεσθαι too gets this constr., as it began to do in late Attic. Λαμβάνεσθαι is never used, but ἀντιλαμβ. has, as always, a gen., so ἐπιλ. generally, but comparing Acts xvi. 19, xviii. 17 with xvii. 19, xxi. 30, 33, it appears that St. Luke sometimes allowed himself to use it in the acc., in places where κρατεῖν would be so used. In Matt. v. 28 ἐπιθυμεῖν probably has an acc. : this is said to be found as early as Menander. In Matt. v. 6, also, a gen. of the thing hungered and thirsted for would have been more classical. Μέλειν (τινί) has its classical constr. with the simple gen. only in 1 Cor. ix. 9—elsewhere it has περί c. gen.

(b) *Adjectives.*

As a rule, there is no difference between the N. T. constr. of adjectives and that of earlier Greek, in such respects as their concord with substantives, their use absolutely or as predicates, and the like. Perhaps the absolute or substantival use of neut. adjectives with the art., both sing. and pl., is commoner than in earlier Greek : so (as already mentioned, p. 45), is the position of the adj. after its subst., the art. being used with both : at least this order seems to imply a less degree of emphasis on the adj. : see *e.g.* Rev. xii. 14, and the solecistic xiv. 19. But except in the Apocalypse, the difference is hardly appreciable : it is at most one of degree.

It is otherwise, when we compare the N. T. use with the classical of the degrees of comparison. Here we seem to find N. T. Greek suffering from both its common sources of corruption, the internal decay of Greek grammatical usage, and the influence of Semitic languages which, in this as in other respects, were less highly organised than the Greek. The piling up of emphasis, till expressions originally emphatic become commonplace, shows itself in the more frequent use of comparatives and superlatives "of eminence": and partly perhaps from this cause, more certainly from the native tendency of the later language to become "analytical," and multiply little words—partly also from the fact that this tendency would be encouraged by assimilation to Hebrew idiom—we get the pos., comp., and sup. degrees each used in places where one of the others would seem more appropriate.

The pos., indeed, is never used absolutely in a comp. sense. In Matt. xviii. 8, 9, καλόν σοί ἐστιν (or in the parallel Mark ix. 43-5 καλόν ἐστίν σε) is not exactly equivalent to κάλλιόν σοί ἐστιν: rather, there is an omission of μᾶλλον before the ἤ, so that the case is like the third parallel, Luke xvii. 2, λυσιτελεῖ . . . ἤ: cf. xv. 7, χαρὰ ἔσται . . . ἤ, also xviii. 14, if ἢ ἐκεῖνος or ἢ γὰρ ἐκεῖνος be read. In all these phrases, ἤ is treated as of itself expressing a comparison—an extension of such idioms as θέλω . . . ἤ, which we get in 1 Cor. xiv. 19. Within limits, this use is quite classical (*e.g.* even *Il.* i. 117): and perhaps the extension of it is rather characteristic of colloquial than of late Greek: at least the extreme instance of it, καλόν ἐστιν . . . ἤ has a parallel to it quoted from Menander.

But the use of παρά and ὑπέρ after adjectives to

express comparison is more certainly a symptom of decay. In some sentences, of course, the use of these prepositions in comparisons is legitimate. In a verbal phrase like κατέβη οὗτος δεδικαιωμένος ... παρ' ἐκεῖνον (Luke xviii. 14, best text) we have a genuine Greek idiom, or at most an extension of one: and similarly ἁμαρτωλοί or ὀφειλέται ἐγένοντο παρὰ πάντας (xiii. 2, 4) would be defensible. But in xvi. 8 (φρονιμώτεροι ὑπέρ), Heb. iv. 12 (τομώτερος ὑπέρ), or Heb. xi. 4, xii. 24 (πλείονα, κρεῖττον ... παρά) it is plain that we have gone beyond the precedents of a few classical passages, where παρά is used pleonastically with a word like ἄμεινον, μείζων, or μᾶλλον. It may not be easy to say exactly where the bounds of pure Greek were passed: Heb. ii. 7 (from LXX.), iii. 3 are intermediate cases: but already we are on the road to the usage of modern Greek, in which παρά is the ordinary word for "than" after a comp., and even loses its constr. as a prep., being followed by the nom.

The extension of this use of the prep. in later usage almost amounts to a proof that it was the result of a tendency native to the Greek language itself. But that it showed itself earlier in biblical than in other Greek (both παρά and ὑπέρ are often used in the LXX.) may be partly due to the fact that in Hebrew there are no degrees of comparison, and that the sense of them has to be expressed by the help of prepositions. Certainly we find a vagueness in the use of the degrees in certain passages of the Gospels, which seems to have a Hebraistic origin. It is paradoxical to deny that the pos. μεγάλη* in Matt. xxii. 36, the comp. μικρότερος

* We may notice in passing the anomalous ἐντολὴ πρώτη πάντων of the parallel, Mark xii. 28 (true text).

in Matt. xi. 11=Luke vii. 28, μείζων in Matt. xviii. 1 (hardly in 1 Cor. xiii. 13) are practically equivalent to superlatives; even in Mark ix. 34, Luke xxii. 24 the distinction of comp. and sup. is not kept clear. In John i. 15, 30, and perhaps even xv. 18, there may well be a reason why πρῶτος is used rather than πρότερος. St. John wants to express an absolute First, not a mere priority in degree; and there are signs that in the Gospel, as still more in the Apocalypse, he does not mind straining the rules of language, if it fails to suggest such thoughts as this without straining.

The use of the comp. where there is no comparison, as a sort of milder sup. of eminence, is of course a genuine Greek idiom: any one might have written the καινότερον or δεισιδαιμονεστέρους (whatever be the exact shade of meaning of the latter) which we get in Acts xvii. 21, 22. Yet we may doubt whether a purer classical writer would have used the two in adjacent sentences: and when we come to τάχιον in John xiii. 27, 1 Tim. iii. 14 (*si vera l.*), or κάλλιον in Acts xxv. 10, βέλτιον 2 Tim. i. 18, it seems as though the comp. were losing its distinctive force.

CHAPTER V.

CHARACTERISTICS OF N. T. GREEK IN THE SYNTACTICAL USE OF VERBS AND PARTICIPLES.

(a) Of the Voices.

THE idiomatic use of the middle voice—esp. the transitive use, where the active might for the most part have stood, but the middle introduces a modification of the sense—is one of the refinements in Greek idiom, which is perhaps beginning to be blurred in some of the N. T. writers, but is preserved to a greater or less extent in most. Thus αἰτεῖν and αἰτεῖσθαι are used quite interchangeably in James iv. 2, 3, 1 John v. 14, 15, 16. But in Mark vi. 23-5, though there is no difference of sense, the difference of voice corresponds to that of constr. with the single or double acc.: so x. 35 (true text), 38; while in the parallel passage, Matt. xx. 20, 22, it seems to correspond with a difference of sense—the mother asks for her sons, but the family for itself as a whole. In the use of ὑστερεῖν, -εῖσθαι, there seems to be no correspondence between the variations of voice and those either of sense or of constr.: the act. in Heb. iv. 1, xii. 15 means exactly the same as the mid. in Rom. iii. 23, and in 2 Cor. xi. 5, xii. 11 it has the same general sense, and exactly the same constr. The most of a distinction traceable is, that where the sense is "wanting" a possession, not "coming short of" a standard, the act. is used c. gen., the mid. absolutely.

So far as the use of the middle shows signs of decay, it is that it is simply disused, not that it is used incorrectly. Πληρουμένου in Eph. i. 23 is perhaps the only case where the sense seems to be merely the same as the act. (the Attic usage of the middle for "manning" a ship is no real parallel). But εὑρίσκεσθαι "to get" as distinct from εὑρίσκειν "to find" has all but disappeared, though, if the verb is to stand in Rom. iv. 1 at all, the middle would be just in place: in fact, we find it in Heb. ix. 12 only. The act. is common throughout the N. T., whether in its plain and classical sense, as Matt. ii. 8, or in Hebraistic phrases like Luke i. 30.

More interesting are such points as these. St. Paul (the rule would also hold good of James v. 16, but not of Matt. xiv. 2=Mark vi. 14) uses ἐνεργεῖν with a personal subj. (1 Cor. xii. 6, 11,* Gal. ii. 8 *bis*, iii. 5, Eph. i. 11, 20, ii. 2,* Phil. ii, 13), ἐνεργεῖσθαι with an impersonal (Rom. vii. 5, 2 Cor. i. 6, iv. 12, Gal. v. 6, Eph. iii. 20, Col. i. 29, 1 Thess. ii. 13,† 2 Thess. ii. 7). Again, "to be baptized" is naturally expressed as a rule as a pass.: of course it is only in the fut. or aor. that this is distinct in form from the mid., but in those tenses as in others it is the rule. We have however the mid. in Acts xxii. 16, and perhaps (authorities are very evenly balanced) in 1 Cor. x. 2. In view of 1 Cor. i. 14 *sqq.*, we cannot say that the person

* We note that πνεῦμα, good or evil, ranks as a personal agent.
† Here however we *might* take Θεοῦ, not λόγον, as antecedent to ὅς.

of the baptizer was, in the apostolic Church, a question of no importance, or that the *ego te baptizo* of Western ecclesiastical usage implies a change from the apostolic point of view: but we do see that the convert in "getting baptized" was conceived as doing something, not merely having something done to or for him.

(*b*) *The N. T. Use of the Tenses of the Indicative.*

The Greek verb possesses, in its large variety of inflected forms, a very full apparatus for the expression of all time relations; and most of the languages of modern Europe are able to express the same relations, by means either of such inflexions as survive in them, or of auxiliary verbs. In the N. T., the modern student finds that hardly any of the classical Greek inflexions of the verb have fallen out of use, and that as a rule each of them retains the force that it had in classical Greek. Yet it would be over hasty for him to assume without enquiry, that the writers of the N. T. regarded the temporal conditions of action from exactly the same point of view as classical Greek writers: we have to ask, How far does the Greek of the N. T. preserve unimpaired the classical use of the various tenses? is there a tendency either to confound some of them among themselves, or to limit or extend the use of some, according to Hebraic analogies?

Perhaps the latter influence is traceable to some extent, but if so it is only within narrow limits. The Semitic tense system (if indeed the word Tense be properly applicable to it) was so utterly different from the Greek that assimilation of one to the other was impossible, unless by downright solecism. One solecism probably traceable to this source we have in Rev. x. 7, where καὶ ἐτελέσθη seems to mean practically τελεσθήσεται, like a so-called "preterite with ו conversive" in Hebrew. It is indeed said that, except that the apodosis is introduced by καί, we have here only a parallel to John xv. 6, 1 Cor. vii. 28, where an aor. stands in the apodosis to a conditional sentence as here to a temporal: but this seems to be a stronger case of non-Hellenic constr. Perhaps also the transition from futures through presents to preterites in Rev. xi. 7-11 (cf. xx. 7-9), may be partly ascribed to Hebraic habits of expression, though the psychological condition of a "seer of visions" is probably explanation enough.

Nowhere however in the N. T. outside the Apocalypse do we get any confusion about the straightforward use of the Greek tenses to indicate past, present, and future time. If there be any change in their use due to foreign influence, it is confined to a certain slight extension of the use of the pres., the tense which may be considered the most general, and most capable of having its use extended without violence to the language. The historical pres. is very much commoner in the N. T. than in ordinary Greek; and though this is in no sense a Hebraism, it does appear to be a Hellenistic peculiarity. In the LXX. it has been observed that, while historical presents as a rule are rare, they are very common in the case of two verbs—λέγει and ὁρᾷ. In the N. T. ὁρᾶν is not a very common word—βλέπειν is much oftener used, and θεᾶσθαι and θεωρεῖν each nearly as often; as a hist. pres. ὁρᾷ occurs only in Luke xvi. 23. But λέγει is very common in all the historical books, except St. Luke,—most so in St. John, who has λέγει some 113 times, and λέγουσιν 7. In Matt. they occur 49 and 16 times respectively, in Mark 54 and 12, in Luke *never* in the narrative of the Gospel, and only twice (xvi. 29, xix. 22) in parables, once (xxi. 37) in Acts. Now the difference of proportion between the sing. and pl. is prob. only an accident, the sing. being more common—εἶπεν, which is practically the preterite of λέγει,* occurs in St Matthew about 119 times, εἶπαν or -πον 21. But that the pres. of this verb is more frequently used than that of others can be roughly shown by this calculation. The passages from the Gospels containing εἰπεῖν and λέγειν occupy 36 columns in Bruder's Concordance, those containing ἔρχεσθαι and ἐλθεῖν about 9½. Now ἔρχεται and ἔρχονται are used as historical presents only 4 times in St. Matthew, 23 times in St. Mark, only once (viii. 49) in St. Luke, 15 times in St. John. We may say then that the idiom is (1) specially common with the particular verb λέγειν,† (2) specially common with other verbs in the crudest and least literary of the N. T. writings.

More interesting and suggestive are the cases where the sense of the pres. tense seems to shade off into that of the fut. This sometimes arises, in part at least, from the nature of the verb's meaning: as in

---

* In the rather numerous cases where one is a v. l. for the other, the one for which MS. evidence decidedly preponderates is counted: if there be fair room for doubt, it is reckoned to neither side.

† One may compare the use of φησίν in classical Greek: also *inquam* and "quoth he," though defective, may be called presents.

classical Greek the pres. εἰμι "I am going" is said to have a fut. sense, so in the N. T. ἔρχομαι may be said to have one, with perhaps better right. Not only does the ptcp. ἐρχόμενος practically mean "future" in such phrases as ὁ Ἐρχόμενος of the Messiah, still more ἐν τῷ αἰῶνι τῷ ἐρχομένῳ, and ὁ Ὤν καὶ ὁ Ἦν καὶ ὁ Ἐρχόμενος of the Eternal: the indic. has more or less of a future sense in Matt. xvii. 11,* xxiv. 42-3-4 (xxv. 6, T.R.), Mark i. 7, xiii. 35, Luke xii. 39, 40, 54, xvii. 20 *bis*, xxiii. 29, John i. 30, iv. 21, 23, 25, 35, v. 24, 25, 28, vii. 41-2, ix. 4, xi. 20, xii. 15 (fr. O. T.), xiv. 3,* 18,* 28,† 30, xvi. 2, 25, 32, xvii. 11, 13, xxi. 3,† Acts xiii. 25,‡ 1 Cor. xv. 35, 2 Cor. xiii. 1, Eph. v. 6, Col. iii. 6, 1 Thess. v. 2, Heb. viii. 8 (fr. LXX.), 1 John ii. 18, iv. 3, Rev. i. 7,* ii. 5,* 16,* iii. 11, ix. 12, xi. 14, xvi. 15, xxii. 7, 12, 20; in by no means all of which is a supernatural visitation spoken of: in several (*e.g.* John xxi. 3) the sense is merely "(some one or some event) is coming."§

Yet even in some of these passages, *e.g.* Luke xxiii. 29, John xvi. 32, the pres. seems to have a deeper significance than this—one that can be traced where the pres. of other verbs, less akin in meaning

* In these passages the word is actually co-ordinated with futures.
† Here, and in John vii. 33, viii. 21-2, xiii. 3, 33, 36, xiv. 4-5, xvi. 5, 10, 17 ὑπάγω is used as exactly correlative to ἔρχομαι: cf. also iii. 8, viii. 14. In the other three Gospels, ὑπάγειν is rare except in the imperative.
‡ This passage, and others parallel with some previously cited, are not grouped with them as forming only one instance: because it is characteristic, if one reproducer of a saying avoids an idiom which another retains.
§ Cf. 1 Cor. xvi. 5, Μακεδονίαν γὰρ διέρχομαι: which has been misunderstood (in the subscription to the Ep.) "*I am passing through* M.," while it really means "I do pass through M.," that is the way I am going.

to futurity, is used in a sense that may be called not only prophetical, but strictly predictive. In Matt. xxvi. 2, γίνεται is parallel to ἔρχεται in its most secular sense, "The Passover is coming on:" but παραδίδοται surely means, like ὑπάγει in ver. 24, that His delivery and departure were part of the eternal counsel, and while yet future were as sure as if actual. So Matt. ii. 4, and John vii. 52 probably.

Any deviation from classical usage, then, that there may be in the use of the pres. tense is traceable, partly perhaps to the merely linguistic influence of Hebraised Greek, but more unquestionably, and perhaps more largely, to the special requirements of the Scriptural order of thought. So far, there are no traces of mere linguistic decay, of loss of accuracy in the use of Greek grammatical forms. It is hard, however, to be equally confident that the same may be said of the use of the different past tenses. But we must keep the question separate, "Are the uses of the perf. and the aor. confounded in N. T. Greek?" from the question, which it is much easier and safer to answer with a decided affirmative, "Is not the aor. often used in N. T. Greek, where in English we should use the compound perf.? and conversely the perf. (sometimes though more rarely) where we should use the simple preterite?" Even in languages so similar in their syntax as English and French, the occasions where we should say " he did it " or " he has done it " are not respectively identical with those where one would say " *il le fit* " * or " *il l'a fait*,"—still less does " he was doing it " coincide exactly with

---

* Not to mention that this tense is tending to drop out of use in elegant and modern French.

"*il le faisait.*" Much less then can we expect the use of the two Greek inflected tenses to be so absolutely identical with those of our inflected and compound ones, as to be mechanically interchangeable with them.

Before approaching this question, however, it may be as well to state the case of the other past tenses, the impf. and plupf. With neither of these, on the whole, is there any real deviation from classical usage. The first is used oftener, the second less often, than its distinctive meaning can be traced, or than the corresponding English tense would be used in translation: but the same is equally the case in the purest Greek, and the fact is due, partly to the smallness of the distinction, and partly perhaps to euphony. The plupf. was always a rare form, perhaps because (see p. 33) it was a cacophonous form, and so the aor. is often used where the plupf. would suit the sense: on the other hand, the impf. is often used where the aor. might have been, because the sense it is desired to give is that of a simple preterite, and neither impf. nor aor. is this and nothing more, for while the one represents the action as continuous or habitual, the other represents it as individual or instantaneous. Esp. it has been noticed that ἐκέλευεν is used where we should have expected ἐκέλευσεν: and perhaps the same will be found to hold good with vowel verbs as a class—that their impf. is often used in what we may call the sense, not of an aor. but of a simple pret. It may be a converse process that leads to the use of the impf. ἀνῆκεν, καθῆκεν in apparently a pres. sense in Acts xxii. 22, Eph. v. 4 (true text), Col. iii. 18: the word *looks* like an aor. or perf.

But perhaps we may rather illustrate by the English use of "ought" (strictly the preterite of "owe": "shall" and "should" have a similar etymology). As this sense of the verb is late, we have no direct illustration from classical usage.

Coming now to the comparison of the perf. and aor., there is no question at all that each is often correctly used in its distinctive sense: sometimes indeed they occur side by side, and are correctly distinguished. Thus in the LXX. of Isa. lxi. 1, quoted in Luke iv. 18, ἔχρισέν με is "He anointed Me"—He did it once;—but ἀπέσταλκέν με "He *hath* sent Me"—and here I am now. Or in Luke xiii. 2, ἁμαρτωλοὶ .... ἐγένοντο, ὅτι ταῦτα πεπόνθασιν;* may be translated either "*Did it make* these Galileans sinners...., that they *have* [now] suffered these things?" or "*Were* these Galileans [at the time of their life's end] sinners? are you entitled to say so on the evidence of the fact that they *have* so suffered?"—the former being the stricter and more logical interpretation, the latter the simpler and more natural, though involving some extension of the force of ὅτι.

Even in passages where the aor. might easily have been substituted for the perf. or conversely, this does not prove that the tense actually used has not its proper force. In 1 Cor. xv. 4, it would have been more natural to write ἠγέρθη, like ἀπέθανεν and ἐτάφη before, and ὤφθη afterwards: but the very fact that

* Though it is a matter of exegesis, not of grammar, I cannot pass this verse without a protest against a popular optimist misapplication of it. The argument is not. "They suffered, but that does not prove that they sinned:" it is, "They suffered for their sins, but they were no worse sinners than you:" "except ye repent, ye shall all likewise perish."

St. Paul has not done what was most natural, shows that he intends to couple things that happened once for all and are over, and the thing that *has* happened, and its result is eternally present: the contrast is stated more emphatically in the ἐγενόμην and εἰμί of Rev. i. 18. (In Rom. xiv. 9, where there are aorists only, the point of view is somewhat different.)

In Mark xv. 44, there is hardly a difference of sense, but an intelligible difference of treatment of the same sense. Pilate may have said to St. Joseph Μὴ ἤδη τέθνηκεν; and to the centurion, Ἄρα πάλαι τέθνηκεν; but the second is, and the first is not, thrown into the past tense, because the second is more obviously a case of *oratio obliqua*: thus ἀπέθανεν is more nearly equivalent to a plupf. than a perf. In 2 Cor. xi. 25, the perf. in the midst of aorists goes quite naturally into English. Ibid. xii. 9 (to come to instances where the perf. stands alone, and it is not its association with aorists, but the *prima facie* sense, that makes us doubt if it retains its proper force), εἶπεν would be merely, "He said," and would leave room for a reply of the Apostle's: while εἴρηκεν intimates, "I have had my answer, and the matter is at an end." Even in i. 9 we can feel what is the effect of the perf. ἐσχήκαμεν, though it may be harder to express its force in an English gloss. On the other hand, ibid. ii. 13, the force of the perf. is surely evanescent, if not quite vanished. And no one but a doctrinaire special pleader is likely to deny that in Rev. v. 7, viii. 5 εἴληφεν, and in vii. 14 εἴρηκα, are mere preterites in sense: it is hard to see what else the perfects can be in Heb. xi. 17, 28,[*] James i. 24.

[*] Cf. the use of κεκάθαρκε, Jos. *Ant.* III. viii. 3.

If the three instances from the Apoc. stood alone, we might say that an incorrect use by this one writer proved nothing as to N. T. usage generally, esp. when it is found only in verbs of exceptional form : * but can we say the same, when we find the usage paralleled in Heb. and St. James, whose grammatical knowledge and power of language are above, not below, the level of the rest?

And it seems uncalled for to deny, that the aor. is used where the perf. would express the sense more accurately, somewhat more frequently than *vice versa:* though far less often than where the auxiliary "have" would be a more idiomatic translation of the aor. than the simple preterite. If in Isa. lxi. 1 (already quoted from Luke iv. 18) the perf. ἀπέσταλκεν is in place, what difference of sense is there in xlviii. 16, where we have ἀπέστειλεν? In Rom. xiii. 12, what distinction of sense can there be between προέκοψεν and ἤγγικεν? or in Phil. iii. 12 between ἔλαβον and τετελείωμαι? In the latter passage, the equivalence of the tenses (and here there is no doubt that the perf. at least has its proper force) is brought out by the use of κατειληφέναι, coupled with the aor. κατελήμφθην,—the perf. form being in the pass. rarer and perhaps more cumbrous. Or to take instances from one Ep. only, are not the aorists equivalent to perfects in Rom. iii. 23, 27 (ἥμαρτον, ἐξεκλείσθη), viii. 15 (ἐλάβετε *bis*), xi. 1, 4, 7 (ἀπώσατο, κατέλιπον, ἐπέτυχεν)? In iii. 23, viii. 15 they are coupled with

* The form also may help to explain the use of the perf. ἑώρακαν in Luke ix. 36. There the sense is plainly plupf. but no one would be surprised at an aor. being used: and ἑώρακαν *looks* like an aor., though really a (late) form of the perf.

presents: in xi. 1, 4 we notice that the tense is St. Paul's own choice, for in both places the parallel passages of the LXX. have the fut. But perhaps as convincing an instance as any in the N. T. is John xi. 14, where Λάζαρος ἀπέθανεν can only mean "Lazarus is dead."

On the whole then it seems necessary to admit that the distinction between aor. and perf. is beginning to be obliterated in the N. T., whether we ascribe the fact to spontaneous loss of accuracy among Greek speaking people, or to the influence of languages, Semitic and perhaps Latin, that had not this distinction of tense. But the obliteration has not proceeded very far—hardly beyond the avoiding of the use of either tense when the form of it, in a particular verb, was rare, doubtful, or cacophonous.* The student ought, in every case, to *look for* a reason for one tense being used rather than the other: though he must not expect always to find one, still less, even when he does, to be able to represent the point in idiomatic translation.

(c) *The Subjunctive and Optative Moods, and the Indicative in Relative Sentences.*

We have nothing more to say of the expression, in the N. T., of merely temporal relations. Any irregularities that there are in the use of the fut. are not in its use as a real direct indic. tense, but in its relation to other moods and types of sentence: so also of the hypothetical and kindred uses of past tenses. In other moods than the indic., the distinc-

* In Heb. xi. 17, it is likely enough that προσενήνοχεν was used as more sonorous than προσήνεγκεν.

tion between the pres. and aor. is not so much that between present and past time, as between continued and instantaneous action : and for this purpose the tenses appear to be used quite regularly, on exactly the same principles as in classical Greek.

The independent uses, moreover, of the different moods are equally correct. We get the deliberative or cohortative subj. rather often, the opt. in the strictly *optative* sense not seldom. It is otherwise, when we come to the use of the moods in subordinate sentences with various relations to the principal one : here we find some vagueness of constr. and relaxation of rule, and still more change in the proportionate frequency of modes of expression, compared with classical Greek.

The most important of these changes is, that the opt. mood is rapidly tending to become obsolete, as it has become in the modern language. Its most frequent use in ordinary literary Greek—that in final sentences dependent on a past tense—is completely obsolete : the subj. being used, probably, in all such cases. The only ones where it can be argued that the opt. is retained are in certain cases where verbs are used whose stems end in ο : *e.g.* δοῖ in Mark viii. 37, and compounds elsewhere, γνοῖ *ibid.* ix. 30 etc. These are undoubtedly the best attested forms (the T. R. substitutes more regular ones), and they have an optative look : but they probably are really meant for subjunctives, formed on the analogy of δηλοῖ from δηλόω -οῦν * : when we have a real

---

* On the other hand, φυσιοῦσθε in 1 Cor. iv. 6, ζηλοῦτε in Gal. iv. 17 are in all probability subjunctives. This suggests the possibility that διαβεβαιοῦνται in 1 Tim. i. 7 may be one :

opt. aor. from διδόναι, as in Rom. xv. 5, 2 Thess. iii. 16, 2 Tim. i. 16, 18, we find δῴη. But where we find ΔΩΗ the best attested form in Eph. i. 17, 2 Tim. ii. 25, have we the right to say that here it is *not* opt., and write δώῃ instead of δῴη, the only possible form in the former passages? (It must be remembered that the oldest N. T. MSS. are without the ι subscript or adscript to either vowel.) Perhaps the truest answer is, that the N. T. writers always meant (so far as they were conscious about the matter at all) to use the subj.: but that, owing to the exceptional form of words of this type, and to the fact that there had been an idiom admitting or requiring the opt., words like these that were really of opt. origin were allowed to be used. Or, to put the matter differently, we may say that the regular forms of the opt. in -οιμι or -οίην were felt to have an exclusively optative meaning: but that δῴη, though it could be used optatively, "sounded right" when used in final sentences also.

Yet there is a want felt by the N. T. writers of a distinction corresponding to that between subj. and opt. in final sentences, where this was not a mere matter of grammatical sequence, the one after primary and the other after historical tenses, but where the one suggests, more forcibly than the other, the notion that the purpose was a certain or actual result. In such cases, the N. T. writers use the fut. indic. where classical writers would put the subj., and the subj. where they would put the opt.

we then get a more distinctive sense for the two clauses, "knowing neither what the things are that they say, nor about *what things to make* assertions."

Curiously, this constr. is seldom or never found (Rom. iii. 4 is the best attested instance: there some MSS. of the LXX. also have νικήσεις, but the best -σῃς) with ὅπως, which can take the fut. in classical Greek, but much oftener with ἵνα—*e.g.* Gal. ii. 4;* so μή or μήποτε in Mark xiv. 2, Col. ii. 8, Heb. iii. 12 (with βλέπετε μή . . . ἔσται in the two latter places, cf. σκόπει μή . . . ἐστίν in Luke xi. 35). The fut. however approximates so closely in form, and still more according to modern (and not very modern) Greek pronunciation in sound, to the aor. subj., that we have almost always more or less interchange of reading between them, even where this introduces the anomaly of a fut. subj. different from the aor. In 1 Cor. xiii. 3, καυθήσωμαι is almost as likely to be right as anything: in John xvii. 2, δώσει seems better supported than -σῃ: but in Luke vii. 4 critical editors agree in reading παρέξῃ. The same may be said of the much rarer case of ἵνα with a pres. indic. If MS. evidence is to prevail in such a matter, we must allow that ἵνα γινώσκομεν is found in 1 John v. 20: and there is considerable authority for ἵνα γινώσκουσιν in John xvii. 3. See also critical notes on John iv. 15, Gal. vi. 12, Tit. ii. 4, and Westcott and Hort's Appendix, pp. 171-2.

There is no doubt that this constr. became frequent in later Greek, as the use of ἵνα widened: we have it as early as St. Ignatius (*ad. Eph.* c. 4), if the sole

* This instance deserves the more notice, because there a past tense precedes, and the fut. must be used to express a modification of the sense. It suggests that the traitors still entertain the design for which they then "came in privily to spy out our liberty": translate therefore "that they *may* bring us into bondage."

Greek MS. may be trusted. We can hardly decide whether it was beginning to come in in N. T. days, or was introduced by early scribes: the scholarly scribes of the middle ages, certainly, eliminated such forms where they found them.

In hypothetical sentences, the constr. is generally in accordance with classical rules. In Luke ix. 13 ($εἰ\ μήτι\ \ldots\ ἀγοράσωμεν$), 1 Thess. v. 10 ($εἴτε\ γρηγορῶμεν\ εἴτε\ καθεύδωμεν$) the use of $εἰ$ c. subj. is not an irregularity but a refinement. In the former place, the subj. is deliberative: the sense is "unless we are to buy," or perhaps "unless — are we to buy?"—in the latter, the verbs in the protasis are, quite correctly, attracted into the mood of the apodosis. But we note that here too the opt. has all but passed out of use: except for the phrase $εἰ\ τύχοι$ twice in St. Paul (1 Cor. xiv. 10, xv. 37) the only instances are in the last chapters of Acts and in 1 Pet. iii. 14, 17 (true text).

Hypothetical sentences are, however, only a particular case of *relative* sentences, and come under the same rule with them, that the subj. will be used if the relative (pron. or particle) that introduces the protasis has $ἄν$ with it, and not otherwise. And this rule is broken in the N. T.—rarely in hypothetical sentences, oftener in temporal, perhaps only once (James ii. 10) with a rel. pron. The use of $εἰ$ c. subj. in 1 Cor. xiv. 5 has parallels even in Attic, and is quite exceptional in the N. T., as in Attic: but the $ἐὰν\ οἴδαμεν$ of 1 John v. 15 would be impossible in classical Greek, while in the N. T. it is only the extremest case of four or five. In the other cases, however (Matt. xviii. 19 [?], Luke xix. 40, Acts viii. 31,

1 Thess. iii. 8); the verbs being presents or futures, the difference of form from the subj. is slight, and it appears as a *v. l.* In Mark vi. 56, Acts ii. 45, iv. 35, 1 Cor. xii. 2, we have a rel. with ἄν joined to an impf. indic., in a frequentative sense.

Of temporal sentences, there are a few where ὅταν is used with the indic.: but perhaps they are confined to the two least correct of the N. T. writers, St. Mark (iii. 11, xi. 19, 25) and Apoc. (iv. 9, viii. 1). The only other case where there is much evidence for the constr. is Luke xiii. 28, and there it is not decisive (as indeed it hardly is in the other cases cited, except the first): if it be admitted there, we have another case where the fut. ind. approximates in usage as in form to the aor. subj. The converse case, of the use of the subj. without ἄν, is confined to the case of words meaning "until" (Luke xiii. 35 comes under this principle, even if we omit ἄν, which is uncertain, and retain ἥξει ὅτε, which is improbable), and this is much commoner. But this is not to be called incorrect, hardly even post-classical: with ἄχρι and μέχρι it is at most non-Attic, with ἕως it is, in good Attic, confined to poetry. We note, however, that Luke ii. 26 is unique in the N. T. as an instance (if it be indeed one*) of the classical constr. of πρὶν ἄν c. subj. after a negative: unique likewise is the undoubted πρίν c. opt. in Acts xxv. 16, where a sentence of this type is spoken of hypothetically—we can hardly say in *oratio obliqua*.

* Perhaps the best attested text is πρὶν ἢ ἂν ἴδῃ: the most widely attested is πρὶν ἴδῃ or πρὶν ἢ ἴδῃ: πρὶν ἂν ἴδῃ is found in B, and *was* found in F, only. πρὶν ἢ ἄν is never found in good Greek: but πρίν and πρὶν ἤ with the subj. are, though the rule is to use ἄν.

It is only in St. Luke, moreover, that we get the opt. in indirect questions: with him it is fairly frequent, both with ἄν (Ev. vi. 11, Acts v. 24, x. 17—not xvii. 20, true text), and without it (Ev. i. 29, iii. 15, viii. 9, xxii. 23, Acts xvii. 11, xxi. 33, xxv. 24). In Acts viii. 31 * (not ii. 12, nor in John xiii. 24, true text), we have the opt. with ἄν in a direct question. We get the subj. in indirect questions (including instances of ἔχειν τί . . ., εἰδέναι τί . . ., and the like), in Matt. viii. 20, xv. 32 = Mark viii. 2, Mark vi. 36, viii. 1, Luke xii. 5, John xii. 49, etc.: and this even after past tenses—Mark ix. 6, xiv. 1, 11, 40; also Luke xxii. 2, 4, Acts iv. 21, preceded by τό. We have not included here Matt. vi. 25 = Luke xii. 22, Matt. x. 19 = Mark xiii. 11, Luke xii. 29, where the subj. may be explained as having a deliberative sense.

One use of the opt. that tends to disappear from N. T. Greek is that with ἄν where it does not form an apodosis to an actual conditional sentence, but is used categorically, only with a suggestion of hypothetical tone. *E.g.* in Mark iv. 13, Rom. v. 7 we should probably in classical Greek have had the opt. with ἄν, whereas in the N. T. we find the fut. indic.

The use of οὐ μή is decidedly commoner in the N. T. than in earlier Greek. Though we may ascribe this to the tendency (p. 42, etc.) of a declining language to heap up emphatic words till emphasis is lost, the combination always retains more or less of real

---

* The sequence of moods here is remarkable, but not meaningless. The eunuch first asks in despair, "How is it possible that I *should?*" then comes the afterthought, "unless some man *will* guide me." The fut. indic. thus improves the sense, though with ἐάν it is an irregularity.

emphatic force. As usual in constructions where either the fut. indic. or the aor. subj. may be used, the one constantly appears as a v. l. for the other: but there is no doubt of the fut. in Matt. xv. 5, xvi. 22, and not much in xxvi. 35, John iv. 14, x. 5, Gal. iv. 30. In Luke x. 19 the reading is doubtful: elsewhere, the subj. should generally stand. There seems to be no distinction of sense between the two: it is always (unless possibly in Matt. xv. 5) predictive, not prohibitory. In John vi. 35, if we follow MS. evidence, we get πεινάσῃ and διψήσει side by side. With this we may compare the more anomalous use of the aor. subj. in Luke xi. 5, ἕξει. . . . καὶ πορεύσεται . . . καὶ εἴπῃ, where there is no negative preceding, but a question equivalent to one.

There seems to be no deviation from classical usage in the employment of past tenses of the indic. to express the unreal and unattainable, either in conditional sentences strictly so called, or with verbs of hypothetical meaning, such as ηὐχόμην (Rom. ix. 3), ἤθελον (Gal. iv. 20), ἐβουλόμην (Acts xxv. 22), ἠδύνατο (Mark xiv. 5): perhaps one may add ἔδει (Matt. xxv. 27), though there the process of thought that leads to the use of the tense is clearer, " it *was* thy duty," at the past time when thou couldest have done it, and didst not: cf. the use of the imperfects ἀνῆκεν and καθῆκεν noted on p. 102. This constr. serves to explain one occurring several times in the N. T.— the use of ὄφελον c. *indic.* to indicate a wish. In good Greek ὤφελον (in Ionic ὄφ.) is used c. inf.: but here we have it with past indic. tenses (1 Cor. iv. 8, 2 Cor. xi. 1, Rev. iii. 15 true text) in a wish which is not realised, with a fut. indic. (Gal. v. 12) in one that is conceived as attainable. The former constr. is found in late but not bad Greek, the latter is condemned as a solecism.

The same half-hypothetical use of past tenses illustrates a constr. like that of Matt. xxvi. 24, καλὸν ἦν αὐτῷ εἰ οὐκ ἐγεννήθη (in Mark xiv. 21 ἦν should prob. be omitted). Here however, being a formally hypothetical sentence, it would have been more regular to have put ἄν in the apodosis: so Acts xxvi. 32 (ἐδύνατο). But this type of sentence serves to illustrate the omission of ἄν in John ix. 33, xv. 22, perhaps viii. 39, xix. 11: also Gal. iv. 15, perhaps 2 Cor. xi. 4.

Different from these, and less defensible grammatically, is the use of past tenses of the indic. with μή in Gal. ii. 2, iv. 11, 1 Thess. iii. 5. One may almost say that in these places St. Paul feels the want of a perf. subj.; that he does not remember that there was a rare but recognised form for it, and that he does not choose to use the cumbrous periphrasis with the ptcp. and ὤ.

(d) *The Imperative and Infinitive Moods.*

The use of the Imperative Mood in the N. T. preserves all the refinements of the classical language. For the distinction of sense between the aor. and pres. tense, note Acts xii. 8, ζῶσαι . . . ὑπόδησαι . . . περιβαλοῦ . . ., but ἀκολούθει: also John ii. 16, ἄρατε "take them away and have done with it," . . . μὴ ποιεῖτε "cease to make." . . . Even in 1 Pet. ii. 17, though we should not have expected a distinction between τιμήσατε and τιμᾶτε, the fact of the juxtaposition of the two forms shows that the author meant something by it: and we can see why varying acts of "honour to all men," whom one may meet at different times, and who have different characters and positions, are called for; but a constant habit of "honour to the king," whose position and relation to his subjects is permanent.

After μή the distinction of the tenses appears sometimes to be the same—*e.g.* Luke x. 4, " do not [habitually] carry" . . . " do not salute" [if you meet any one, as you occasionally may]. But generally μή with the pres. indic. has the sense " Do not [go on doing so and so, as you are doing now]:" so John ii. 16 already cited, Luke vii. 13, viii. 50, 52, etc. All this is quite regular. So too is the use after μή of the pres. imper., but of the aor. subj. always in the second person: in Attic as in the N. T., the aor. imper. is occasionally found in the 3rd.

What deviation there is from classical usage is not in the use of the imper. itself, but of certain equivalent constructions. The indignant οὐ παύσῃ . . .; of Acts xiii. 10 ought not to be watered down into such an equivalent. But there seems no doubt that οὐκ ἔσεσθε in Matt. vi. 5 is just equivalent to the μὴ γίνεσθε of ver. 16: so constantly where the Commandments are quoted. The reason of this is no doubt, that in Hebrew the fut. is regularly used after a negative; though there is a prohibitive particle, distinct from the categorical negative as μή from οὐ. We get the fut., however, without a negative in what at least approaches an imperative sense, in Matt. v. 48: we note that the LXX. has likewise futures in the passages of the old Law which this recalls—Lev. xi. 44, Deut. xviii. 13.

Not a Hebraism, but a post-classical constr., is the use of ἵνα c. subj. in an imperative, or perhaps rather precatory sense—Mark v. 23, 2 Cor. viii. 7, Eph. v. 33. This is exactly equivalent to the classical use of ὅπως, usually c. fut. indic.

Another idiom of the late language is seen in the beginning of the use of ἄφες, ἄφετε as an auxiliary. In Matt. viii. 22 = Luke ix. 60 every one can see that the word keeps its independent verbal meaning and constr., "*leave* the dead to bury . . .," "let them alone that they may . . .," so John xi. 44, though less emphatically, Matt. xiii. 30, Mark vii. 27, and even Matt. xix. 14 = Mark x. 14 = Luke xviii. 16. But in Matt. vii. 4 = Luke vi. 42, ἄφες ἐκβάλω is no more than "*Let me* cast out :" like ἄφες or ἄς in modern Greek, the word has sunk into a mere auxiliary. Such, no doubt, is its use also in Matt. xxvii. 49 = Mark xv. 36: though the two accounts differ as to the speaker, and consequently as to the use of sing. or pl., both mean to convey the same general sense of ironical scepticism.*

Lastly, we may note under this head the few N. T. instances of infinitives used in a sense more or less close to the imper. If in Luke xxii. 42 we read παρενέγκαι or παρενεγκεῖν,† we have an instance of the classical (and mostly poetical) use of the inf. in prayers. It is hardly of any use to discuss how nearly the use of the inf. in Rom. xii. 15, Phil. iii. 16 is

---

* The discrepancy of sense therefore disappears which is supposed by Dr. Abbott (*Encycl. Brit.*, art. "Gospels"), who takes the words in Matt. to mean "Desist from giving the drink," in Mark "Desist from mocking."

† Παρένεγκε, however, has the high authority of BDT, though παρενέγκαι comes nearest to the character of a reading that will account for both the others. That -κε in D at least is a mere itacism, is made likelier by the fact that *d*, the parallel Latin version, has the inf.

identical with this: it is at any rate analogous to the quite classical epistolary use of χαίρειν or ὑγιαίνειν—we remember we have the former of these in Acts xv. 23, xxiii. 26, James i. 1.

This use of the inf., in fact, is only a slight extension of one of its proper uses, which we get in Acts xxi. 4, 21, Tit. ii. 2. Here we must not say that λέγειν—still less λαλεῖν—has the sense of commanding: we have simply the common inf. of *oratio obliqua*, only it represents an original imper., not an indic.—*e.g.*, the Tyrian disciples τῷ Παύλῳ ἔλεγον " Μὴ ἐπίβαινε," which St. Luke reports by ἔλεγον . . . μὴ ἐπιβαίνειν.

Already in the N. T. we see the beginning of the tendency which has prevailed in modern Greek, to use ἵνα c. subj. as a substitute for the inf., in almost all its relations except that of simple *oratio obliqua*, and for that to use ὅτι c. indic., which the classical language always offered as an equivalent. Opinions may differ as to the number of cases in which ἵνα is thus to be explained: see this question discussed below, p. 176. As to ὅτι, it is probably relatively more frequent than in earlier Greek *—especially before a speech given otherwise in *oratio recta*, so that the ὅτι is almost Greek for inverted commas: notice Luke vii. 16, where the repeated ὅτι serves to mark that we have two sayings of the people, not one saying in two clauses. In Rom. iii. 8 we have ὅτι as a quotation mark to a cohortative subj., in John ix. 11 (true text), 2 Thess. iii. 10 to imperatives: with the last cf. Epict. Diss. I. ii. 18, τί οὖν μοι λέγεις ὅτι 'Εξομοιώθητι τοῖς πολλοῖς.

* The anacoluthon in Acts xxvii. 10, where ὅτι stands redundantly before an acc. and inf., is not without classical precedent.

Nevertheless, there is no sign in the N. T. of the inf. tending to become obsolete: it is used very freely, and on the whole quite correctly: if there be any deviation from classical usage, it is rather in the extension than in the restriction of its use.* Phil. iv. 10, where τὸ ὑπὲρ ἐμοῦ φρονεῖν stands as a sort of cognate acc. after ἀνεθάλετε, is hardly to be called such an extension: it is simply a looseness of constr. such as a writer who is no grammatical purist, but is at home in the language he is using, will allow himself occasionally but rarely. But the inf. in a final, consecutive, or epexegetical sense is more frequent, and is found in a larger class of cases in biblical than in classical Greek. No one would be surprised at a use like Matt. ii. 2, ἤλθομεν προσκυνῆσαι, or Mark iii. 14, ἵνα ἀποστέλλῃ αὐτοὺς κηρύσσειν; though κηρύξοντας in the latter case would be commoner, and προσκυνήσοντες in the former not uncommon. But would any classical author have written a sentence like Ex. xxxii. 6, *ap.* 1 Cor. x. 7, ἐκάθισεν ὁ λαὸς φαγεῖν καὶ πεῖν, καὶ ἀνέστησαν παίζειν? or Heb. v. 5, οὐχ ἑαυτὸν ἐδόξασεν γενηθῆναι ἀρχιερέα? or ib. vi. 10, οὐ γὰρ ἄδικος ὁ Θεὸς ἐπιλαθέσθαι? So Acts v. 31 (if τοῦ be omitted), xv. 11, 2 Pet. iii. 2. Or, if any or each of these might individually be justified, still we may say that we should not get such extended use of the inf. so often in classical writers. St. Paul is especially loose in this use of it; see *e.g.* 2 Cor. x. 13, 16, xi. 2, Col. i. 22, iv. 6. Sometimes, on the other hand, an inf. of this kind, even one which would be quite regular, and in harmony with the nature of the governing verb, has its constr.

* We should mention, however, that neither infin. nor ptcp. is used in the N. T. with ἄν.

INFINITIVE IN FINAL SENSE. 119

helped out or emphasised by the use of ὥστε (Matt. xxvii. 1) or ὡς (Luke ix. 52, Westcott and Hort; Acts xx. 24, T. R., Tisch. etc). The cases cited are the only ones where ὡς is used c. inf., except the classical ὡς ἔπος εἰπεῖν of Heb. vii. 9 : ὥστε, of course, is common —perhaps as common as in other Greek. The constr. of ὥστε c. imper. is perhaps relatively commoner; though that is quite classical.

Where the inf. has a distinctly final sense after a verb which is not, in a wide sense, causative, it is usual, and we may say regular, to employ with it the gen. art. τοῦ. (Ἕνεκεν τοῦ c. inf. is peculiar to 2 Cor. vii. 12, where the context accounts for its use.) This constr. is pure Greek, but is far more frequent in the later literary language than in the classical. In the N. T. it is most frequent in St. Luke, least in St. John, doubtful in Mark and Apoc.; it is the tendency of the T. R. to introduce it, as more regular, where the apparently oldest texts have the simple inf.: *e.g.* Mark iv. 3, Luke xii. 42. Exceptional extensions of its use are found in Luke xvii. 1, Acts x. 25, Rev. xii. 7. In the last, it is impossible to represent the constr. as regular, and useless to speculate what regular constr. would come nearest to the sense intended: the process in the writer's mind is apparently, "There was war in heaven—Michael and his angels making war. . . ." or "so that they made war." In Acts x. 25 the sense is much the same as in the common (and especially Lucan) ἐγένετο τὸν Π. εἰσελθεῖν, on which see p. 166.

Where an inf. with the art. forms the subject to a sentence, the predicate is usually a subst. (*e.g.* Phil. i. 22), adj. (Acts x. 28), or pron. (Matt. xx. 23)—

rarely a verb, as in Matt. xv. 20, Rom. vii. 18, Phil. i. 29. An inf. preceded by τοῦτο or the like (distinguish Matt. xx., Phil. i. 11. cc. where τοῦτο follows) generally has not the art. when it is subject (Eph. iii. 8, 1 Thess. iv. 3, 4; but in ver. 6 τοῦτο has been left so far behind that the art. reappears; James i. 27); but has when predicate (Rom. xiv. 13, 2 Cor. ii. 1: yet see 1 Cor. vii. 37).

While the use of the inf. with the proper case of the art. in dependence on a prep. is no doubt good Greek, its frequency in the N. T. must be considered a Hellenistic feature. Most decidedly, the use of ἐν τῷ c. inf. as a note of time may be called a downright Hebraism, being a literal translation of a common Hebrew idiom: for this see p. 144. With this mainly Lucan use we may co-ordinate the mainly Pauline one of εἰς (Rom. iv. 18, 1 Cor. x. 6 etc.), and the rarer one of πρός c. acc. (Matt. vi. 1, 2 Cor. iii. 13): though these are rather Hellenistic in spirit than Hebraistic in origin. See below, on the various prepositions.

The tenses of the inf. are as a rule used correctly, the subtle or at least untranslatable difference between the pres. and aor. being preserved wherever the sense allows it to be perceptible. But perhaps less use is made of the fut. inf. than in classical writers. It is never used in the N. T. with μέλλειν, except in the one phrase μέλλειν ἔσεσθαι in Acts (xi. 28, xxiv. 15, xxvii. 10: in xxiii. 30 om. μέλλειν, and in xxiv. 25 ἔσεσθαι), never with ἐλπίζειν, except in Acts xxvi. 7 according to Cod. B only. Μέλλειν (when not used absolutely) almost always has a pres., but an aor. in Rom. viii. 18, Gal. iii. 23, Rev. iii. 2, 16,

xii. 4 (not ii. 10)*. Ἐλπίζειν has ὅτι with pres. (necessarily for the sense) in Luke xxiv. 21, with fut. in Acts xxiv. 26, 2 Cor. i. 13, xiii. 6, Philem. 22, neither having classical precedent, though there is for ὅπως c. fut. Its usual constr. when followed by a verb (ἐλπίζειν ἐν, εἰς, or ἐπὶ is an exclusively biblical constr.) is c. inf. aor., as most editors even in Acts xxvi. 7; we even get it c. perf. inf. in 2 Cor. v. 11— never c. acc. et inf., ὅτι serving to replace this. So ἐπαγγέλλεσθαι takes an aor. inf., and so ὀμνύειν in Acts ii. 30, but a fut. in Heb. iii. 18—not without reason, the former passage being "He swore *to*" do something, the latter "He swore *that*" something should happen, not directly an act of His.

One is a little surprised, therefore, to get the acc. and inf. after verbs similar or parallel in sense to these, even where the subject of the inf. is the same as of the principal verb; as in Luke xx. 20, Rom. ii. 19, Rev. ii. 9. But in Phil. iii. 13 we see that the expression of the subject may be necessary for clearness, or at least greatly conducive to emphasis. In Eph. iv. 22 ἐδιδάχθητε ... ἀποθέσθαι ὑμᾶς is hardly quite the same as ἐδιδ. ἀποθέσθαι: St. Paul *assumes* here that they have learnt what they *should* do, and in vv. 25 *sqq.* bids them learn to do it.

Words of request or command have some peculiarities of constr. Κελεύειν always is followed by an inf., as in pure Greek: but we have both in SS. Matthew and Luke (the only N. T. writers who use this word) the unclassical constr. with the inf. *pass.*, the subject to which, of course, is not the

* The force of the aor., singularly, is more distinctly traceable in the Apoc. than in St. Paul.

object of the verb (except in a place like Matt. xiv. 19, where the sense is really med.). See Matt. xiv. 9, xviii. 25, xxvii. 58, 64, Luke xviii. 40, Acts xii. 19, xxi. 33, 34, xxii. 24, xxiii. 3, 35, xxv. 6, 17, 21. So προστάσσειν, Acts x. 48: παραγγέλλειν never has this constr. but usually the regular inf. act.: it is followed however by ἵνα in Mark vi. 8, 2 Thess. iii. 12 (in 1 Tim. v. 7 ἵνα does not depend immediately on the verb), and in 2 Thess. iii. 10 by ὅτι c. imper. With other verbs of this class, ἵνα or ὅπως is often used: and so with θέλω—see c. VI. (c.).

(e) *The Participles.*

The Greek language differs from and surpasses most others, in possessing a complete set of participles, corresponding to almost all the tenses which it distinguishes in the indic. mood. Of this richness none has been lost as regards variety of form, and not much as regards freedom of usage, in the stage of the language represented by the N. T.: though the more "analytical" character of the language leads to participles being less frequently used, at least by some writers. In Luke xxiv. 18, John vi. 50, vii. 4 etc., we have clauses connected by καί where it would have been more natural to a Greek to express one by a ptcp.; perhaps the same may be said of co-ordinate imperatives, as in John i. 47.

But though participles may be less used than in earlier Greek, when used they are used in the same way. Or if there be any loss of accuracy in their use, it is, as in the case of the infin., in the rarer and more limited use of the fut., not in the loss of the distinction between pres. and aor., nor (whatever we may think is the case in the indic.) between aor. and perf. This last distinction * perhaps requires some insistence, because, though there is nothing distinctive in the N. T. usage in the matter, the point is one which English scholars are apt to miss. We translate both ποιήσας and πεποιηκώς by "having made": we hardly ever realise that in so doing we are obliterating as real a distinction as a Latin translator who uses *feci* both for ἐποίησα and πεποίηκα.

For though in most of the unaugmented moods the *temporal* character of the aor. disappears, and even in the inf. is by no means the most prominent or important feature in its use, in the ptcp. the sense is as strictly temporal as in the indic., and just the same † as it is there. We show our sense of this, by the frequency with which in translation we break up an aor. ptcp. agreeing with the subject of the sentence either into a relative clause or into a finite verb co-ordinated by a conj. with the principal one. We ought to recognise that the temporal relation is exactly the same when the ptcp. agrees with the object or some other dependent case, though it may be convenient in translation to represent it otherwise, or may not be worth while to represent it at all. Thus Luke x. 18 gives the sense "Satan fell like lightning: I was there beholding:" it is neither "I beheld him *fall*" (ἐθεώρουν πεσεῖν) nor "I beheld him *fallen*" (ἐθ. πεπτωκότα), still less of course "I beheld him *falling*" (ἐθ. πίπτοντα). In

* A suggestive and instructive discussion on this point, if not always convincing, is to be found in a paper in the *Expositor* (2nd Series, vol. iii. pp. 161 sqq.) by Dr. T. S. Evans.

† [Except that participles express time only in relation to the verbs on which they depend.]

Acts ix. 12, Ananias is told that Saul "saw a man by name A.: the man in his vision came in and put his hands on him." If it be worth while in translation to be more accurate than the A. V., which substitutes present participles for aorist, we might put a relative clause, as in xi. 13, where (so far as there is a right and wrong in such niceties) the A. V. is right and the R. V. wrong: if it was worth while to make the constr. the same as in the parallel passage x. 3, the assimilation ought to have been the other way. We have perf. and aor. participles set side by side, each with its proper sense, in 2 Cor. xii. 21, where the πρo emphasises the force of the perf.; and still more pointedly in 1 Pet. ii. 10, where both forms belong to the same verb, and where the choice of tense is the more clearly seen to be deliberate, because there is nothing corresponding to it in the LXX. of Hosea. In *translating* either passage, we can hardly express the distinction better than the A. V. does in the latter—representing the perf. by (what we call) a plupf., and the aor. by a perf.: "who *had* sinned, and *have* not repented," "who *had* not obtained mercy, but now *have*." But if we desire to analyse what was in the Apostles' mind that led them to vary the tense, we may say that they speak of an *act* of repentance, an *act* of God's mercy (whether the latter be that shown in redemption or in conversion) as contrasted with the *state* that men were in before it. An angel or other watcher of those to whom St. Peter writes might have said of their former state Οὐκ ἠλέηνται, "they have not obtained mercy:" of their *entrance into* their present state, Νῦν ἠλεήθησαν, "now mercy was shown to them." Similarly, in Gal. iii. 13, 17, γενόμενος and γεγονώς are correctly distinguished: they are correlative respectively to the historical tense ἐξηγόρασεν and the pres. ἀκυροῖ with which they are associated. And (to pass from cases where both tenses are used to a case where one is used and the other might have been) in Acts xiii. 12 we learn that what astonished and convinced the ἀνὴρ συνετός was not τὸ γενόμενον "the event," but τὸ γεγονός "the state of things produced." Elymas was not only frightened into thinking he was blinded, but was *left* blind, though (as we understand) only ἄχρι καιροῦ.

But the aor. ptcp., though not perfect in sense, is distinctly preterite: in pure Greek, when it is used with a verb, we may assume that the action expressed by the ptcp. precedes that of the verb in the order of time or thought. In N. T. Greek it seems that the constr. can be used if the two are contemporary sometime even when, if we resolved it into two co-ordinate verbs, that expressed by the ptcp. would necessarily come first. In Rom. iv. 20 *sq.*, Phil. ii. 7, the adoring confidence, the assumption of the servant's form, did not precede the vigorous faith or the κένωσις, but was what it consisted in. Perhaps we may say the same of Heb. ii. 10, translating ἀγαγόντα "when He brought:"—"in bringing" would necessarily be ἄγοντα.* But we are somewhat surprised at Acts i 24, προσευξάμενοι εἶπαν, if it means "they prayed and said," so as to be equivalent to προσευχόμενοι εἶπαν "they said in their prayer:" and we almost

---

* It hardly makes any differen.c as to the difficulty or the proper force of the tense, whether we connect it with the subject or the object of τελειῶσαι.

refuse to believe that in xxv. 13 St. Luke wrote κατήντησαν ... ἀσπασάμενοι "they arrived ... and saluted," though MS. evidence proves it, if there be no limit to what it can prove. Perhaps we may say that the N. T. rule is, that of two contemporary acts in past time, the principal is expressed by the verb, the secondary by the ptcp.

The rarity of the fut. ptcp. in the N. T. may be partly due to its simplicity of ethical tone, which gives us plenty of plain narrative of the past, and not a little direct prediction of the future, but rarely mentions people's sayings or doings in regard to future events—Matt. vi. 34.* Partly however it must be ascribed to the existence of words which mark future time but are not technically future tenses—the Greek μέλλων, and the Hellenistic ἐρχόμενος (see p. 100). But for the use of these words, it would hardly have been possible that we should find ἐσόμενον nowhere but Luke xxii. 49, γενησόμενον nowhere but 1 Cor. xv. 37. The constr. of the fut. ptcp. with ὡς is found nowhere but Heb. xiii. 17. And the form is nowhere used in a final sense, as often in classical Greek, except a few times in the Acts, mostly in the last chapters: viii. 27, xxiv. 11, 17, xxv. 13— if we there read ἀσπασόμενοι (with T. R.). In an earlier writer we should have had the constr. much oftener even in that book—certainly in many places where we get an inf. with or without τοῦ, probably in some where we have a pres. ptcp. *E.g.* in xv. 21 τοὺς κηρύξοντας would have seemed more natural and more

* From this point of view, συναντήσοντα in its context in Acts xx. 22 may almost be called an exception that proves the rule.

elegant; still more ἀπαγγελοῦντας, ib. ver. 27; and perhaps σαλεύσοντες καὶ ταράξοντες in xvii. 13. So Rom. xv. 25, διακονῶν; where indeed the progressive sense of the pres. πορεύομαι helps a little to the treatment of the object of the journey as already in execution.

Except, however, in the case of words of this sort of progressive meaning (like ἐρχόμενος), there does not appear to be any tendency, such as sometimes has been suspected, to use the pres. ptcp. in a sense approximating to the fut. Οἱ σωζόμενοι and οἱ ἀπολλύμενοι in the Acts and in St. Paul are "those in a state of salvation" or "of perdition,"* which states begin in this life: βαλλόμενον in Matt. vi. 30 is not "which *will be* cast," but "which habitually is growing one day and being taken for fuel the next." One hardly likes to discuss the force of ἐκχυννόμενον in the eucharistic passages, Matt. xxvi. 28, Mark xiv. 24, Luke xxii. 20: but the *quod effundetur* of the Latin versions is perhaps rather a liturgical tradition than a gloss on the evangelical text; in St. Matthew the true text of St. Jerome's version appears to have the pres. The pres. is certainly used by him for διδόμενον in St. Luke in the verse before; and of course in 1 Cor. xi. 24 the fut. *quod pro vobis tradetur* is as legitimate a gloss as the pres. κλώμενον in the Greek T. R. on the true text, τὸ ὑπὲρ ὑμῶν.

There is one pres. ptcp. however, of which it is hardly to be said that it always keeps the proper present, or rather imperfect, meaning of the tense: viz. that of the verb substantive, which stands almost alone in having no aor. or perf. ptcp. Of course no one is surprised at a sentence like John xi. 49, which

* See p. 35, and note there.

we can translate quite literally, "*being* high priest ..., he *prophesied*;" •his high priesthood was present at the time of the prophecy, though τοῦ ἐνιαυτοῦ ἐκείνου tells us, if it needed telling, that it was past at the time of writing. But in 2 Cor. viii. 9 it would be too much to think that the Apostle speaks (as John iii. 13 does, *si vera l.*) of—

> Verbum supernum prodiens,
> Nec Patris linquens dexteram :

the ptcp. is used as in Eph. ii. 13, Col. i. 21, 1 Tim. i. 13, where the sense of ὤν is defined by the use of ποτέ or πρότερον. One may doubt whether these are quite good Greek,* though in *late* literary Greek at least we get parallels to them ; of John ix. 25, τυφλὸς ὢν ἄρτι βλέπω, we may say that it is certainly a straining of language. It is difficult however to see what else the Evangelist should have written, intending, as he did, exactly the sense of the A. V.: whether he was or was not the same person who wrote ὁ Ὤν καὶ ὁ Ἦν five times in the Apoc., he knew that here as there γενόμενος would give quite a wrong sense. Here it would mean "whereas I *was born* blind," which is not what he wants to insist on, or else "whereas I *once was blinded*," which was not the fact: he wants a strictly *preterimperfect* ptcp., and uses the nearest approach to one that exists.

It is different from an improper use of the tense of a ptcp., when the ptcp. becomes so far adjectival, that the idea of tense hardly belongs to it. Ἐβδελυγμένοις in Rev. xxi. 8 is just equivalent to βδελυκτοῖς :

* Gal. i. 23 no doubt is: it is "our former persecutor" (Moulton's Winer), the pres. being used to *make abstraction* of the conception of time.

ψηλαφωμένῳ in Heb. xii. 18 is "palpable," A.V. excellently "that might be touched": "but in both cases the tenses used are correct, giving the point of view from the word started on its way to become adjectival. In Gal. ii. 11, κατεγνωσμένος is hardly adjectival: the sense is really plupf., "had condemned himself, stood self-condemned" (Moulton).

We note, as not infrequent in St. Paul and writers influenced by him, a tendency to use participles instead of and co-ordinately with finite verbs—the sense sometimes being that of an indic., sometimes of an imper. or cohortative subj.: possibly sometimes the ptcp. was preferred, as leaving the question open whether he states what ought to be or what was. For instances, more or less certain, see Acts xxiv. 5, Rom. v. 11, xii. 6-19, 2 Cor. v. 6, vii. 5, 1 Thess. ii. 11, 12, Heb. vii. 1, xiii. 5, 1 Pet. ii. 18, iii. 1, 8-9, iv. 8-10. Most of these, however, if real irregularities, are rather cases of anacoluthon, or incomplete structure, than of extended use of the ptcp., and are peculiarities rather of the writer's style than of N. T. grammar.

Different from this are the cases of anacoluthon, where a transition is made from a ptcp. to a finite verb, as though the former were equivalent to a relative clause, the rel. pron. in which would serve as subj. to both—John i. 32, 2 Cor. vi. 9, Eph. i. 20 *sqq.*, Col. i. 26, Heb. viii. 10. (from LXX., repeated x. 16), 2 John 2, and constantly in the Apoc.—*e.g.* ii. 2, 9, 18. 1 Cor. vii. 37 *can* be read as another instance: ib. vii. 13 is somewhat analogous, and so are Luke xix. 2, John xv. 5.

It is doubtful if the ptcp. is used proleptically in

1 Tim. v. 13. The easiest sense is to translate as the A.V., but it is harder to make the adj. proleptic than the ptcp. Certainly in classical Greek μανθάνουσι περιερχόμεναι cannot mean "they learn to go about," and what it could mean ("They learn that they are going about") will not make sense. Buttmann thinks the words as they stand must mean, "idle as they are, going about from house to house, they learn"—the Apostle does not say what. But this gives no sense to φλύαροι καὶ περίεργοι in the next clause: so we are driven back to the A. V.

There remain to be mentioned two uses of the ptcp., both of which may, in very different degrees, be called Hebraisms. The conjunction of the ptcp. with the finite verb for emphasis, common in the LXX. as a representation of the so-called absolute infinitive of the Hebrew, is confined to the O. T. quotations in Matt. xiii. 14, etc., Acts vii. 34, Heb. vi. 14, unless we understand Acts v. 4 *init.* as an instance: though we get an equivalent constr. in Luke xxii. 15, John iii. 29, Acts (iv. 17 T. R.) v. 28, xxiii. 14, James v. 17, and a similar though not formally identical use of the ptcp. in Acts xiii. 45 T. R.

This of course is a Hebraism in the strictest sense: it is otherwise with the use of the verb substantive with pres. or perf. participles (never aor. unless in Luke xxiii. 19) as a periphrasis for certain tenses. This constr., most frequent in St. Luke, corresponds to one found in Aramaic and late Hebrew: but it was native to the Greek language, which could not express otherwise certain perf. and plupf. forms, and presumably would have become commoner as time went on, without any but native Greek influences;

HEBRAISTIC PERIPHRASES. 131

We subjoin a table of instances of this constr., as, from the arrangement necessary in Bruder's Concordance, it is rather laborious to trace it there through any one book. And (what is more important) he does not distinguish cases of this constr. from those where a ptcp. with the art. stands as subject or predicate; where the verb subst. is used absolutely, being itself the primary predicate, and the ptcp. being only a secondary one; or where, though a copula, it has another predicate, so that the ptcp. is still secondary. As the line is hard to draw in the second and sometimes in the third case, we admit some instances that may be held to fall under them, marked with a ? (? *after* a reference means, as usual, that the reading is doubtful).

COMBINED WITH SOME PERSON OF PRES. INDIC.	Part. Pres.	Part. Perf.
		? Matt. x. 26 = Luke xii. 2.
		x. 30.
		? xviii. 20.
	? Luke vi. 43.	Luke xii. 6.
		xx. 6.
		xxiii. 15.
		xxiv. 38.
		John ii. 17, ἔστιν
		vi. 31, 45, x. γεγραμ-
		34, xii. 14, μένον
		xx. 30. (vel -να).
		iii. 21, 28.
		? Acts v. 25.*
		xxi. 33.
		xxv. 10.*
		xxvi. 26.
		Rom. xiii. 1.
		1 Cor. iv. 8, v. 2, ? viii. 5,
		xv. 19.
		† 2 Cor. ii. 17.
	2 Cor. ix. 12.	iv. 3 bis.

* Perfects in form but pres. in sense.

	Part. Pres.	Part. Perf.
COMBINED WITH SOME PERSON OF PRES. SUBJ.	Gal. iv. 24. [Eph. v. 5 T. R.] Col. i. 6. ii. 23. ? James i. 17. iii. 15. Rev. i. 18.	Eph. ii. 5, 8. Col. iii. 1 * Heb. vii. 20. ? 23. 2 Pet. iii. 7. 1 John iv. 12.
PRES. SUBJ.	[James ii. 15. T. R.]	Luke xiv. 8. John iii. 27 = vi. 65. xvi. 24. xvii. 19. 23. 1 Cor. i. 10. 2 Cor. i. 9. ix. 3. James v. 15. 1 John i. 4 = 2 John 12.
IMPER.	Matt. v. 25.	
INFIN.	Luke ix. 18 = xi. 1.	
PARTICIPLE		Eph. iv. 18. Col. i. 21.
FUT. INDIC.	Matt. x. 22. = xxiv. 9 = Mark xiii. 13 = Luke xxi. 17. Matt. xiii. 25. Luke i. 20. v. 10. ? xvii. 35. xxi. 24. 1 Cor. xiv. 9.	Matt. xvi. 19 bis. = xviii. 18 bis. ? Luke vi. 40. ? xii. 52. Heb. ii. 13* (fr. LXX.).
IMPERF. INDIC.	Matt. vii. 29 = Mark i. 22. xix. 22 = Mark x. 22. ? xxiv. 38. ? xxvii. 55. ? Mark i. 13. 39. (?)	Matt. ix. 36. xxvi. 43. Mark i. 6. 33.

* Perfects in form but pres. in sense.

HEBRAISTIC PERIPHRASES. 133

COMBINED WITH SOME PERSON OF IMPF. INDIC.	Part. Pres.		Part. Perf.
	Mark ii. 18.		Mark ? ii. 6*
?	iv. 38.		
	v. 5.		
?	11.		
	[40 T. R.]	?	ii. 6*
	ix. 4.		vi. 52.
?	x. 32.		
	x. 32 iterum.		
	xiv. 4.		xiv. 40.
?	49.		
	xv. 43.		xv. 46.
?	Luke i. 10.		Luke i. 7.
	21.		
	22.		
	ii. 8.		ii. 26.
	33.		
	51.		iv. 16.
	iv. 31 (cf.		17.
	Matt. vii. 29).		
?	33.		
	38.		
	44.		Matt. v. 1*
	v. 16.		
	17.	?	17*
			17 iterum
	29.		18.
	vi. 12.		viii. 2.
	viii. 40.		ix. 32.
	ix. 53.		
	xi. 14.		
	xiii. 10.		
	11 [bis T. R.]		
	xiv. 1.		
	xv. 1.		xv. 24, 32.
	xix. 47.		xviii. 34.
?	xxi. 37.		
	xxiii. 8.		xxiii. 19.†
		?	38. (?)
?	xxiii. 53.		51.
	xxiv. 13.		55.

* Perfects in form but pres. in sense.

† Here, and here alone, the best texts have the aor. ptcp βληθείς instead of βεβλημένος.

134 LANGUAGE OF THE NEW TESTAMENT.

COMBINED WITH SOME PERSON OF IMPF. INDIC.	Part. Pres.	Part. Perf.
	Matt. xxiv. 32.	
?	53.	
?	John i. 9.	
?	28.	
?	ii. 6.	
	iii. 23.	John iii. 24.
?	x. 40.	
	xi. 1.	
	[41 T. R.]	xii. 16.
?	xiii. 23.	xiii. 5.
		xviii. 18,* 25.*
		John xix. 11.
		19, 20.
		[xx. 19 T. R.]
	Acts i. 10.	
	13.	
	14.	Acts i. 17.
	ii. 5.	ii. 2 *
	42.	
	viii. 1.	iv. 31.
	13.	viii. 16.
	28.	
	ix. 9.	
	28.	ix. 33.
	x. 24.	
	30.	
?	xi. 5.	
	xii. 5.	
	6.	? xii. 12.
	20.	xiii. 48.
	xiv. 7.	xiv. 26.
?	xvi. 12.	
	xviii. 7.	xviii. 25.
	xix. 14 (non T. R.)	
		Acts xix. 32.
		xx. 8.
	Acts xxi. 3.	13.
	xxii. 19.	xxi. 29.
		xxii. 20.*
		29.
	? 2 Cor. v. 19.	
	Gal. i. 22.	Gal. ii. 11.
	23.	iv. 3.
	Phil. ii. 26.	? Eph. ii. 12.
		Rev. xvii. 4 (non T. R.).

* Perfects in form but pres. in sense.

In many of these cases (those with perf. pass. participles especially) the phrase is a mere periphrasis for a mood or tense rarely used or ill sounding. But as a rule it will be seen that there is a sense of *permanent or habitual* action implied by the use of it: note *e.g.* Mark ii. 18, xiii. 25, Luke xxi. 24, Gal. i. 23, of cases with the pres. ptcp., and Matt. x. 30, Luke xx. 6, Gal. iv. 3, with the perf. It will be observed that the impf. is the tense oftenest associated with both participles: and the resemblance of the resulting phrase with the perf. to the Latin compound tenses of passive and deponent verbs is a real one. But that of the impf. with the pres. ptcp. to the English so-called impf. must not be exaggerated. In Mark ii. 18 the sense is prob. as the A. V., not "were keeping a fast," which called their attention to the diversity of practice: in Matt. vii. 29 and parallels, Luke ii. 51, we see that the sense is of habitual action rather than continued, and that the English idiom would be quite out of place.

Besides this verbal use of the ptcp. we should notice the substantival use of the *aor.* ptcp. with the art., which we get substituted for a verb, *e.g.* in Luke viii. 45 compared with Mark v. 30, Luke xx. 2 with Matt. xxi. 23, Mark xi. 28. See also Matt. xxvi. 68= Luke xxii. 64, John v. 12, 15, Acts vii. 38, ix. 21; though here there is more intentional insistence on the *person* of the doer, so that the notion is less purely verbal. We have *present* participles used like these in John iv. 10, 37, v. 32, 45, xiv. 21, xxi. 20; perhaps one or two more: a fut. in John vi. 64, and a perf. in Luke xxii. 28, Acts x. 42.

We may conclude by noticing the curious way that the ptcp. is made to agree with an attracted rel. in Acts xxvi. 22, Rev. xvii. 8.

CHAPTER VI.

USES AND MEANINGS, CHARACTERISTIC OF THE N. T., OF PARTICLES.

(a) *Prepositions.*

AS already mentioned (p.75-76), the N. T. language often uses prepositions where in classical Greek simple cases would have sufficed: and this is in part through the influence of a foreign language, but partly—perhaps more largely—from an internal tendency in the Greek language itself, which might be called rather a development than a corruption, as it would lead to a gain in accuracy greater than any possible loss in brevity and vigour. But we perceive a process of corruption going on at the same time: if prepositions are used to define more exactly the force of the cases with which they are associated, there is a counter tendency to obscure the distinction of the prepositions among themselves, and between their meaning associated with various cases. In modern Greek εἰς c. acc. has almost superseded ἐν c. dat., while retaining its old classical sense too: μετά for "with" still takes a gen., but is apocopated into μέ c. acc.: and in the vulgar language *all* prepositions can be used with that case.* In view of these facts, it is

* Geldart's *Guide to Modern Greek*, p. 247.

needless to look for classical accuracy in the use of prepositions and cases in the N. T., when the simple and natural sense of a passage is that which supposes the tendency dominant in later times to have already begun.

Of the eighteen Greek prepositions strictly so called, ἀμφί does not occur in the N. T. except in two or three compounds.* 'Aνά is rare, being confined to the phrase ἀνὰ μέσον (which is pure but late Greek, and receives a Hebraistic extension of usage: 1 Cor. vi. 5 is an extreme case), and the distrib. use with numerals. The adverbial use c. nom., which we get in Rev. xxi. 21, ἀνὰ εἷς ἕκαστος, though late seems not to be exclusively Hellenistic; but there is no classical parallel to this exact phrase.

'Αντί has none but classical uses: but we note as Hellenistic (oftener in LXX. than N. T.) the relative frequency of ἀνθ' ὧν; though it is quite classical both in the sense of "because" (Luke i. 20) and of "wherefore" (Luke xii. 3). 'Αντὶ τοῦ c. inf. is peculiar to James iv. 15. The remarkable use of the word in John i. 16 is clearly explained in the passage of Philo quoted as a parallel (I. 254, *De Post. Cain*, § 43.) χάριτας ἀεὶ . . . νέας ἀντὶ παλαιοτέρων . . . ἐπιδίδωσι. The earlier parallel alleged, Theogn. 344, is doubtful: reading δοίην (with Bergk) the sense will be the plain one, "unless I give *pain for pain*," avenge myself.

'Από gives special illustrations of the double tendency to define more accurately than is done by the use of simple cases, and to obscure distinctions between prepositions. On the one hand it is used

* It is hardly necessary to say that the rare use of ὡς as a prep. does not occur at all.

where in earlier Greek the simple gen. would have been held to suffice: on the other, it is often used interchangeably with ἐκ, where there ought to be a distinction between them. Thus we get ἀθῷος ἀπό in Matt. xxvii. 24, ἐσθίειν ἀπό, xv. 27=Mark vii. 28, διδόναι ἀπό, Luke xx. 10: but side by side with the two last phrases we have διδ. ἐξ in Matt. xxv. 8, 1 John iv. 13, and φαγεῖν ἐξ in John vi. 26, 50, 51, Rev. ii. 7 (cf. ver. 17, T. R.). Here no doubt, if a prep. was to be used instead of the simple partitive gen., either was equally appropriate; but it is hardly so in Matt. xxvii. 21, τίνα . . . ἀπὸ τῶν δύο by the side of xxi. 31, τίς ἐκ τῶν δύο: here in good Greek one would say simply τούτων πότερος . . .; πότερον τοῖν δυοῖν . . .; but if any prep. be used it should surely be ἐκ. In Luke ii. 4 there is a real distinction between ἀπό and ἐκ—the first telling the *direction* from which he came, the second his *starting-point*: though we might have had them reversed, with the sense that He came *from* Nazareth *out of* Galilee. But in John xi. 1, Acts xxiii. 34, the two stand side by side with apparently identical meanings.

The relation of ἀπό to ὑπό, on the other hand, seems not to be other than is found in classical Greek (*e.g.* Thuc. I. xvii. 1, III. lxxxii. 13, IV. cxv. 2): often, in the N. T. as elsewhere, the one is a v. l. for the other. In James i. 13 the sense is "My temptation *comes from* God": in v. 4 the sense "on your part" is not inappropriate: even in Acts ii. 22 one can feel if not express the shade of meaning given. Neither in Luke vii. 35 nor xvii. 25 does it appear that the notion is exactly that of agency: and in vi. 18 (if we read ἀπὸ πν.) we may perhaps

PREPOSITIONS: ἀπό, διά. 139

suspect a sort of zeugma, the constr. being half ἀπὸ πνευμάτων ἀκ. ἐθεραπεύοντο, like ἰαθῆναι ἀπὸ τῶν νόσων just before. Rev. xii. 6 is perhaps the only place where the difference from ὑό really vanishes.

But there is an extension of the use of ἀπό, where it is used of cause, like the Latin *prae*. There is nothing to surprise one in a use like those in Matt. xiv. 26, Acts xii. 14, or again xx. 9 : but Matt. xviii. 7 is plainly Hellenistic : and the use in Luke xix. 3, John xxi. 6, Acts xxii. 11 seems not to be quite good Greek.* Winer seems to think that this last extension of meaning only occurs in "negative combinations," *i.e.* where ἀπό indicates what *prevents* a thing being done, not what causes it.

The constr. to express local distance (John xi. 18, etc.), is late but pure Greek : in a better age the measure of distance comes in the acc. before ἀπό, so that that would run ὡς σταδίους ιε΄ ἀφ' Ἱερ. Perhaps the word, though bearing quite its commonest sense, is used with rather unusual freedom of constr. in Acts xvi. 33, Rom. ix. 3, 2 Cor. xi. 3, Col. ii. 20 (where ἀποθανεῖν ἀπό seems to be a clearer equivalent to the ἀποθανεῖν c. dat. of Rom. vi. 2 etc.). If we decline to rank Heb. v. 7 with these, it is on account of the limitations of N. T. use of εὐλάβεια, not of ἀπό.

Διά c. gen. in a local sense is used of extension or motion through, not of the limits of intervals. Of time, on the contrary, it has the latter sense in Mark ii. 1, Acts xxiv. 17, Gal. ii. 1 : so Matt. xxvi. 61= Mark xiv. 58, "at an interval of three days," *i.e.*

---

* In Plut. *Timol.* c. 27 we have σύνοπτον οὐδὲν ἦν ἀπὸ τῶν πολεμίων : but further on in the same c. read ὑπὸ τῶν ἁρμάτων . . . εἰς χεῖρας ἐλθεῖν τοῖς Καρχηδονίοις οὐ δυναμένους.

practically "after three days"; equivalent to the ἐν τρισὶν ἡμέραις of Matt. xxvii. 40=Mark xv. 29, John ii. 19.* It also is used of time passed through, in Luke v. 5, Heb. ii. 15, and so no doubt in Acts i. 3: if it be the fact that the Lord did not stay with the Apostles *through* the forty days, but was seen by them at intervals *during* forty days, that fact is inferred from the Gospels, not stated in this place. But this use is comparatively rare, except in almost adverbial phrases—διὰ νυκτός "by night" four times in Acts (v. 19, xvi. 9, xvii. 10, xxiii. 31) and διὰ παντός constantly.

One knows not whether to refer to this sense of "passing through," or to the instrumental one, the exclusively Pauline use of διά to denote the *state in which* a thing is done: Rom. iv. 11, xiv. 20, 2 Cor. ii. 4: in iii. 11 we see that διὰ δόξης must be almost but not quite equivalent to ἐν δόξῃ. Rom. viii. 25, 2 Cor. v. 10 (hardly 7), Gal. v. 13, seem to bridge the interval between this use and the instrumental: a few passages, like Rom. ii. 27, may be assigned to either: but in Heb. ix. 12, 1 John v. 6, it seems quite a mistake to bring in this sense. It is different from the Attic use of διὰ δίκης, διὰ μάχης ἰέναι, δι' ὀργῆς ἔχειν, etc., "to come into" or "to have some one in, a relation of . . . ," to have that as the medium *through which* you deal with him: but διὰ πένθους τὸ γῆρας διάγειν in Xen. *Cyr.* IV. vi. 6 comes very near to it. It is a question whether we can give this meaning to δι' ἀσθένειαν in Gal. iv. 13: it certainly seems a little rash to get, as modern commentators do, an interesting biographical fact out of a grammatical

---

* There is some authority in St. Mark, and rather better in St. John, for the omission of ἐν.

refinement of this sort, and say that it must mean that St. Paul was detained in Galatia by illness. We need not dwell on the strictly instrumental sense of the word, which is often as clearly and definitely used as in Aristotle: but we must remember that, though the N. T. writers know what this usage is, they are less careful than Aristotle to use words with technical accuracy, and less apt to assume (of course they have better reason for not assuming) that words are adequate to the accurate expression of their meaning. Thus in Gal. i. 1 we get ἀπό and διά distinguished, and expect, but do not get, ἀπὸ $\overline{\Theta Y}$ distinguished from διὰ $\overline{IY}$ $\overline{XY}$: in iv. 7 the T. R. actually glosses $\overline{\Theta Y}$ διὰ $\overline{XY}$. for διὰ $\overline{\Theta Y}$ of the primitive text. In Heb. ii. 10 δι' οὗ τὰ πάντα καὶ δι' ὃν τὰ πάντα refers to a different Person from the δι' οὗ of i. 2, the δι' αὐτοῦ of John i. 3, or the δι' αὐτοῦ καὶ εἰς αὐτόν of Col. i. 16, but in all probability the same as ἐξ αὐτοῦ καὶ δι' αὐτοῦ καὶ εἰς αὐτόν in Rom. xi. 36. We should here notice in passing the Hebraistic use of διὰ χειρός, δ. στόματος, the former at least hardly being more than equivalent to the simple διά.

Διά c. acc. is used just as in classical Greek—sometimes meaning "for" of the final cause, sometimes "because of" in a more general sense: which may approximate to, or rather be exchangeable with διά c. gen. Thus in John xv. 3 διὰ τὸν λόγον is "because of the word," not "by the word:" but if they were clean *because of* it, the phrase proves that they must have been cleansed *by* it. In the Apoc. we should not be surprised if there were a confusion between the cases: but in fact iv. 11 is "for Thy will" (A. V. is an excellent gloss), xiii.

14 "by reason of the signs:" even xii. 11 ascribes the victors' strength to the cause they fought for, not to the arms they fought with. In Luke xvii. 11, but nowhere else, διά in a local sense has the acc., if, with the best critical editors, we feel bound to bow to the consent of B ℵ L.—supported, in some measure, by two good groups of cursives. If this be right, the constr. is an inadvertence, rather than a revival of a classical but only poetical use.

Εἰς and ἐν are best considered in connection with each other, being originally connected etymologically, and tending, as they do, to approximate more in usage in the late language. The approximation is however on one side only: as in modern Greek εἰς can be used for "in," but ἐν cannot be used for "into," so in N. T. Greek there is, to say the least, better reason to doubt whether the proper sense of εἰς is remembered than whether that of ἐν is, in the cases where they appear to be "used for" each other. Probably on the whole, each does retain something of its proper form. Εἰς, when immediately depending on a verb of action done *in* a place, is sometimes actually explained by a verb of motion standing co-ordinately with that on which it depends, so that the sense of the one colours the other, *e.g.* Luke xxi. 37, where ηὐλίζετο εἰς belong together, but the sense is ἐξερχόμενος εἰς . . . ηὐλίζετο ἐν τῷ ὄρει. So Matt. ii. 23, iv. 13, and from this the transition is easy to Heb. xi. 9, and not difficult even to Acts viii. 40. Acts (xviii. 21 T. R.) xxi. 13, similarly may be held to imply a journey, though speaking only of what is to be done at its end. We should certainly read κηρύσσων εἰς τὰς συναγωγάς in Mark i. 39, and almost certainly in Luke iv. 44 : in the former passage the best text has ἦλθεν κ., in the other we may, if we please, say that the sense "preaching *to* the synagogues" is included. In John ix. 7 we may either look to ὕπαγε as explaining εἰς, or may say that, in washing, he would dip his hand, perhaps his face: into the pool, cf. Mark i. 9. But it is best not to look for far-fetched justifications in places like Mark xiii. 9, Acts xix. 22, xxv. 4; as it is certain that in late writers (Ælian is the earliest quoted) εἰς means no more than "in," we are prepared to admit that it *may* be so in the N. T. See esp. the parallel passages Matt. xxiv. 18 ἐν τῷ ἀγρῷ, Mark xiii. 16 εἰς τὸν ἀγρόν.

We have one use of εἰς which may fairly be called Hebraistic, the constr. γίνεσθαι εἴς τι which we get in Luke xiii. 19. That this is its nature is proved by the fact, that while it is common in the Apoc. (viii. 11 etc.) and in quotations from the O. T. (Matt. xxi. 42 and many parallels, Heb. i. 5 etc.), it is decidedly rare elsewhere. Yet the constr. had roots in the Greek language itself. Apart from the plainly Hebraic passages, Luke l. c. is perhaps the only one where we feel the phrase to be Hebraistic. Γίνεσθαι εἰς οὐδέν (Acts v. 36), or even εἰς κενόν (1 Thess. iii. 5), seem quite possible Greek, and John xvi. 20 ἡ λύπη ὑμῶν εἰς χαρὰν γενήσεται, has a perfect precedent in Theogn. 162, οἷς τὸ κακὸν δοκέον γίγνεται εἰς ἀγαθόν. It is possible too that this use of εἰς was commended to late generations of Greek-speaking people by its analogy with the Latin double dat.: 2 Sam. vii. 14 *ap.* Heb. i. 5 is exactly *ille mihi filio erit*.

Ἐν has a wider range of non-classical and mainly Hebraistic use. Both εἰς and ἐν, it is true, are used often to express spiritual relations, *e.g.* in the phrases βαπτίζειν εἰς, ἐν (Acts x. 48), or ἐπὶ (ii. 38 *si vera l.*), πιστεύειν εἰς, once or twice (Mark i. 15 : John iii. 15 is ambiguous) πιστεύειν ἐν, ἐν Χριστῷ, ἐν τῷ ὀνόματι. But these are (p. 74) extra-grammatical points : as a rule, they are only applications in a special relation of a familiar use of the prep., though in some of them (the last especially) we may trace a Hebraistic element. More necessary for us to notice are the use of ἐν τῷ c. inf., not only where it means " in the course of " the action (which would be classical) but where it is "at the moment" of it, ἅμα τῷ. (Notice this specially Lucan constr. in Luke ix. 36, where the Greek aor. is used correctly, defining the use of the prep. as *not* pure Greek.)

Still further from classical use is the instrumental ἐν, where in pure Greek we should have the simple dat.,* common esp. in the Apoc. (*e.g.* ii. 16 etc.), but not very rare in the Gospels (Matt. v. 13 etc.). This shades off, no doubt, into the local meaning—*e.g.* βαπτίζω ἐν ὕδατι, Matt. iii. 11 (which well illustrates one of the starting-points of a spiritual use of the prep.—see the end of the verse), Heb. ix. 22; and, where the local meaning remains, we get ἐν even in classical Greek with an instrumental sense at least suggested. Ἐν of price (Rev. v. 9, and prob. i. 5, reading λύσαντι, as we should) is only a special case of this use: ἐν χειρί, like διὰ χειρός noticed above, is a still more Hebraic form of it. Akin to it, but not quite identical, is the sense of *accompaniment*, 1 Cor. iv. 21, 1 Thess. iv. 16, Heb. ix. 25. This may be

* [This idiom is an extension beyond all classical precedent of a construction as old as Homer.]

illustrated by the physical use of the word of garments, Matt. vii. 15 etc.; or we may compare Luke xiv. 31, which we must translate "*with* 10,000," with Enoch *ap.* Jud. 14; which quite possibly means "among." In 1 Cor. vi. 2, xiv. 11 the sense seems to be *apud vos, apud me:* ib. iv. 6, ix. 15, "in my case," which is quite classical.

A Hebraistic use, apparently independent of the instrumental, is that of ὀμνύειν εἰς or ἐν, Matt. v. 35, .34-6, xxiii. 16 *sqq.*; with which cf. ὁμολογεῖν ἐν in Matt. x. 32, Luke xii. 8.

Ἐξ and ἀπό are, as noted above, used more promiscuously in the N. T. than they should be: it is noticeable how often they appear as variant readings. In Matt. vii. 4 the ἐκ of the critical texts is, one would have thought, obviously more appropriate than the ἀπό of the T. R.: in xvii. 9 the reverse is the case: in Mark xvi. 3 ἀπό is old, and seems more appropriate, but ἐκ is better attested, and has remained more popular.

The thoroughly causal sense of ἐκ, rare but not unknown in classical Greek, is in the N. T. confined to St. John's writings—perhaps indeed to the Apoc. (viii. 13, xvi. 10, 11), but many so take Ev. vi. 66, xix. 12, though in the former place at least the temporal meaning seems more natural. The only important use of ἐξ that can be considered Hellenistic is an extension of what may be called its partitive use. John iii. 1, vii. 48, ἐκ τῶν Φαρισαίων, ἀρχόντων, do not go beyond ἐκ τῶν δυναμένων εἰσίν, "are of the number of the powerful," in Plat. *Gorg.* 525 *e*: but in xvi. 17, perhaps iii. 25, we feel the constr. to be harsh: even Ep. II. 4, Rev. ii. 10, seem to give a non-Hellenic force to the prep. And often it seems to add nothing to the force of the simple gen. We have already noticed that ἀπό is used interchangeably with ἐξ in this sense among others.

Perhaps it is a development from Greek germs, but it is hardly a Greek usage, when we have ἐξ used for "at the rate of . . ." (Matt. xx. 2, cf. the simple gen. in ver. 13), or "at the price of" (ib. xxvii. 7, Acts i. 18: so still more directly Ep. Jer. [Bar. vi.] 24). The mental process leading to this use is illustrated by Luke xvi. 9, where the mammon is conceived almost as raw material, at any rate as means and starting-point, for "making friends:" also by comparing the use of ἐξ in Matt. xxvii. 7 with that of εἰς (as apparently understood by the Evangelist) in ver. 10: they get the field *out of* the money, by a process correlative to that of (as we say) sinking the money *in* the field.

Unique is the use of νικᾶν ἐξ in Rev. xv. 2. Some suggest that it may be a Latinism, equivalent to *triumphare de*, or still more exactly to the *victoriam ferre ex* of Liv. VIII. viii. 15. But perhaps the sense is more comparable with the N. T. constructions, themselves natural enough, of μετανοεῖν ἐκ, σώζεσθαι ἐξ, and the like: the victors are conceived as fighting their way clear from the enemy.

Ἐπί differs less than most prepositions in its sense when joined with different cases: and in the N. T. we meet with remarkably direct proof of the consciousness that, in its primary local sense of "upon," it is almost a matter of indifference what case is joined with it. For we get it joined with different cases in the same or in adjacent or parallel sentences, to express obviously identical relations—Matt. xix. 28,

Luke xii. 53, Acts v. 9, 23 (cf. Matt. xxiv. 33=Mark xiii. 29, Rev. iii. 20), xxvii. 44, Rev. iv. 2, 9, 10, xiv. 9, xix. 11, 14 (18), 20, etc.: or compare the best texts of Matt. xxiv. 2=Mark xiii. 2 with Luke xxi. 6. But it has special meanings with each case: all these are found in classical Greek, and are not confused in the N. T., except where (as in Luke l. c.) either case may correctly be used in the sense intended: *e.g.* in 2 Tim. ii. 14 (true text), ἐπ' οὐδὲν χρήσιμον "to no useful end," is correctly distinguished from ἐπὶ καταστροφῇ "so as to overthrow." In Phil. ii. 27, however, the λύπην ἐπὶ λύπῃ of the T. R. is better Greek than ἐπὶ λύπην of the critical text. Perhaps the chief divergence from classical use with this prep. is, that it has apparently ceased to bear the sense "towards" c. gen. And the use is post-classical of ἐπί c. acc. to indicate a point of time, as it apparently does in Luke x. 35, Acts iv. 5, perh. iii. 1 (*not* Mark xv. 1, true text). Βασιλεύειν ἐπί c. acc., "to reign over" (Luke i. 33, xix. 14, 27, Rom. v. 14), is not a classical constr., though the prep. has in classics the sense implied. In Matt. ii. 22 the best text has the simple gen. after βασιλεύειν, which is classical, instead of β. ἐπί c. gen. of the T. R.: in Rev. v. 10 ἐπὶ τῆς γῆς prob. has a merely local sense, and does not depend on β. We notice that, while ἐπὶ τῷ ὀνόματι (in its distinctive Biblical sense) is apparently interchangeable with ἐν τῷ ὀν. (see Acts iv. 10, 17), we do not get ἐπὶ τὸ ὄνομα to correspond with εἰς τὸ ὄν. —though ἐν and εἰς are as nearly synonymous as in Acts x. 48, xix. 5. But we get πιστεύειν ἐπί c. dat. in 1 Tim. i. 16, as well as in the quotation in Rom. ix. 33, x. 11—where it is worth remembering that the Vatican text of the LXX. omits ἐπ' αὐτῷ—, by the side of the commoner π. ἐπί c. acc. In Luke xxiv. 25 the constr. is no doubt different, "to believe *in view of*" . . . : Rom. iv. 16 is even plainer. Notice the frequency of this phrase ἐπ' ἐλπίδι (or ἐφ' ἐλπ.).

Κατά is used upon the same lines as in classical Greek, but its use has in some respects become more vague as well as more extensive. In some respects, the change is less than one might expect. In the best ages, the quasi-adverbial phrases καθ' ὅλου and κατὰ παντός were the only ones in which κατά c. gen. seemed to have the sense "throughout," as c. acc. : but in Polybius (I. xvii. 10, III. xix. 7, lxxvi. 10) one constr. seems quite equivalent to the other. Now in the N. T. we never get the gen. in this sense, except in St. Luke (iv. 14, xxiii. 5, Acts ix. 31, 42, x. 37), and in him always with the adj. ὅλος; the phrase seeming to "sound right," because the adv. καθόλου (also peculiar to him in the N. T., Acts iv. 18) had become so common since Aristotle.

Ὀμνύναι κατά τινος is quite classical, but is used of the objects sworn *on*, or pledged to execration by the oath, not of the God sworn *by*, as in Matt. xxvi. 63, Heb. vi. 13, 16. In James v. 12 we have the classical ὀμνύειν c. acc. : in the Gospels, as already noted, the Hebraistic ὀ. ἐν or εἰς. Ἐγκαλεῖν κατά in Rom. viii. 33 is a familiar classical sense of the prep., but the classical constr. of the verb is c. dat., as Acts xix. 38, xxiii. 28.

Κατά c. acc. perhaps goes a little beyond classical precedent in its local use : any Greek writer might have written κατὰ Κυρήνην in Acts ii. 10, perhaps κατὰ τὸν τόπον in Luke x. 32, but one may doubt κατ' αὐτόν in the next verse. Κατὰ πρόσωπον is good Greek (see Polyb. III. xix. 7, where curiously we have τῶν μὲν κατὰ πρόσωπον τῶν δὲ κατὰ νώτου), but there is a Hellenistic element in its sense in Luke ii. 31, Acts iii. 13, and even Gal. ii. 11. More decided is the extension of its vaguest and most general use, "in relation to," though often we may render "according to," "by way of," and so bring it within recognised meanings of the word. Τῶν καθ' ὑμᾶς ποιητῶν in Acts xvii. 28 is literary, even elegant, Greek, but of a late period: and the use of τοῖς κατ' ἐξοχήν in xxv. 23 is, so far as we know, unique, the phrase itself being anyhow late. Still more may one doubt whether κατὰ πᾶσαν αἰτίαν (Matt. xix. 3), or even κατὰ ἄγνοιαν (Acts iii. 17) is quite good Greek. But of St. Paul's κατὰ Θεὸν, κατὰ χάριν and the like, we may say that it is the thought rather than the word that is beyond the limits of Hellenism.

Μετά has for its primary meaning "among," whether it be etymologically cognate with μέσος or not: and this sense survives more or less in some N. T. passages, Luke xxii. 37 (the LXX. has ἐν τοῖς ἀνόμοις: the quotation is not genuine in Mark xv. 28), xxiv. 5 being perhaps those ones where "with" is most inadequate to translate it; but Mark i. 13 and several other places admit or require the sense to be more or less present. But in general the word means no more than "with," and it seems useless to try to elaborate a distinction between it and σύν: some tell us that it implies a much closer union than it, some say just the reverse.* The fact is, that while in the

* If there be any definable distinction, I should rather say it is that σύν sets the things connected more on a level, while

earliest Greek σύν is the ordinary word for "with," as time went on μετά began to supplant it, and became far commoner than it, even in Attic: vid. Liddell & Scott. *s. v.* In the N. T. σύν is rare, except in SS. Luke and Paul—and perhaps we should add some of the Catholic Epp., which are too short to have frequent occasion for either. As σύν, though never used like our "with" to express the instrumental relation, yet is occasionally used of things that *might* have been regarded as instruments, so we may say μετά is used in Luke xvii. 15, perhaps Acts xiii. 17.

In Rev. ii. 16, xii. 7, xiii. 4, xvii. 14 we find πολεμεῖν μετά used like our "to make war *with*," *i.e.* against. This is exactly the Hebrew נִלְחַם עִם of Judges v. 20, 1 Sam. xvii. 33, etc.: in pure Greek the phrase could only mean "to make war *in alliance with.*" Some have actually so taken the Hebrew in Judges l. c., as though the stars fought for Sisera and the river against him: but in most of the O. T. passages, and all those in the Apocrypha, the sense is unmistakable. Perhaps we may rank also as a Hebraism the religious sense of the word, which we find in Matt. i. 23 (cf. Is. viii. 8—in vii. 14 the LXX. leave the pr. n. untranslated), Luke i. 28, John iii. 2, etc.

Μετά c. acc. is found only in the regular sense "after"

μετά regards the noun dependent on it as an *accompaniment* to the other. *E.g.* in Phil. i. 1 the address is to the whole Church *and* its officers—they being sufficiently important to be considered as co-ordinate with the whole body. Μετ' ἐπισκόπων καὶ διακόνων would have treated them as mere appendages to it. Yet in the LXX. of Judges i. 3, 2 (4) Kings x. 15 we have μετά, though the object is to express association in exactly equal and reciprocal terms.

* [Where σύν is confined to special phrases in prose—except in Xenophon.]

PREPOSITIONS: μετά, παρά. 151

—always of time except Heb. ix. 3, when it is of place, or perhaps rather of order. The only irregularity to be noticed is the Latinism in Acts i. 5, corresponding to that noticed below s. v. πρό. Παρά is, generally speaking, used correctly with all three cases. C. gen. there are a few phrases where, though the case has its proper force, its point is apt to be missed. If we read the gen. in Luke i. 37 (no one reads it in Gen. xviii. 14) it must mean "no word on God's part, no word spoken by God," whether or no we give to ἀδυνατεῖν its classical instead of its Hellenistic sense. In Mark iii. 21, οἱ παρ' αὐτοῦ are "they of his own house," and similarly the neut. in v. 26, "all the substance of her house," all that (literally) *came from* the place *where she was:* so Luke x. 7, "what the household supplies," though the A.V. gives a suitable sense.

Παρά c. gen. is in Greek prose always used exclusively of *persons*, so it is in the N. T. c. dat. also, with the one exception of παρὰ τῷ σταυρῷ in John xix. 25. Among many idiomatic usages we get an ethical one, for which there is hardly classical precedent, though it is quite in harmony with the meaning of the word—παρ' ἐμοί 2 Cor. i. 17, "with me," *i.e.* "in my character" or "habits:" so oftener παρὰ τῷ Θεῷ, Rom. ii. 11, ix. 14, Eph. vi. 9, James i. 17. (Different and commoner is παρὰ τῷ Θεῷ in Rom. ii. 13, "*before* God," "in His *judgment*.") C. acc., the chief point to notice is the extension of its sense in comparison, causing it to be used (see pp. 92-3) after comparative degrees, and in other ways for which the sense "beyond" or "above," which it has no doubt in classical Greek (in Plat. *Theæt.* p. 144 *a*, we even get it with an adj., ἀνδρεῖον παρ' ὁντινοῦν, "braver than any one"), gives a starting-point, but hardly a full justification. Of particular phrases, Rom. i. 25 is naturally translated "beyond" or "above," *i.e.* "more than the Creator," for which it is quite good Greek. Some try to make it mean "passing by the Creator" —more possible would be "in contravention of His rights:" but without a verbal phrase defining one of these senses it seems hardly possible to get either out of the prep. In xiv. 5 ἡμέραν παρ' ἡμέραν is certainly good Greek for "one day above another:" one might hesitate a little about the use of κρίνειν, but it is so used in pure Greek with πρό, if not with παρά.

Περί c. gen. goes some way beyond classical usage towards becoming synonymous with ὑπέρ, the two being often interchanged as vv. ll., *e.g.* Mark xiv. 24. It is sometimes doubtful which is really best attested, and at any rate it cannot be said that the later texts have any consistent tendency to substitute either for the other. In Eph. vi. 18, 19, they stand side by side in the same constr., as almost synonymous. One may derive this sense of acting *on behalf of* a thing from a combination of the common sense, of telling or thinking *about* it, and the equally classical sense of striving *for* the thing, *i.e.* to get or save it. (Luke iv. 38 shows how easy the transition is from the former sense.) It does not mean, quite as distinctly as ὑπέρ, *in the interest, for the benefit* of the dependent noun: *e.g.* the characteristically Hellenistic phrase περὶ ἁμαρτίας means that, by the sin-offering, there is a *remembrance made* of sin; but it is that sin may be abolished, not retained. At the same time we have περὶ καθαρισμοῦ (Mark i. 44=Luke v. 14), which is the same in principle. See also 1 Pet. iii. 18, where περί and ὑπέρ have distinguishable senses. If there be a difference between the two in Eph. l. c., it probably is "making mention of all God's people, and working for my aid"—making the most of what they are to do for himself, partly from the sense of his need under trial, and of his helplessness in imprisonment, and partly as a delicate recognition of their dignity as his intercessors. But John xvi. 26, xvii. 9, 20 show that the most exalted intercession may be worthily expressed by περί. Hardly classical is the use of περί in John x. 33, where it appears as practically equivalent to διά of ver. 32: but Acts xxvi. 7 explains how this sense is reached. (That constr. is classical, except for the pass. use of ἐγκαλοῦμαι; which does not seem to occur, but is paralleled by the use of the pass. of other verbs governing a dat.).

Περί c. dat. does not occur in the N. T., though the sense of it is involved in the compounds περιπείρειν and περιπίπτειν. Of περί c. acc., most of the uses are regular enough. We notice the use of οἱ περὶ αὐτόν in Mark iv. 10, Luke xxii. 49 in the most literal sense, "they that were about Him": but in Acts xiii. 13 οἱ περὶ Π. is idiomatically "Paul and his company." The alleged further modification, as meaning only the person named, is certainly not found in the N. T.: John xi. 19 would seem like it if the T. R. were genuine, but even then it would be good sense "to comfort Martha, Mary, *and their family* concerning their brother.

Πρό needs no remark, except that the constr. with a double gen., of an interval of time elapsing before an event (*e.g.* John xii. 1), is late but not exclusively biblical: it is explained as a Latinism. We notice also the Hebraistic pleonasm, πρὸ προσώπου c. gen. meaning no more than πρό: generally of a person, so that the phrase gains somewhat in picturesqueness or vigour, as in Luke ix. 52, x. 1, as well as the many more or less direct quotations of Mal. iii. 1: but in Acts xiii. 24, still no doubt under the influence of that passage, we get the phrase used where it can mean no more than the simple prep.

Πρός c. gen. occurs once only in the N. T. (Acts xxvii. 34) in the (quite classical) sense " for," " in the interest of." C. dat. it is not much more frequent— Mark v. 11 (true text), Luke xix. 37, John xviii. 16, xx. 11 (true text), 12, Rev. i. 13. In all these places the meaning is obviously "close to," never "in addition to." But in general, even in this sense πρός is used c. acc.—not only in places like Mark xi. 4, where we might say "tied to the door," but in Mark ii. 2, iv. 1, xiv. 54=Luke xxii. 56, where it is of place, with no notion of motion. Matt. xiii. 56=Mark vi. 3, xxvi. 18, Mark ix. 19=Luke ix. 41, xiv. 49, and several other places where it is used of persons, are on a somewhat different footing: there is no notion of motion necessarily involved (see esp. 1 Cor. xvi. 6, 7, Gal. i. 18), but the sense seems not to be merely local, but to suggest active personal relations: note the use in Gal. ii. 5, shortly after the last of the passages cited, or in Rom. iv. 2, 1 John ii. 1. In St. John Ev. i. 1, Ep. I. i. 2, πρὸς τὸν $\overline{ΘΝ}$, πρὸς τὸν $\overline{ΠΡΑ}$, certainly means much more than "closest," "in contact with:" it is rather "in living relation with:" of ὁ ὢν εἰς τὸν κόλπον in Ev. i. 18—which differs from ἐν τῷ κόλπῳ just as, in xiii. 23-5, ἀναπεσὼν ἐπὶ τὸ στῆθος is more than ἀνακείμενος ἐν τῷ κόλπῳ. The other uses of the word seem to need no comment, except in relation to its distinction from εἰς in certain ethical relations. We have the two prepositions used side by side in Rom. iii. 25-6, Eph. iv. 12, and perhaps Philem. 5. In the first two passages, the relations and connexion of the clauses are too doubtful to give us a fair start for discussion of the difference, if any, between the prepositions. But in the third, the only doubtful question (assuming that the reading with both prepositions is the true one, as is likely *a priori*, MS. evidence being ambiguous) is whether the two are to be taken as correlative with the two nouns—saying with Bishop Lightfoot "there is a propriety in using πρός of the faith which aspires *towards* Christ, and εἰς of the love which is exerted *upon* men;" or whether, if this separation seem uncalled for, we shall say that Philemon's faith and love went *to* Christ as to one object, but went *among* men, dispersing their good gifts to each.

Σύν needs no comment, further than what has already been said of its relation to μετά, and its rarity as compared therewith.

Ὑπέρ is never used in a merely local sense, either with gen. or acc., ἐπάνω, or more rarely ὑπεράνω, c. gen. being available for this purpose. As already mentioned, it tends to approximate to and become confused with περί; and indeed ὑπέρ has the better right to approximate to the other, for the sense "concerning," found *e.g.* Rom. ix. 27, 2 Cor. i. 8 (?), viii. 23, is a legitimate and classical one, though rarer in good Attic than in earlier or later Greek. (See Plat. *Leg.* p. 776 *e*, where the language has a half epic colouring.)

Uses like 2 Cor. i. 6, 7, 2 Thess. ii. 1 are modifications of this meaning; 2 Cor. xii. 8 may be held to mark a transition to the next. The commonest N. T. sense of the word, and a common one in all Greek, is "on behalf of," sometimes "on the side of," as Mark ix. 40=Luke ix. 50, Rom. viii. 31. To this we must refer Rom. xv. 8 (="by His ministry it was secured that God should be true"), Phil. ii. 13—where, taking ὑπὲρ τῆς εὐδ. with ὁ ἐνεργῶν, as is usual, it is "in order to carry out His gracious will:" if we connect it rather with the two infinitives, it will be "that your will and action may be *on the side of* His gracious will." 1 Cor. iv. 6 is no doubt used of men boasting of their party leaders or their party following, and so is like 2 Cor. vii. 4 etc.: but some take it "that ye be not puffed up one *over* another"—which would be natural Greek enough, but unique in the N. T., as well as less suitable to the context.

It is a question how near ὑπέρ in this sense, "on behalf of," approximates to the meaning of ἀντί "instead of." Of the many passages where ὑπέρ is used of the Atonement, Gal. iii. 13 is almost the only one that suggests the equivalence. If we desire to approach the theological question on its grammatical side, we had better start from Philem. 13, where ὑπὲρ σοῦ "as your representative" comes practically to the same thing as ἀντὶ σοῦ "as your substitute," but is not quite the same. And 2 Cor. v. 14 illustrates the extent of the difference, corresponding to that between the true translation of the aor. and that of the A.V. Ὑπέρ c. acc. has only the sense, in the N. T., of "beyond" or "above," of measure or degree. Besides its classical uses in this sense, it is used like παρά (as already mentioned, pp. 92-3) in comparative sentences where a prep. cannot be considered classical: in fact, there is less classical precedent for so using ὑπέρ than for παρά.

The adverbial use in 2 Cor. xi. 23 is unique: but ὑπερλίαν in xi. 5, xii. 11, though we know of no precedents, has as good a right to exist as ὑπεράγαν (whether we write either as one word or two).

Ὑπό c. gen. is only used of agency, its commonest classical sense. There is nothing to surprise us in its use with neut. verbs, as in Matt. xvii. 12 etc., hardly in 2 Cor. xi. 24. But the use receives an extension which is hardly good Greek in Rev. vi. 8, though there we see the reason for using ὑπό of the living agents, as distinct from the instrumental ἐν of lifeless causes. Hdt. VII. xxii. 2, lvi. 1, ὀρύσσειν, διαβαίνειν ὑπὸ μαστίγων, are not really parallel to this—rather to id. I. xvii. 3, with perhaps a sarcastic reminiscence of that use.

The poetical use of ὑπό c. dat. of course is not found in the N. T. That c. acc. is comparatively rare, and does not differ from the classical.

We may conclude with one or two general remarks about the use of prepositions. Besides the compositions for the sake of redundant emphasis, noted on p. 42, we find combinations of a prep. and an adv. of time very much commoner in late Greek than in classical, and prob. in biblical Greek commoner than in secular. A few such phrases, *e.g.* εἰς ἀεί, παραυτίκα, are quite classical, and even approached or assumed the character of compound adverbs: but ἀπάρτι (in the sense of "henceforth"—in a different sense ἀπαρτί is older), ἐφάπαξ appear first in comedians, and in no classical Greek is as common as in the N. T. St. Matthew's ἀπὸ τότε (also Luke xvi. 16) may be instanced: so ἀπὸ πρωὶ, ἀπὸ πέρυσι (which is unique, 2 Cor. viii. 10, ix. 2), ἔκπαλαι.

When a prep. has more nouns than one depending on it, the prep. is repeated with each of them more frequently in the N. T. than in pure Greek. In Luke xxiv. 27, the second ἀπό almost spoils the sense of the first—the sense is "going on through all the prophets," and perhaps the repetition adds the idea of *drawing from* each, but it would not have occurred in a pure Greek writer. In 1 Thess. i. 5, the second ἐν was of course required after ἀλλά, but the third and (*si vera l.*) fourth have at most a rhetorical value. Mark xiii. 32 (true text), 1 Tim. ii. 9, v. 19, Heb. x. 28, are said to be the only cases where nouns separated by disjunctive conjunctions have only one prep. between them; and every one will see that in all these cases—in the two last especially—the repetition would have been impossible, or have altered the sense. In clauses where there is a comparison (*e.g.* Acts xi. 15 ἐπ' αὐτοὺς ... ὥσπερ ἐφ' ἡμᾶς) the prep. is always repeated: always after an adversative, except sometimes where (as 1 Pet. i. 23) it is adjectives belonging to one subst. that are distinguished (so ibid. ver. 11 after a disjunctive). In Acts vii. 4, xx. 18 we get the prep. repeated with the rel., though by no means the most suitable prep. to its place in the sentence, by a curious extension of the principle of attraction. In xiii. 2, 39 we have, far more classically, the prep. omitted with the rel., being understood from the antecedent clause. In

vii. 38, there is perhaps a point in the omission of μετά before τῶν π. ἡμῶν—the privilege of "our fathers" is heightened, when one may speak of being "with the Angel and them." But in xxvi. 18, 1 Cor. x. 28, Heb. vii. 27 the repetition of the prep. would have been more natural: in the two former places, there is just enough MS. testimony for it, to show that early scribes felt it so.

Besides these prepositions commonly recognised as such, the N. T. makes very extensive use of the adverbs and other words that take the constr. of prepositions; including some peculiar to late Greek, or even to the Hellenistic dialect. Thus besides the classical ἄντικρυς and ἐναντίον, we get ἔναντι, ἀπέναντι, κατέναντι, ἐνώπιον, κατενώπιον: of which ἀπέναντι alone is found in pure if late Greek, as is the adj. ἐνώπιος, but not the adverbial neut. Being common in the LXX., it looks as though it were conceived as a literal translation of בְּעֵינֵי. Besides ἔμπροσθεν and ὄπισθεν, we find ὀπίσω c. gen.: besides ἐπέκεινα, with which we may couple πέραν and ἀντίπερα, which is late only in form, ὑπερέκεινα: besides ἐκτός and ἔξωθεν, παρεκτός: besides the simple ἕως c. gen., we get such phrases not only as ἕως τοῦ νῦν, but the direct combination with notes of time, ἕως ἄρτι, ἕως πότε, ἕως σήμερον (2 Cor. iii. 15), with local words, ἕως ὧδε. (Luke xxiii. 5), ἕως ἄνω (John ii. 7), ἕως κάτω (Matt. xxvii. 51=Mark xv. 38), ἕως ἔσω εἰς (Mark xiv. 54), ἕως ἔξω c. gen. (Acts xxi. 5), with a numeral, ἕως ἑπτάκις (Matt. xviii. 21-2), and with prepositions, ἕως εἰς, ἕως ἐπί. Ἐπάνω and (the late) ὑπεράνω have received extensions of meaning, as well as become relatively more frequent. Ὑπερεκπερισσοῦ, which is used adverbially in 1 Thess. iii. 10, v. 13 (?), is perhaps hardly quite prepositional in Eph. iii. 20: but ἄτερ, ἐγγύς, ἐντός, μεταξύ, πλήν, πλησίον, ὑποκάτω, χωρίς are all found in the N. T. as virtual prepositions c. gen.: so are the less local ἕνεκα and χάριν: and so are ἅμα, ἐγγύς, παραπλήσιον c. dat.

(b) Conjunctions.

Conjunctions in the strictest sense—particles that serve, not to articulate the structure of a sentence, but to couple together co-ordinate sentences, or words or clauses that hold co-ordinate places in a sentence— are in the N. T. comparatively wanting in variety, and are made to do a good deal of duty. Of the two common Greek copulatives, τε is rare, except in the semi-classical language of Acts and Hebrews. In St. Paul and St. Luke's Gospel the correlative τε καί is less rare than the simple τε; but the latter never has τε for "and," and the former only in 1 Cor. iv. 21, Eph. iii. 19, (the double τε only in Rom. i. 26): the use of τε γάρ in Rom. vii. 7 (2 Cor. x. 8 ? is different, and late though not exclusively Hellenistic). St. Mark and the Apoc., as well as some of the shorter Epp., never (according to their true text) use τε at all.

Καί, on the other hand, is used very extensively, and most so in the most Hebraic books, the Synoptic Gospels and the Apoc. Even in the Acts, we get it more frequently than we should in a classical narrative, and there is no doubt that this frequency is more or less directly a reproduction of O. T. style, and so in some sense a Hebraism.

In what sense and to what extent it is so, is a

further question, and not free from doubt. Not only is it characteristic of biblical Hebrew * to link every successive sentence in a narrative to the preceding one by the same conj., but that conj. is what has been called " a conjunctive general "—it is used to *suggest* various relations between clauses which, in any European language, we should *express* by different particles. *E.g.* in Ps. li. 16 (Heb. 18) a " literal " translation would be " For Thou desirest not sacrifice and I [will] give it : " the meaning is, in all likelihood, that of either the text or the margin of the English Bible, " else would I give it," or " that I should give it," but a few take it to be "though I will give that too : " in any case, we should use something more distinctive than a simple copulative.

Now it would certainly be wrong to suppose that the N. T. use of καί covers as wide a range of meaning as this : at most, it may perhaps be credible that the Seer of the Apocalypse, with his mind steeped in the language of the O. T. Prophets, in one passage (x. 7 ; see p. 98) unconsciously followed Hebrew idiom in the use of the simplest and commonest conj. As a rule, we get καί not only more frequently used, but used with a somewhat wider range of meaning, than would be the case in classical Greek : but we do not get it used except in cases where it would be just admissible in Greek, or where the LXX. has (with or without some native Greek analogy) established its use as idiomatic in the Hellenistic dialect. As examples of

---

* *Not* of Aramaic, as even the English reader of the Book of Daniel may notice. The A. V. often there inserts an "and" in italics, feeling it to be necessary for assimilation to the ordinary biblical style.

the latter kind we may take the use of καὶ ἐγένετο followed by an indic.; of a second καί or καὶ ἰδού after this (or, in St. Luke, after the equivalent ἐγένετο δέ); of καί or καὶ ἰδού at the beginning of the apodosis to relative sentences * (Luke ii. 21; Rev. xiv. 10, etc.): of the former, the use with notes of time in places like Matt. xxvi. 2, 45, Mark xv. 25,† Luke xix. 43, Acts v. 7, Heb. viii. 8 (which differs more or less from any independently known text of the LXX., but agrees with it in this constr.), and some—it is hard to say how many—of the cases where we may translate καί "and so," "and then" or the like, or where we might have expected an adversative rather than a copulative. It will be worth the student's while to examine the uses of καί ranked in Bruder's Concordance under the heads, not only of I. 2 "ubi magis recedere videtur particulæ usus ab dicendi Occidentalium ratione, aliis particulis sententiarumque conformationibus utentium," but of I. 1. C. "καί rhetoricæ indolis: in sententiis strenue oppositis, in

---

* The few classical passages where καί stands redundantly, introducing an apodosis, usually to a ptcp., are not really parallel to this. And when it introduces the apod. to a relative clause (e.g. Thuc. II. xciii. 3) it seems to have a more distinctively emphatic sense than in the Hellenistic passages.

† Winer points out, that this constr. covers two cases different in principle. Luke xxiii. 44 is no more than an exact parallel to Soph. *Phil.* 354-6 or to Plat. *Symp.* 220 *c*, (in the story of Socrates' trance before Potidæa), ἤδη ἦν μεσημβρία καὶ ἄνθρωποι ἠσθάνοντο: but in Mark l. c. the point is not "such an hour came, and then something happened:" we have been told in ver. 24 σταυροῦσιν αὐτόν, and now what we learn is, *when* this was done. St. Mark's sentence is a non-Hellenic way of saying "It was the third hour *when* they crucified Him:" St. Luke's is a vivid and perfectly Hellenic way of following the day through its course, and noting its events as they came.

presse dictis," and D. "καί initio apodoseos positum." But generally it will be right to translate it simply "and," even in passages like Mark xii. 12, Rom. i. 13, 1 Thess. ii. 18, where the English sentence would be clearer with "but." The Greek conjunctions, copulative and adversative, correspond fairly enough to the English: and it is a fact which we have to acknowledge, that in Hellenistic Greek the copulative not the adversative are here used. Of course this will not apply to the other case, where there is a real Hebraism or anacoluthon in the structure of the sentence: there no one disputes that we must translate "And it came to pass *that* . . ." "For if I grieve you, who *then* is he, etc." (2 Cor. ii. 2), and the like.

The use of τε, in the books that do use it, does not materially differ from the classical. Only it may be thought that some writers are too fond of it, and put it in where, if not redundant, it suggests a false view of the structure of the sentence. Thus in Acts xix. 27, xxi. 28 τε καί are not correlative, but mean "*and* that she should *even* be deposed," "and further hath brought Greeks *also*:" while in xxvi. 10 we get καὶ πολλούς τε together, as though καὶ . . . τε stood like καὶ . . . δέ for "and . . . also," whereas really πολλούς τε . . . κατέκλεισα is co-ordinate with ἀναιρουμένων τε . . . ψῆφον. And whereas in classical Greek τε καί often serve to mark a slight *opposition,* of the same sort as μὲν . . . δέ though milder (nearly like the English "as well . . . as . . . "), in the N. T. it does not seem to have this force—a double καί sometimes comes nearer to it, as Rom. xiv. 9, 1 Cor. vi. 14, Phil. iv. 12 etc. So perhaps in John xvii. 25 the first καί is correlative, not to the immediately following δέ but to the second καί: the effect being something like, "While the world knew Thee not, though I knew Thee, these on their part knew. . . ."

There is not much to be said of what may almost be called the adverbial use of καί—that which we represent by the words "also," "even," or the like. Perhaps the most distinctive type of this use is where it occurs in comparisons—sometimes in the relative clause, as 1 Cor. vii. 7, sometimes in both, as Rom. i. 13 (last two clauses), more commonly in the antecedent clause, either emphasising an adv., as Matt. vii. 12, or alone as in Matt. vi. 10. For all of these, however, there are classical parallels.

Of disjunctive conjunctions, we need only notice the correct use of ἤτοι in Rom. vi. 16. The word is regularly used with the *first* of two or more alternatives, which it is desired to emphasise—sometimes as the more desirable, sometimes, as here, as the more probable.

The negatives οὐδέ and μηδέ, οὔτε and μήτε, though commonly ranked as disjunctives, have almost more affinity in use with copulatives. We are here concerned with the difference, not between the negative particles, but with that between the conjunctions combined with them, the rules for the use of each pair being much the same. Of course in the case of words so similar both in form and meaning, confusion of reading between them is common: but according to the best textual evidence it appears that οὔτε and μήτε are indeed sometimes used beyond the limits allowed in pure Greek, but that such cases are rarer in the original than in the later texts of the N. T.

The single οὔτε in James iii. 12, and the μή . . . μήτε . . . μήτε of Acts xxiii. 8 are perhaps the only certain cases of incorrect use;—for the latter is not parallel to Matt. v. 34-6, 1 Tim. i. 7, etc., where we have a general case stated with μή, and then broken up into a number of subordinate alternatives with μήτε's: perhaps μήτε εἶναι ἀνάστασιν μήτε ἄγγελον μηδὲ πνεῦμα, "that there is *neither* resurrection *nor* angel *or* spirit," would have expressed most correctly the writer's meaning. For the use of οὐ (1 Cor. vi. 9, 10 best text) or οὐδέ in the last clause after one or more οὔτε's there is classical precedent, though mostly in poetry, *e.g.* Æsch. *Prom.* 450-1: οὐδέ in Luke xx. 35, 36, Acts xxiv. 12 needs no justification. Οὔτε . . . καί in John iv. 11, 3 John 10 is late (at least, the only classical instance cited, Eur. *I. T.* 591-2, is doubtful): but it is just equivalent to the classical οὔτε . . . τε. In James iii. 14 we have, as in Hebrew, two verbs joined by the simple καί, and the negative that goes with the former applying to both—καί in fact being used where μηδέ would be more obvious. Here the change of conjunction perhaps modifies the meaning a little, but it may be really due to the influence of Hebrew idiom: it is different in 2 Cor. xii. 21, where we have verbs connected with καί after φοβοῦμαι μή, and in the passages where Isa. vi. 9, 10 are quoted.

Of adversatives, the simple and common use of ἀλλά is most frequent, at least in the Gospels, after negatives—Matt. v. 15, 17, etc.: but we also get it before negatives, as in Mark x. 27, or in other relations, as in Mark xiii. 24, 1 Pet. iii. 15: occasionally after μέν, as (Mark ix. 13?), Acts iv. 16. Besides this, we have to note its use (1) in pathetic appeals (not however, in the N. T., where a strictly adversative force is excluded), Matt. ix. 18, Mark ix. 22 : (2) in stating or meeting an objection, Lat. *at*, Rom. x. 16, 18, 19, xi. 4, etc. : (3) in St. Paul only, in the apodosis to concessive or even hypothetical sentences, Rom. vi. 5, 1 Cor. ix. 2, 2 Cor. v. 16, (xiii. 4, T. R.), Col. ii. 5 ; and this sometimes after another ἀλλά, 2 Cor. iv. 16, or before one, xi. 6 : (4) in answering one rhetorical question by another, Heb. iii. 16 : (5) where the adversative form almost disappears, the point being a climax, Phil. i. 18.

We notice with this word the tendency of the declining language to combine and accumulate particles: we get twice (Luke xii. 51, 2 Cor. i. 13—not 1 Cor. iii. 5) ἀλλ' ἤ, one or other particle being redundant; twice (Luke xxiv. 21, 1 Cor. ix. 2) ἀλλά γε ; once (Phil. iii. 8) ἀλλὰ μὲν οὖν [γε], as well as the frequent and natural ἀλλὰ καί.

Δέ by itself is something between a copulative and an adversative conj., or at least its natural English equivalent is almost equally often " and " and " but." Perhaps it stands oftener in the N. T. than in classical Greek for a mere note of *transition*, at the beginning of a sentence, where we in English should put no conj. at all, or at most the particle " Now." Its use is somewhat freer in the writers whose style is more nearly classical, but it can hardly be said to be markedly more or less frequent in one than in another. At least, if we think its greater rarity in St. John's Epp. and in the Apoc. not to be accidental, it yet is due less to want of familiarity with the particle than to deeper characteristics of their style. St. Luke's substitution of ἐγένετο δέ for the more purely Hebraic καὶ ἐγένετο is perhaps the most important point to be noticed under this head. The combination καὶ ... δέ, "and ... also," is used just as in pure Greek, and not much more frequently.

The characteristically Greek form of antithetical sentence, with its balanced words or clauses marked by μέν and δέ, has by no means become obsolete in the N. T.: we find it in every writer;—unless we refer 2 Peter and the Apoc. to separate authorship; for it occurs in neither of them (nor in St. John's Epp.).

Like other pure Hellenic idioms, it is most frequent in SS. Luke, Paul, and Heb.: but perhaps it is in 1 Peter that its use is freest, and contributes most to the sense: certainly every time that he uses it (five times, not counting ii. 14, where omit μέν) the antithesis is emphatic. In the Gospels, μὲν ... δέ is rare (though not unknown in any of them), except in the phrase ὁ (or ὅς) μὲν κ.τ.λ. (see p. 52): notice especially Matt. xxiii. 2-12, where μέν does not occur at all, though there are many phrases where it would be forcible. Nowhere in the N. T. do we get the emphatic idiom, where something is said about the conjugate sentence which properly refers to the δέ clause only; so that we in English have to recast the antithetical sentence into a concessive one, and represent μέν by "while" or "though," and the δέ clause by an apodosis. The disuse of this idiom is the more remarkable, that in Rom. vi. 17 we actually have a sentence of this type and meaning, but the μέν is omitted. In John iii. 19, again, we might naturally have had this constr.—ὅτι τὸ μὲν φῶς ... οἱ δὲ ἄνθρωποι: see also p. 187, on 1 Pet. i. 8. Otherwise, we have little variation from classical usage,

and much variety in harmony with it. Μέν is occasionally answered, not by δέ but by other particles (Mark ix. 12, Acts iv. 16 ἀλλά, Luke xxii. 22 πλήν, John xi. 6, etc. ἔπειτα: even καί in Acts xxvii. 21): occasionally also it stands absolutely, not only in the combination μὲν οὖν (which itself passes by imperceptible degrees from a combination of the two independent particles to become itself an adversative particle), but of the simple μέν, having lost its second clause by an aposiopesis or anacoluthon (Acts i. 1, iii. 21, xxviii. 22, and several times in St. Paul).*
Μὲν οὖν is used quite in the classical manner by St. Luke, esp. in Acts, and now and then by St. Paul (1 Cor. vi. 4, 7: in Rom. xi. 13 it is perhaps questionable if it has exactly the classic force) and in Hebrews (vii. 11, ix. 1). But it is peculiar to the N. T. to use μενοῦνγε (Luke xi. 28, Rom. ix. 20, x. 18) at the beginning of a sentence—whether we write it as one word, or as two, or three. Μέντοι is not very frequent, but is used correctly—oftenest by St. John, who once (xii. 42) has the somewhat redundant ὅμως μέντοι. Καίτοι is correctly used, as an adversative conj. in Acts xiv. 17, as a concessive particle (rarer, but not unknown, in good Greek) in Heb. iv. 3. The use of καίτοιγε in John iv. 2, and those of καίγε in (Luke xix. 42?) Acts ii. 18 (from O. T., but not in LXX.), xvii. 27 (true text) are further from classical use. Of καίγε without an intervening word the only good Attic instance cited is Lysias *in Theomn.* ii. 7; and that is not really parallel to any of these—most nearly to Acts ii. 18.

* Rom. i. 8, iii. 2, vi. 21, (*v. l.*), x. 1, xi. 13 (T. R.), 1 Cor. xi. 18, 2 Cor. xi. 4, xii. 12, Col. ii. 23, 1 Thess. ii. 18.

(c) Relative Adverbs—Conditional, Final, etc.

Above, in c. V. (c), we had occasion to mention the principle, which runs through the technical and seemingly arbitrary rules for the sequence of moods and tenses in dependent sentences, that almost all their main types are particular cases of the *relative* sentence: that as the rel. pron. can be used in causal, concessive, or final sense, or the like, so the particles that ordinarily introduce them are *relative* particles —ὡς and its compounds, and ὅτι, most obviously, but also ἵνα, and even εἰ, whether this be a mere phonetic variant of ᾗ, or represent another relative root.

In view of this principle, we have been able to say above as much as seems needful, for the purposes of this work, of the way that these (in the widest sense) relative particles modify the structure of sentences, and how far N. T. usage deviates in this respect from classical. But the present will be the proper place to mention what particles have in the N. T. a new or an extended sense, and how their use there affects not merely the form but the meaning of the sentences that they serve to introduce.

In the chapter referred to, we noted the chief deviations from classical usage in the choice of moods and tenses associated with ἄν and particles embodying it. While these deviations are not unimportant as regards its use in relative clauses, there is hardly any irregularity in its use in the apodosis to conditional sentences. Only, whereas the use of the plupf. indic. with ἄν, of the result possible from an unrealised hypothesis, is classical though rare, in

Attic the tense is not used without a reason*: while in the only certain N. T. case, 1 John ii. 19, there can be no meaning in the plupf. as distinct from the aor.—even the impf. would not have been quite inappropriate. (The only other instances of the constr. are also in St. John—xi. 21, xiv. 7: in neither is the reading certain, and though in the latter it may be probable, nothing can be said of ᾔδειτε being treated as an aor.). The rhetorical omission of ἄν in sentences like Rom. vii. 7, Gal. iv. 15 (ii. 21 is somewhat different: that X̄Ū ἀπέθανεν is a certain fact— it is only His Death being δωρεάν that depends on the hypothesis) does not go beyond classical precedent.

We observe also, that ἄν is never used with infinitives or with participles. On ὡς ἄν see below, p. 175.

The redundant use of κἄν " if it be [were] but ..." in Mark vi. 56 (cf. v. 28), Acts v. 15, 2 Cor. xi. 16 should be noticed, but is not unclassical: see *e.g.* Soph. *El.* 1483. Ἐάν, which in pure Greek was always a conditional particle, is in Hellenistic Greek (according to the best critics, not in even late secular writers, at least till Byzantine times) used interchangeably with ἄν after rel. pronouns or adverbs. This is a mere matter of form, and readings often vary between the two: as sometimes in the converse case, where ἄν if read has its (late Attic) sense, as a shorter form of ἐάν.† But the fact that ἐάν is not strictly confined to a conditional use has some bearing

---

* *E.g.* in Plat. *Euthyphr.* 14 c. ἱκανῶς ἂν ἤδη παρὰ σοῦ τὴν ὁσιότητα ἐμεμαθήκη, ἤδη explains the plupf.: it is not only " I should be sure to have learnt; " but " I should *have* been sure to have learnt *before now.*"

† The older ἤν, which still survives in Attic, never occurs in the N. T.

upon the exegetical question, whether it ever is used as a temporal particle. It is argued that this sense is required in certain passages of the LXX. (Isa. xxiv. 13, Amos vii. 2, Tobit iv. 3, vi. 17, perhaps Ps. xcv. 7 (xciv. 8) quoted in Heb. iii. 7, 15), and of St. John's writings Ev. xii. 32, xiv. 3, 1 Ep. ii. 28* (true text), iii. 2). We cannot here examine all these in detail; but it seems on the whole that they are too small a foundation to establish the exceptional sense of the word. In the O. T. passages it is likeliest that the translator, rightly or wrongly, meant the sense "if:" in the former passage (at least) from Tobit, and in those from St. John, that sense seems equally, if not more, appropriate; in some the conditional form need not imply uncertainty, and in others there is no reason why it should not.

Besides the simple εἰ and ἐάν, we get in the N. T. the compound conditional particles εἴγε (Rom. v. 6??, 2 Cor. v. 3?, Gal. iii. 4, Eph. iii. 2, iv. 21, Col. i. 23), εἴπερ (Rom. iii. 30, viii. 9, 17, 1 Cor. viii. 5, xv. 15, 2 Cor. v. 3?, 2 Thess. i. 6, 1 Pet. ii. 3 T. R.), and ἐάνπερ (Heb. iii. 6, T. R. 14, vi. 3). It is plain that εἴπερ has its proper force, "if, as is the fact," so that it approximates to the sense of ἐπείπερ (which appears as a *v. l.* in Rom. iii. 30), in most of these passages; and we can see the reason for its use in the others. Rom. viii. 17 gains in pathos, when we see that the share of the disciples in the Master's sufferings was felt to be a fact of which there was no question. 1 Cor. xv. 15 is more forcible, when

* The *v. l.* ὅταν in these places is evidence, no doubt, of what transcribers felt to be the easiest sense—and not to be the sense of ἐάν.

the Apostle throws himself so fully into his opponents' point of view as to say " If, *as is admitted*, the dead rise not ": though at the same time he half corrects the admission by ἄρα, " if *we find the unexpected result, that* the dead rise not." Εἴγε seems to have the same force as εἴπερ in the two passages of Eph., and in 2 Cor. if it be read there—so too in Rom., for if we read it with Westcott and Hort, we must punctuate as they do. But in Gal. it is used of a supposition which the Apostle is loth to believe possible, and in Col. of one which, he apparently means to intimate, is not certain. We see therefore that the force of this word varies a good deal, though its primary meaning " if at least " or " if indeed " covers all its uses. Εἴ πως is used, as in pure Greek, for " to see if . . ." "in hopes that "—c. fut. ind. in Rom. i. 10, xi. 14, Phil. iii. 11 (unless we prefer to regard the two latter as aor. subj.), c. opt. in Acts xxvii. 12, where the hopes and the action prompted by them are only related historically. Ἐπεί and ἐπειδή, and St. Luke's ἐπειδήπερ, are used just as in classical Greek—the first having the sense " else " ("*for*, if it were not so ") several times in St. Paul and Heb. (Rom. iii. 6, xi. 6, 22, 1 Cor. v. 10, vii. 14, xiv. 16, xv. 29, Heb. ix. 26, x. 2). Γάρ also preserves its idiomatic uses—epexegetical in Matt. i. 18 [T. R.]—connecting and so enlivening the progress of a dialogue in Matt. xxvii. 23, John vii. 42, Acts viii. 31, xvi. 37, xix. 35, 1 Cor. xi. 22, Phil. i. 18, where we represent it by the interjectional " What ? " or " Why "—the latter showing * that we also feel that

---

* We are helped in the analysis of our own instincts in the use of this word, by the fact that the old English " Forwhy "

there is something of *causality* in the connexion. Perhaps in all other places it is a mistake to look for more than its common sense, as giving a reason for what precedes; though the way in which it accounts for it is sometimes no doubt obscure, as in John iv. 44. In some places the connexion is at first obscure, not from subtlety of thought but from conciseness of expression: *e.g.* in Mark v. 42 (she walked, *for*, though we call her θυγάτριον and παιδίον, she was not a mere infant), xvi. 4 (the greatness of the stone explains both the expressed anxiety of the women about its removal, and their implied emotions at the sight of it).

Γε is rare in the N. T. We have ὅς γε in a causal sense (like *quippe qui*) in Rom. viii. 32, διά γε c. acc., "yet because of . . ." in Luke xi. 8, xviii. 5 : elsewhere it is only used to emphasise or modify other particles.

There is not much to be said of the N. T. use of διότι, which from its primary sense "for this cause, that . . ." sinks into that of our "because," but is just as far above a mere equivalent to γάρ as "because" is above "for." Of the simple ὅτι the use is more varied. As we have said (p. 117), its use in introducing an *oratio obliqua* is somewhat more extensive than in older Greek; and no very sharp line can be drawn between this use, and that in which we translate it "because" instead of "that." One can hardly say which translation is more appro-

—almost exactly equivalent to the Latin *quippe*—is now usually written and read as if it were a translation of τί γάρ; without material injury to the sense of passages where it occurs.

priate in 2 Thess. iii. 7—the sense is "how ye ought to imitate us, *in our conduct of* orderly behaviour." Similarly in John ii. 18, ix. 17, ὅτι is "in relation to the fact that . . ."—or at least in these places, and also vii. 35, the word is used to express a very vaguely conceived relation between the main sentence and that which accounts for or explains what is said in it. A more definitely explicable use of the same sort is Rom. v. 8, where ὅτι is "*by* the fact that. . . ."

We do not get in the N. T. the classical but colloquial ὅτι τί; "because why?" like ἵνα τί; but in (Mark ii. 16?) Luke ii. 49, Acts v. 4, 9 we have (as often in the LXX.) τί ὅτι . . . "why is it that . . . ?"—explained by τί γέγονεν ὅτι, John xiv. 22, or τίς ὁ λόγος οὗτος ὅτι, Luke iv. 36—cf. Matt. viii. 27 = Mark iv. 41. Οὐχ ὅτι "not that," in John vi. 46, vii. 22, 2 Cor. i. 24, iii. 5, Phil. iii. 12, iv. 11, is a distinctively N. T. phrase: for the classical sense of οὐχ ὅτι "not only," or in Plato "not but that . . ." is quite different. Οὐχ οἷον ὅτι, "not as though," in Rom. ix. 6 is nearly but not quite the same.

The transposition into an object of the subject of the clause introduced by ὅτι (*e.g.* Matt. xxv. 24), is very common in the N. T., and not rare in Attic. But the constr. is worth mentioning, as its principle serves to explain the rather harsher constr. of Acts v. 26, Gal. iv. 11, and even Rev. iii. 9.

Of ὡς, the most remarkable uses are ὡς ἄν c. inf. in 2 Cor. x. 9, the sense of ὡς ἄν ἐκφοβεῖν being apparently that of the Attic ὡσπερανεὶ ἐκφοβοίην— with this cf. ὡς ἐάν c. subj. in 1 Thess. ii. 7: and ὡς ὅτι in 2 Cor. v. 19, xi. 21, 2 Thess. ii. 2, of which we can only say the force is "as though:" we cannot explain the second passage, as we might the first and third, as a fusion of ὡς ὄντος and ὅτι ἦν, of ὡς ἐνεστῶτος and ὅτι ἐνέστηκεν. The temporal use of ὡς, very common in SS. Luke and John, is perhaps confined to them: in Matt. xxviii. 9, we must omit the clause, and in Mark ix. 21 the reading is not certain. St. Paul however has ὡς ἄν for "whensoever" in Rom. xv. 24, 1 Cor. xi. 34, Phil. ii. 23.

Ὡς ἄν c. impf. ind. in 1 Cor. xii. 2 has been mentioned already (p. 111). Ὡς is used c. inf. in doubtful but not impossible readings in Luke ix. 52, Acts xx. 24, and in the phrase ὡς ἔπος εἰπεῖν in Heb. vii. 9 only: c. ptcp. fairly often in SS. Peter (both Epp.), Paul, Luke, and Heb., but elsewhere only Matt. vii. 29 = Mark i. 22, James ii. 12.

Perhaps this may be the best place to notice the use of οὕτως, the correlative to ὡς, almost in the sense *quae cum ita, sint (essent)*: Acts vii. 8, xxviii. 14, 1 Cor. xiv. 25, 1 Thess. iv. 17—possibly also 1 Cor. ix. 24, compare the use in Acts xx. 11. Ὥστε has the same constructions as in classical Greek. But the constr. c. indic. "so that (the result) is or was (attained)" is become rare (John iii. 16, Gal. ii. 13 only), compared with the case where ὥστε comes at the beginning of a sentence, virtually meaning "wherefore," and often followed by an imper. Moreover the constr. c. inf., properly consecutive, though differing from that c. indic. as our "so as to . . ." from "so that . . ." approximates to a final sense in a few places—Matt. xxvii. 1, and still more Luke iv. 29 (true text) being the clearest instances. In both these places there is a *v. l.*, showing that early scribes felt the final sense to be intended, and Luke ix. 52

may be a similar case : xx. 20 hardly, for though ὥστε is the right text, the final sense has already been expressed by ἵνα, and a consecutive ὥστε is in place after it.

Ὅπως is only used in final sentences (taking, it must be said, a wide view of what are such : for it shares the lax use of ἵνα) except in Luke xxiv. 20, where it is "how," introducing an *oratio obliqua*.

We have referred already (p. 117) to the extension in the N. T. of the use of ἵνα : we now have to examine the nature and the limits of that extension. We note that the classical usage with past tenses of the indic., of an object now hopeless, has disappeared : and it is doubtful (see p. 109) whether the corrupt use with the present indic., found in the less educated Greek ecclesiastical writers, has yet come in. The regular constr. is c. subj., occasionally c. fut. indic., which in form and meaning is akin thereto : the main question is, how far has ἵνα advanced towards its use in modern Greek, where (in the apocopated form νά) this word c. subj. has superseded the infin. ?

Certainly it cannot be contended that it can be used in all cases where it might in modern Greek, where the English *that* or the French *que* might represent it. The limits of its use would far more nearly coincide with those of the Latin *ut :* but as *ut* c. subj. can be used in a consecutive or ecbatic sense, we have still to ask whether ἵνα can. Very often, we have it where the final sense is obviously unimpaired : very often, where the final sense is *not* obvious, but where to deny its existence is only a piece of exegetical laziness, or incapacity to conceive things from a point of view not natural to us, perhaps because too spiritual for us. Of this sort is St. Matthew's ἵνα πληρωθῇ τὸ ῥηθέν, and the corresponding phrases of St. John: so too is surely Luke ix. 45, which presents less difficulty than John xii. 40: and with which cf. 1 Thess. v. 4. But sometimes, beyond doubt, ἵνα is used where the final element in the sense is very much weakened—sometimes where it is hard to deny that it has altogether vanished.

In the first place, it is not unnatural that verbs of *desiring*—both θέλω, and such as express entreaty, or even command—should have their "object" expressed by the same constr. as the "object" of the action of other verbs. In Matt. iv. 3 εἰπέ, ἵνα . . . γένωνται, is strictly "Speak, that these stones may become bread:" it practically means, "Command them to become . . . but as these are equivalent, we can understand xvi. 20 διεστείλατο (or ἐπετίμησεν) . . . ἵνα μηδενὶ εἴπωσιν. In vii. 12 we might translate "whatsoever things ye desire, that men may do them to you:" this in the same way prepares us for Mark vi. 25, and even for Matt. xviii. 14.

Almost easier is it to see the final sense in ποιεῖν ἵνα. In Rev. xiii. 15, "to cause that they be killed" is, in regard to the agent's attitude, much the same as to order that they be killed, or to contrive that they may be: and again it may be uncertain, and is indifferent, whether ποιεῖν ἵνα or θέλειν ἵνα is the constr. of Matt. xx. 33 = Mark x. 51 = Luke xviii. 41. So in 1 Cor. iv. 2, "that a man be found faithful" is the "object" of the seeking.

And then it is impossible to draw a line between cases like these, and constructions like that with συμφέρει in Matt. v. 29, 30, ἱκανός εἰμι viii. 8, ἀρκετόν x. 25 (cf. John v. 7), etc.: see the series of passages marked * in Bruder *s. v.* So then one might almost as fitly add a few more—*e.g.* 1 John v. 20, 2 John 6, and the many cases of δοῦναι ἵνα, more or less like ποιεῖν ἵνα, in the Apoc.: Acts viii. 19 again connects itself with these.

We observe that ἵνα is very frequent in (all) St. John's writings; he only uses ὅπως and ὥστε once each, (Ev. xi. 57, iii. 16), while this word has with him some peculiar extensions of use, both as to form and sense. He often has the elliptical ἀλλ' ἵνα (i. 8, ix. 3, xi. 52, xiii. 18, xiv. 31, xv. 25), to which the only complete parallel elsewhere is Mark xiv. 49, and perhaps Eph. v. 27.* Notice other elliptic uses of the word, marked (as these are) ** in Bruder: also Gal. ii. 10 (as well as 9) should be included. Philem. 19 may be explained as a Latinism—the sense is just *ne dicam*: but 2 Cor. ii. 5 is just the same constr. We may distinguish one class of cases as epexegetical —of which we may take as subordinate types (1) cases like Luke i. 43, John xv. 8, where we get τοῦτο ἵνα directly connected (*unde hoc mihi ut veniat . . .* Vulg. Luc. l. c.). (2) John iv. 34, and others where the clause with ἵνα serves to explain the nature of a subst.: 3 John 4, is no doubt a (somewhat elliptical) example of this. (3) Intermediate are cases like John vi. 29, 2 John 6, where τοῦτο stands so to speak in apposition to the ἵνα clause, to enable it to stand as subject to the sentence identifying it with a subst.

---

* 2 Thess. iii. 9 is quite normal, "not because . . . but in order that . . . , giving a wrong and a right way of accounting for the fact stated just before.

Now that we have recognised that ἵνα *can* be used in other than a strictly final sense, we can consider on their merits alternative schemes of interpretation: *e.g.* in 1 John iv. 17 we see that grammatically ἵνα ... κρίσεως may be epexeg. of ἐν τούτῳ, though if we prefer to take ἵνα in its final sense, τούτῳ, may refer to what goes before, or to ὅτι ... τούτῳ in the next clause. So with John viii. 56, Rev. xiv. 13.

For the special use of ἵνα in entreaties, like the classical ὅπως, see p. 109. The use in 1 Cor. i. 31 is curious but intelligible: it is of course to be explained as an ellipsis. Ἵνα is not really followed by an imper. instead of a subj., but the sense is " that (things may be) as the Scripture says they ought to be," and then follows the quotation, telling how that is.

Of relative adverbs of place, and their correlatives, one whole series had disappeared, viz. those relating to motion *to* a place, οἵ, ὅποι κ.τ.λ.: just as in modern, or at least in colloquial English, it is an affectation to say "whither" instead of "where." The disuse is however less consistent in Greek: ὧδε* and the rarer ἐνθάδε serve for both "hither" and "here," while ἐνταῦθα has disappeared, but ἐντεῦθεν not: ἔνθεν is used twice demonstratively (Matt. xvii. 20, Luke xvi. 26, true text). Ἐκεῖ can have the sense of "thither" (Matt. ii. 22, xvii. 20, etc.); but ἐκεῖσε occurs twice in Acts—once (xxi. 3) with something of

---

* Ὧδε in the N. T. has never its oldest sense of "thus." The sense "hither" is first found in Sophocles (and that in passages where something of a colloquial use would not be out of place): "here" not before Theocritus. In 1 Cor. iv. 2, Rev. xiii. 10, 18, xiv. 12, xvii. 9, the sense seems to be "herein"—a metaphorical extension of the latest local meaning.

its proper force, but in xxii. 5 this cannot be traced —even ἐκεῖθεν would have been more appropriate. The pregnant use of this last word with the art. is found in Luke xvi. 26 only, and there is at least doubtful. Ὅθεν is used both in a local sense (Matt. xii. 44 = Luke xi. 24, Matt. xxv. 24, 26, Acts xiv. 26, xxviii. 13, Heb. xi. 19), and in an illative, "from which" coming to mean "for which cause"—so Matt. xiv. 7, nearly so 1 John ii. 18, and so five times in Heb.

Of other illatives, διό (twice in 1 Cor. διόπερ) alone is a rel. in form : of it we have only to note its rarity in the Gospels (Matt. xxvii. 8, Luke i. 35, vii. 7 only), and its total absence from St. John. But we may mention in this connexion the other N. T. illatives— οὖν (once, John xviii. 37, οὐκοῦν), ἄρα, τοίνυν, τοιγαροῦν. As regards the first, it is impossible to draw a very sharp line between its strictly illative use, and that where it is merely continuative, like our "then" or "so." It is this latter use that is so frequent in St. John; perhaps elsewhere the passage where it is most fully developed is Luke xx. 29 (for in several places in St. Luke οὖν disappears from critical texts) : while we have transitional cases in Matt. xxvii. 17, Mark xii. 6, etc. And this continuative use passes, through sentences like Luke iii. 7, into what may be called the *resumptive*, of which we have an instance in Rom. xii. 1, still more plainly in 1 Cor. viii. 4, where the thread of ver. 1 is resumed after a digression, whether we make it an actual parenthesis or not.

The sense of ἄρα, as in classical Greek, is at least as much that of *discovery* (often of surprise) as of *inference:* see on the one hand Matt. vii. 20 (where it is emphasised by γε), 2 Cor. v. 15, on the other Matt. xii. 28=Luke xi. 20. Luke xi. 48, Acts xi. 18, show how one passes into the other, " it follows, little as you may think it," or "little as we had expected it." So where ἄρα stands after an interrogative (Matt. xix. 25, Mark iv. 41, Luke i. 66, and, in an *indirect* question, xxii. 23) it gives a tone of surprise or anxiety: and so in hypothetical sentences, as Acts viii. 22, xvii. 27 (where εἰ ἄρα is practically=*si forte*, but it is utterly misleading to say that ἄρα means *forte*). All these modifications of sense are classical; but not so the N. T. usage of putting the illative ἄρα at the beginning of a sentence, still less the way that St. Paul emphasises it by the combination ἄρ οὖν (often in Romans, and in Gal. vi. 10, Eph. ii. 19, 1 Thess. v. 6, 2 Thess. ii. 15). Heb. xiii. 13 has no known precedent except in the LXX. for τοίνυν at the beginning of a sentence; but in late secular Greek it was allowed there: for τοιγαροῦν it is the correct place.

(d) *Negative and Interrogative Particles.*

The two negative particles οὐ and μή, and the whole series of their compounds and derivatives (οὐδείς, μηδείς κ.τ.λ.), are in use in the N. T. as in classical Greek, and are used, generally speaking, upon the same principles. But there is much more laxity in the observance of the rules for their use, and the rules that are or tend to be observed are not absolutely the same: there are larger classes of cases where either negative can be used with little or no difference to the sense; and there are uses for which one particle only was appropriate, on which we find that the other has encroached.

Thus in Mark xii. 14 the use of the two particles is quite clear and correct. The difference of mood in the verb corresponds to the difference of the negative: "Is it lawful . . . or [*is* it] not? are we to give, or *are we not to* give?" So in 1 John v. 16, " a sin not unto death " is part of the supposition : in the next verse, the existence of such a sin is categorically affirmed : and so we have μή in the former clause, and οὐ in the latter.

But when we compare John iii. 18 with 1 John v. 10, we fail to see any reason, either in the grammar or in the sense, why we should have ὅτι μὴ πεπίστευκεν in the former, and ὅτι οὐ πεπίστευκεν in the latter. And in fact it is a mistake to look to any difference of sense to explain the choice of different particles : the true explanation is simply, that whereas in a classical writer we should certainly have had ὅτι οὐκ, in late [*e.g.*, Lucian] (not only in Hellenistic) Greek the tendency prevailed to use μή after causal particles. In the N. T. it is still exceptional : but we get it in Heb. ix. 17, after ἐπεί, as well as in John l. c. after ὅτι.

On the other hand, it is an all but universal rule in pure Greek, that in conditional sentences the negative shall be μή. The only recognised exceptions are, where the εἰ is virtually equivalent to a non-conditional particle (*e.g.* in the phrase θαυμάζω εἰ, where οὐκ is sometimes but not always used), or where the negative is inseparably connected with a single word, and belongs to it rather than to the sentence ; *e.g.* Soph. *Aj.* 1131, εἰ τοὺς θανόντας οὐκ ἐᾷς θαπτεῖν, "if thou *forbid* to bury." We get no clear instance (though John x. 35, Heb. xii. 25, 2 Pet. ii. 4 might pass for such) of the former sort in the N. T., but Luke xii. 26, εἰ οὐδὲ ἐλάχιστον δύνασθε, 2 Cor. xii. 11, εἰ καὶ οὐδέν εἰμι, fall under the latter. So in the use of participles with the art, ἡ οὐ τίκτουσα, ἡ οὐκ ὠδίνουσα in Isa. liv. 1, quoted in Gal. iv. 27, and τὴν οὐκ ἠγαπημένην in Rom. ix. 25: similarly οἱ οὐκ ἠλεημένοι in 1 Pet. ii. 10.

Perhaps we ought to distinguish from this, as another case in which οὐκ is admissible, even in the purest Greek, that where, though the negative does not coalesce with any one word into a privative phrase, it is placed, for rhetorical or other reasons, in close association with the word which it denies, and at considerable distance from the conditional particle, or equivalent form. Thus in Thuc. III. lv. 4, εἰ δ' ἀποστῆναι Ἀθηναίων οὐκ ἠθελήσαμεν, it is a question whether we say that οὐ θέλειν coalesce into one idea, *nolle*, like οὐκ ἐᾶν: if the order had been different, even without separating the negative from the verb, we should probably have had εἰ δὲ μὴ ἠθελήσαμεν ἀπ' Ἀθηναίων ἀποστῆναι.

On this principle we may justify the use of οὐκ in Luke xiv. 26, xvi. 11, 12, 31, John iii. 12, v. 47, x. 35, Rom. viii. 9, xi. 21, 1 Tim iii. 5, v. 8, 2 Pet. ii. 4, 2 John 10. And in other passages one might find some other plea: *e.g.* in 1 Cor. xv. 13 εἰ δὲ "Ἀνάστασις νεκρῶν οὐκ ἔστιν" gives a quotation, or at least what is treated as one, of what some among the Corinthians said (ver. 12): and the principle might, with a little stretching, cover the repeated instances of εἰ οὐ that follow.

Again, it seems to be the use of late but. pure Greek writers to use οὐ where there is a marked antithesis with the apodosis, or with a positive clause balancing the negative one—"if not one thing, then another," or "if not one thing but the other, then." . . . This would explain Luke xi. 8, xviii. 4, 1 Cor. ix. 2, James ii. 11, besides applying to several of the passages given above. Similarly where a negative clause, equivalent to a ptcp., comes after the art. in Rom. iv. 12, τοῖς οὐκ ἐκ περιτομῆς μόνον, ἀλλὰ κ.τ.λ.: here but for the antithesis, we should certainly have had μή. (In Eph. v. 4 τὰ οὐκ ἀνήκοντα is a *f. l.*: and even that is in a negative clause followed by ἀλλά.)

We believe that in all these cases there is a real reason for the use of οὐ: but it is hardly the right way to regard them, to treat them (as we must treat such parallel cases as we find in classical Greek) as exceptions to the general rule requiring εἰ μή. For if we did so, the exceptions to the rule would outnumber the examples of it. Εἰ μή is used very freely in the N. T.—more extensively than in pure Greek: but its general use is as a compound particle used after negatives, almost=πλήν, "except:" sometimes in St. Paul helped out by ἐκτός (1 Cor. xiv. 5, xv. 2, 1 Tim. v. 19). As introducing a real conditional sentence, we meet it only in Matt. xxiv. 22=Mark xiii. 20, John ix. 33, xv. 22, 24, xviii. 30, xix. 11, Rom. vii. 7, ix. 29 (from LXX.), 2 Cor. xii. 13, 1 Tim. vi. 3.

On the other hand, we have εἰ οὐ, besides the cases above enumerated, and without any of the reasons given for those applying, in Matt. xxvi. 24 (=Mark xiv. 21), 42, Mark xi. 26 [T.R.], John

x. 37, Acts xxv. 11 (οὐδέν), 1 Cor. vii. 9, xi. 6, xvi. 22, 2 Thess. iii. 10, 14.

Can we trace any principle here? If not, it might be worth while to remark that about half the instances of εἰ μή are in a single writer: and we might say that εἰ οὐκ is the rule, and εἰ μή the exception, in all N. T. writers but St. John. But on examining the instances, we shall see that in all the places where μή is used except the last, it is used with a past tense of the indic. of an unrealised supposition: in all where οὐκ is used, either the verb is in a primary tense of the indic., or the sense is "if, as was the fact" (Rom. xi. 21, Heb. xii. 25, 2 Pet. ii. 4), or one of the reasons stated above applies (Luke xvi. 11, 12).

This then appears to be the rule of N. T. usage— that εἰ with the indic. almost always takes οὐ, except with a past tense in the sense specified. Ἐάν however always takes μή c. pres. as well as c. aor. subj. And though εἰ οὐκ is a deviation from classical usage, it may admit of justification on the principles of the classical language. If we resolve the conditional particle into a relative one, εἰ will be "in *the* case in which," . . . and ἐάν "in *any* case in which" . . . : and of these relative sentences, the one would regularly take οὐκ and the other μή. In practice, however, we must not expect always to find an assignable difference of meaning between εἰ οὐκ and ἐὰν μή, any more than between the simple εἰ and ἐάν: compare Matt. vi. 15, ἐὰν δὲ μὴ ἀφῆτε, with Mark xi. 26, εἰ δὲ ὑμεῖς οὐκ ἀφίετε—which, though not part of the genuine text of St. Mark, belongs to the oldest form of the "Western Text," and shows what were the natural variants of language among people who still possessed evangelical sayings in a plastic form. On the other hand, we may notice Matt. xxvi. 42, where we get εἰ οὐ and ἐὰν μή in the same sentence. Here there is a real difference between the two, illustrated by the necessary difference in a Latin or English translation.

In the elliptical sense "if not," "otherwise," we always have εἰ δὲ μή (or εἰ δὲ μή γε, everywhere except in SS. Mark and John). It is noticeable, that in most of the passages (7 or 8 as against Luke x. 6, xiii. 9, John xiv. 2, 11, Rev. ii. 5, 16: Luke xiv. 32 is ambiguous), the supposition which μή excludes is itself a negative one.

Except in this case of εἰ c. indic., the tendency of late Greek is certainly to extend the use of μή rather than to contract it. We may say that in classical Greek οὐκ is used where there is a categorical negation, even in dependent clauses—in relative sentences, with participles, or the like: only that μή can be used where there is any special reason, *e.g.* to give a conditional or (sometimes) a causal sense. In later Greek, the rule and the exception are the other way: the rule is, in fact, almost the same as in modern Greek, where we are told that μή is the particle ordinarily used with subjunctives and participles (Geldart's *Guide to Modern Greek*, p. 254): while in relative sentences μή can be used, even with the indic. —Tit. i. 11, 2 Pet. i. 9. The general practice, however, in relative sentences is to use οὐ c. indic., and μή when the verb is in the subj. with ἄν: cf. Matt. xiii. 12, Mark iv. 25 with Luke viii. 18. We have always οὐκ in the relative sentence that expresses universality by a double negative—οὐδεὶς ὅστις οὐ, and the like: so Acts xix. 35, Heb. xii. 7. Notice however the double οὐ μή in Mark xiii. 2—*not* Matt. xxiv. 2 true text, though Luke xxi. 6 alone has the normal constr. With participles, we may say that μή is always used when the ptcp. is equivalent to a conditional clause, almost always when it is causal, and mostly when it is equivalent to a mere relative: but οὐ sometimes in the last case, and generally where the sense is concessive. So in modern Greek ὄχι (=οὐχὶ or οὐ) δυνάμενος is "*though* he could not," but μὴ δυνάμενος "*because* he could not" (Geldart, p. 73). We have instances of οὐ with participles in Matt. xxii. 11 (cf. 12), Gal. iv. 8, Col. ii. 19, Heb. xi. 1, 35, where it seems to be used simply as being the natural negative. In Luke vii. 6, οὐ μακράν, in Acts xxvii. 20 οὐκ ὀλίγου, are virtually one word—we have μήτε ... ἐμφαινόντων just before the latter. In 1 Cor. ix. 26 we may say something of the same sort— the sense is, "I box, as striking—not the air (but my enemy):" or the parallelism with ὡς οὐκ ἀδήλως may be explanation enough. In Luke vi. 42, Acts vii. 5, xxviii. 17, there may be the difference of sense required by the modern rule: so in Acts xvii. 27, where the concessive sense of the ptcp. is put beyond question by καίγε: In 1 Pet. i. 8 we get both οὐ and μή with participles, and cannot doubt the difference of meaning: ὃν οὐκ ἰδόντες is "whom *though* ye have not seen," εἰς ὃν ... πιστεύοντες "in whom *because* ye believe." But instead of leaving these three last words alone, the Apostle expands them into an antithesis, which in classical Greek (see p. 167) would have been expressed by something like οὐχ ὁρῶντες μὲν ἄρτι, πιστεύοντες δέ: and as the negative introduces, not merely the ὁρῶντες but the whole antithesis, it takes the form suitable to the sense of πιστεύοντες, its more emphatic member. In John x. 12, 1 Cor. iv. 14, 2 Cor. iv. 8, 9, Phil. iii. 3, οὐ may be explained by the existence of an antithesis such as was noted above in hypothetical sentences. But we get μή [and compounds] even in antithesis, as Mark v. 26, Acts ix. 7, 2 Cor. vi. 9, 10—where there seems no difference of principle or even of tone from iv. 8, 9—and constantly elsewhere (*e.g.* Luke xviii. 2), where it is not possible to trace anything causal in the sense, as no doubt we may in Matt. xviii. 25, xxii. 25, 29, Acts v. 7, ix. 26, xii. 19, xvii. 6. The rule seems a sound one, that where we get μή with a ptcp. it does not need accounting for, but that where we get οὐ with one we ought to look for some reason for its use; though it is too much to say that there must always be some assignable reason to be found. It agrees with this principle—that μή is used with a ptcp. where οὐ would be with a verb—that when we have a ptcp. constructed with the verb substantive, the negative is οὐκ or μή, according as it belongs to the verb or the ptcp. See on the one hand Luke vi. 43, xii. 6, xxiii. 53, John iii. 24, Rom. iii. 12, 2 Cor. ii. 17, James iii. 15; on the other Luke i. 20, xiii. 11, Acts ix. 9. The last passage is especially noticeable, because οὐ follows immediately, with verbs.

As in pure Greek, the ptcp. with the art. regularly takes μή: what exceptions there are have been explained above. Even in Rom. iv. 12 we should prob. have had μή, had οὖσι been expressed. Where the ptcp. depends upon a final clause (*e.g.* 1 Cor. vii.

29), μή is equally necessary. Yet we get οὐχ in connexion—not, it is true, immediate—with an imper. in 1 Pet. iii. 3, and οὐδέ with a final sentence in Rev. ix. 4. These are, of course, irregular.

For the inf. also is associated with μή in the N. T. even where it would not be in classical Greek. When it serves to express an *or. obl.*, we should expect, in general, the same negative to be used as would be in the *or. recta*—οὐκ in categorical speeches, μή in prohibitory. Mή therefore is necessary in Matt. ii. 12, Luke v. 14, 1 Cor. v. 9, 11, etc; but is hardly classical in Luke ii. 26, xx. 7, Acts iv. 20, xxiii. 8, Heb. ix. 8. Where the inf. has the art., a negative between them is regularly μή: we find it too in 2 Pet. ii. 21, where the inf., without art., is subject of the sentence. In Acts xix. 27, Rom. vii. 6, Heb. vii. 11, we should hardly have had οὐ (or οὐθέν) except in the second member of an antithesis. In 2 Tim. ii. 14 we have οὐδέν, but should prob. have had ἐπὶ τὸ μὴ χρ., had the simple negative been used. In John xxi. fin., the negative belongs not to the infin. but to αὐτὸν τὸν κόσμον.

Of μήποτε in Heb. ix. 17 we have given above (p. 182) what seems the most probable account: though it is possible to explain its use as a rhetorical question. It is used in a direct question in John vii. 26, in an indirect in Luke iii. 15. The tendency in late Greek to the extended use of this form in particular may have been encouraged by its Aristotelian use in the sense of "perhaps;" of which we have something like an example in Matt. xxv. 9; though perhaps it is not wrong to supply (we must not insert) an οὐ before it. In 2 Tim. ii. 25 μήποτε is of course not "lest," but "in case," "if haply," and so *allied to* the Aristotelian sense. Μήπως in Rom. xi. 21 would be just equivalent to that use—perhaps half dependent on the φοβοῦ preceding: but it is a "Western and Syrian" reading that cannot be regarded as original. For the use of μήπως c. indic. (twice coupled with a subj.) in Gal. ii. 2, iv. 11, 1 Thess. iii. 5, see p. 114. Notice also the use of ὁρᾶν, βλέπειν, σκοπεῖν μή— sometimes c. indic., p. 109, on the analogy of φο, βεῖσθαι μή.

The interrogative use of μή, in questions expecting a negative answer, is perhaps connected (if so, prob. as effect not as source) with this dubitative use of μη. In St. John, and perhaps in St. Paul, the interrogative use is commoner than in pure Greek, but does not materially differ from it, so far as regards its use c. indic.: it is not used c. subj. in the N. T., for in Mark xii. 14 cited above it is a real negative. Μῶν in the same sense is not found. We may notice the use of μή several times in St. John, where the expectation of a negative answer is ironical or hypocritical, and the askers mean to suggest as possible what they profess to reject as incredible—vii. 47, 52, viii. 22 (μήτι).

The use of οὐ where an affirmative answer is expected needs no remark, being just analogous to the practice in English and Latin: only in the latter *non* may seldom be used for *nonne*, and in English we vary the order of words—"is he not?" interrogatively, but "he is not" categorically. In Greek, there is not necessarily—in the N. T. not usually—any difference in form between the two: but it is seldom that the sense fails to make it clear which is intended.

Where ambiguity might arise (*e.g.* 1 Cor. v. 12) it is avoided, not, as in classical Greek, by the use of ἆρ' οὐ, for this combination is not found in the N. T., but of οὐχί—a form appropriated exclusively to *questions* (Matt. always—9 or 10 times: Luke vi. 39, xii. 6, xiv. 28, 31, xv. 8—the two last in questions beginning with τίς,—xvii. 8, 17, xxii. 27, xxiv. 32, xi. 9,* Acts v. 4, vii. 50 (fr. O. T.), Rom. ii. 26, iii. 29, viii. 32—after πῶς,—1 Cor. i. 20, iii. 3, v. 12, vi. 7 bis, viii. 10, ix. 1, x. 16 bis, 2 Cor. iii. 8—after πῶς,—1 Thess. ii. 19—with ἤ,—Heb. i. 14, iii. 17), *answers* (always followed by ἀλλά—Luke i. 60, virtually, xii. 51, xiii. 3, 5, xvi. 30, John ix. 9 (true text), Rom. iii. 27), and *antitheses* (John xiii. 10, which explains the use in 11, xiv. 22, 1 Cor. v. 2, vi. 1). This restriction of the use of the form is not classical; in Attic it seems to be admissible whenever the negative is emphatic, though there are also several examples of its use in questions, in answers, or after ἀλλά.

Direct questions, when not suggesting their own answer, seem to have been less often introduced by a distinct interrogative particle in popular language than in literary: and the N. T. follows the popular use: see *e.g.* John v. 6, ix. 19, 1 Cor. ix. 11, 2 Cor. iii. 1, where the form of the sentence does not show it to be interrogative at all. We find ἆρα only twice, (Luke xviii. 8, Acts viii. 30—ἆρά γε): at least in Gal. ii. 17 ἆρα, however we accent it, is certainly illative and not merely interrogative, though the sentence is rightly taken as a question ("is He therefore. . . . ?" "does it follow that He is. . . . ?")

---

* Also vii. 42 T. R., and several times besides where the best texts have the simple οὐ.

Ἡ (though no one proposes to write it ἤ) seems to have an interrogative force, not a disjunctive, in Matt. xxvi. 53, Rom. iii. 29, vii. 1, xi. 2, 1 Cor. vi. 2, 9, x. 22, xiv. 36, 2 Cor. xi. 7, James iv. 5 : in all these places (for one can hardly correlate 1 Cor. vi. 9 with ver. 2) it stands as the first word of the question. In 1 Thess. ii. 19, also, we have the use in " such direct questions as follow a general question and suggest the answer " (L. & Sc. *s. v.* A. ii. 1). And we have an unclassical use of εἰ to introduce direct questions, often in St. Luke, besides only in Matt. xii. 10, xix. 3, xx. 15, Mark viii. 23 (best text). St. Luke seems not to use εἰ, however, before a direct *double* question, when the texts of vi. 9, xiv. 3 are amended. As a rule, the first clause in such questions stands without a particle, the second being introduced by ἤ. On the use of εἰ and ἤ in indirect questions we have nothing to remark : πότερον occurs only in John vii. 17. We find, however, another peculiar use of εἰ, which may be mentioned here, though prob. connected rather with the hypothetical than with the interrogative use of the word. There is a Hebrew idiom, literally reproduced in the LXX., according to which אִם " if " is used as equivalent to a negative in oaths : *e.g.* Ps. xcv. (xciv.) fin., quoted in Heb. iii. 11 *sqq.* The origin of this is, no doubt, the aposiopesis of an imprecation—one may guess, that of the biblical oath, " God do so to me and more also, *if* . . . : " but it comes to be, in Hellenistic language, simply a very emphatic and solemn negative. In this sense, we get it in Mark viii. 12.

It seems moreover to be connected with this use, that we get εἰ μήν in an affirmative oath, in what seems to be unquestionably the true text of Heb. vi. 14. The same spelling is found in the best extant MSS. of the LXX. in the passage quoted, and in several others: so the evidence is too early and too widespread for it to be a simple itacism: η did not get confounded with $\epsilon\iota$ nearly as early as ι. We may suppose that the classical formula of oath $\mathring{\eta}$ $\mu\acute{\eta}\nu$ was assimilated to or confounded with the Hebraic $\epsilon\grave{\iota}$ $\mu\acute{\eta}$, and that a mixture of the two got established in Hellenistic usage.

CHAPTER VII.

MISCELLANEOUS FEATURES OF NEW TESTAMENT GRAMMAR AND IDIOM.

WE meet with a good deal of inconsistency of practice, in the observance or non-observance of the Greek syntactical rule, that a neut. pl. is followed by a verb in the sing., unless the subject, though formally neuter, really represents living agents —persons, or at least animals. Thus *e.g.* Matt. vi. 33, ταῦτα πάντα προστεθήσεται, ib. 32, πάντα γὰρ ταῦτα τὰ ἔθνη ἐπιζητοῦσιν, ib. 26, τὰ πετεινὰ ... οὐ σπείρουσιν κ.τ.λ., are all quite regular. But ib. 28 we have τὰ κρίνα ... αὐξάνουσιν· οὐ κοπιῶσιν οὐδὲ νήθουσιν: and so Luke xxiv. 11,* John vi. 13, 1 Tim. v. 25, Rev. iii. 2 (?), (*si v.l.*) xvi. 20.* In (Matt. xiii. 4 *v.l.*) John x. 4, 16, xix. 31,* Rev. i. 19 both sing. and pl. verbs are used in the same sentence. In most of these we trace no principle: in John xix. 31 any reason there is for insisting on σκέλη implying two or three *persons* (ver. 32) would apply with greater force to σώματα. In c. x. however, there is a delicate shade of meaning in the change: the sing. is used where the figure is adhered to, without admixture of the thing signified

[* Marks the passages where T. R. does not consistently insert the singular.]

(read ἔστιν in ver. 12); but the pl. where it is distinctly intimated that "the flock of His pasture are men" (vv. 14, 27-8: read ἀκούουσιν in ver. 27), or where the literal sheep are described as acting intelligently, "like Christians," vv. 4, 5, 16. There may be a touch of similar feeling in the personification of the lilies in St. Matthew.

On the other hand the neut. pl. of living agents has a singular verb in Matt. xii. 45=Luke xi. 26, Matt. xiii. 4 (once at least)=Mark iv. 4=Luke viii. 5, Mark iv. 10 (?) cf. Luke viii. 30 (but not 33, true text), Luke (iv. 41?) viii. 2, xiii. 19, Rom. ix. 8, 1 Cor. vii. 14, 1 John iii. 10, iv. 1.* In Rom. iii. 2 St. Chrysostom considered it grammatically an open question, whether τὰ λόγια were subject or object to ἐπιστεύθησαν: but on exegetical grounds there is no doubt that it is object, so that the pl. is regular.

Akin to this variety of use in a special Greek idiom is that common to all languages in the use of a sing. or pl. verb when its subject is either a noun of multitude or a number of individuals coupled by conjunctions. The sing. is commoner with a collective in the N. T. as in classical Greek—in the LXX. it is the other way: but often a verb less directly, though inferentially, connected with the singular subj. will be pl.—*e.g.* Luke i. 21, John vi. 2: so 1 Tim. ii. 15, where the sing. preceding is not a collective, but a representative.

The order of the words has not a little to do with

* Here it may be a question whether the πνεύματα are conceived as personal. This will not apply to the instances in the Gospels where δαιμόνια is the subject: but it may be a question (esp. in Mark iv. 10) how far their action is ascribed to the demoniac.

determining the constr. in this point: compare the two clauses with ὄχλος in Mark iv. 1, John vi. 22 (best text), 24, xii. 9, 12. So it affects the gender and number of a ptcp. standing as a secondary predicate: compare Acts xxi. 36 (true text) with Luke xxiii. 1. An adj. or ptcp. forming a primary predicate would naturally be sing. (Luke i. 10, 21): yet we get the pl., and that before the pl. copula, in John vii. 49.

With a compound subject, the verb can only be sing. if it stand first (Matt. xvii. 2, John ii. 2, Acts xx. 4), so that it is intelligible as constructed with the first only of the nouns, and is supplied with the rest. We notice a slight irregularity in the use of a sing. verb with a pl. ptcp. as primary predicate in Luke ii. 33, and as secondary in Matt. xvii. 2.

In general, the want of clear and straightforward connexion between subject and predicate is the rarest of faults in the style of the N. T.: the simplicity of most of the sentences is a security for their correctness and intelligibility. In the more periodic style of the Acts, however, we get some entanglement: in xvii. 2 it is hardly Greek to leave the subject to be inferred from mention in an oblique case. Of viii. 7 we could at best say the same, if the T. R. were right; but as we must certainly read πολλοί, the only choice is between saying that we have a mixture of two constructions (πολλοὶ τῶν ἐχ. πν. ἀκ. ἐθεραπεύθησαν, and πολλῶν πν. ἀκ. βοῶντα φ. μεγ. ἐξήρχοντο), and taking ἐξήρχ. in a peculiar quasi-transitive sense, "had spirits come out of them."

A converse case to this is the trajection of the subject of clause to the beginning of the sentence, for the sake of emphasis. 1 Cor. xi. 14, where ἀνήρ and γυνή are put each at the beginning of its own clause, are quite natural Greek: so is even John viii. 45: but Luke xxi. 6, John x. 29 (if we read the neut.), still more 1 John ii. 27, or even 24, go beyond what a classical author would be likely to write.

Sentences like these, in fact, though they have a place in their framework into which the nom. can be fitted, really approximate to those in which we get the so-called nom. abs., to designate the subject of the sentence in the popular sense, when it is not the "subject" in the grammatical—*e.g.* Ex. xxxii. 1 quoted (loosely) ap. Acts vii. 40. So Matt. x. 32, Luke xii. 10, Rom. ix. 10: Luke vi. 47 may be regarded as an instance either of this constr. or of that last mentioned. In John vi. 39, πᾶν may be regarded either as nom. or as acc.,—being (if the latter) originally intended to serve as object to ἀπολέσω and ἀναστήσω, but being replaced with the former by ἐξ αὐτοῦ, which makes the statement more absolute: but sentences like Luke xii. 10 tend to show that here too πᾶν is really nom. There is something of a Hellenistic tone in sentences like these. In Exod. or Acts l.c., a classical writer would have been likelier to put an acc., in some sort of dependence on οὐκ οἴδαμεν, "We know not about this M. what is become of him." But though a nom. thus used is a sort of slight anacoluthon John xv. 5 shows how possible it is to have a noun or pron. that cannot, without recasting the whole sentence for the worse, be introduced in any other way.

Similar in principle to this use of the nom. is that of a relative clause without any definite antecedent,

Matt. x. 14, Luke ix. 5. But sentences of this sort shade off into such as Luke x. 8, where the rel. clause has, if not a definite place in the sentence, a coherent construction of its own, and from this into such as ver. 10, where it even gets an antecedent clause at last. In general, when we meet with anacolutha more considerable than these, they are too closely connected with the individual style of the writer to rank as characteristics of Hellenistic New Testament Greek. We may however here notice the change of constr. in Mark vi. 8, 9 from ἵνα to the inf., and this through a ptcp., which seems to presuppose an earlier inf., and in its absence has no proper constr. at all. This case is not unlike the common one (esp. common in St. Luke), where a report of a speech begun in *or. obl.* slides into *or. recta:* so indeed a *v. l.* here. We have a solitary instance of the opposite transition from *or. recta* to *obl.* in Acts xxiii. 23-4. Somewhat similar to this, again, is the case of Rom. ii. 7, 8, xi. 22, where the change from acc. to nom. cannot be explained, like most of St. Paul's anacolutha, either by his losing his way in a long or involved sentence, or by his wanting, before he had finished saying one thing, to bring something else into relation to it. See also p. 77, on Phil. iii. 18, 19. But we throw no light on slight irregularities like these, by correlating them with the mixtures of cases that we get in the Apoc., *e.g.* vii. 9, xviii. 12, 13.

Of course no difficulty is presented by a sentence where—generally with a rhetorical purpose—the constr. is not changed, but left incomplete : *e.g.* Acts xxiv. 19, where the "Jews of Asia who ought to be here" never get a predicate—the Apostle, instead of challenging them, challenges those who *are* here to say the worst they can of him. A familiar case is that where the apodosis of a conditional sentence is suppressed, as Acts xxiii. 9 (true text), Rom. ix. 22. With the true reading in Luke xiii. 9, it becomes doubtful if we have there an instance : εἰς τὸ μέλλον may be, not merely "if it bear fruit *for the future*," but a suggestion of an apodosis, "if it bear fruit, we can leave the question for another day."

The question how far parenthesis is used in the N. T. is partly one of exegesis, partly of definition: but as a rule one may say that it is commoner in the Epp. than in the historical books. In St. Paul the line is not always clearly drawn between parenthesis and anacoluthon: when he has made a digression and returns to his first subject, he very often makes a fresh start, leaving the first sentence unfinished. So apparently Rom. v. 12, 18; and very likely 1 Cor. viii. 1, 4. In Rom. ix. 11 we have a nearer approach to a real parenthesis, though the nom. Ῥεβεκκα . . . ἔχουσα is succeeded by the dat. αὐτῇ : but we seldom get in him as consistent a resumption of the interrupted sentence as *e.g.* Heb. xii. 18-22, at least if the parenthesis is of any length. 1 Cor. xvi. 5 runs smoothly : but an equally unargumentative and hardly more impassioned passage like Rom. xv. 23-8 gets into confusion.

In the historical books, on the other hand, a parenthesis as long as that in Luke xxiii. 51 is exceptional. We get indeed shorter notes inserted in a sentence, in a way more like parenthesis than anything for which there is a grammatical term ; such as the notes of names in John i. 6, iii. 1 (compare, but distinguish

Luke xix. 2, as well as viii. 41), or of time in Matt. xv. 32 (true text), Luke ix. 28. And we get occasional glosses on foreign words (Mark vii. 11, John i. 39, etc.), and more rarely comments on what is related or reported (Matt. xxv. 15=Mark xii. 14, and prob. Mark vii. 19). But in general, notes like these, if not incorporated in the main sentence, are brought in as separate sentences after it (*e.g.* John vi. 59, viii. 20; or again vii. 39, xii. 33, etc). It is characteristic of Hellenistic narrative to proceed without such breaks: even the single words φησίν and ἔφη are rarely inserted *between* the words quoted (only in Matt. xiv. 8, Luke vii. 40 (true text), Acts xxiii. 35, xxv. 5, 22, xxvi. 25, 1 Cor. vi. 16, 2 Cor. x. 10, Heb. viii. 5). One may notice that in the three last passages φησίν (if that be the true reading in 2 Cor.) is used with a vaguely conceived subject: one hardly thinks the Apostle definitely understood ὁ $\overline{\Theta C}$,—rather ἡ γραφή (Rom. xi. 2 etc.) or ὁ χρηματισμός (ib. 4).

There are a good many elliptical adverbial phrases found in the N. T., formed by the use of certain parts of adjectives without their substantives. The adverbial use of the neut. does not indeed go beyond what was usual in late but pure Greek: and of the phrases (mostly fem.) that employ a more definite ellipsis, κατὰ μόνας is quite classical, κατ' ἰδίαν as early as Polybius. But we nowhere find in secular Greek ἀπὸ μιᾶς (it is hard to say what the subst. understood is), as in Luke xiv. 18. In pure Greek we have ἡ σήμερον, ἡ αὔριον, but not τῇ ἑξῆς (Acts xxi. 1, xxv. 17, xxvii. 18—prob. not Luke vii. 11). Ἡ ἐπιοῦσα, however, and ἡ ἐχομένη are used as early as Polybius: so ἐξαυτῆς, which is found much earlier in poets. But we find no precedent for ἀφ' ἧς (Luke vii. 45, Acts xxiv. 11—here no doubt the context helps it out—2 Pet. iii. 4), instead of the common ἀφ' οὗ (Luke xiii. 25). In James v. 7 it perhaps is better not to understand ὑετόν, but καρπόν, which is readily supplied from the context.

We may conclude with the notice of two points—one of Hebrew idiom toned down through the medium of the LXX., and one of Greek idiom, perhaps imperfectly mastered. We get in Hebrew phrases like Gen. xxv. 1, lit. "And Abraham added and took," LXX. προσθέμενος δὲ Αβραάμ ἔλαβεν; xxvi. 18, lit. "and Isaac returned and digged," LXX. καὶ πάλιν Ισαάκ ὤρυξεν; Hos. i. 6, lit. "for I [will] not add further I [will] have mercy," LXX. οὐ μὴ προσθήσω ἔτι ἐλεῆσαι; Dan. x. 18, Theodot. here literally καὶ προσέθετο καὶ ἥψατό μου. So with other verbs, e.g. Judges xiii. 10, LXX. literally ἐτάχυνεν ἡ γυνὴ καὶ [ἐξ]έδραμεν; 1 Sam. i. 12, lit. "as she multiplied to pray," LXX. ὅτε ἐπλήθυνεν προσευχομένη; ii. 3, lit. "Multiply not, talk (not)," LXX. μὴ καυχᾶσθε καὶ μὴ λαλεῖτε, (but Vulg. *nolite multiplicare loqui*).

Now in the N. T. we hardly get any instance of a reproduction of this idiom in its most un-Hellenic form, the co-ordination of two finite verbs: the only clear ones are Acts vii. 42, which though not an actual quotation from the O. T. is in a passage full of O. T. language, and xv. 16, which is a very lax quotation, though founded on the LXX.: the words ἀναστρέψω καί are actually not found there, nor the corresponding ones in the Hebrew. Luke vi. 48 ἔσκαψεν καὶ ἐβάθυνεν καὶ ἔθηκεν, may be taken as such an instance, if we connect ἐβάθ. with what follows, "he laid the foundation deep : " but it is perh. simpler to connect it with ἔσκ., "he dug, and deepened (the trench dug out)."

There are however cases where the N. T. writers use the constructions with infin. or ptcp. into which the LXX. had often softened the Hebrew one, and the former of which actually occurs in Hebrew : we get the constr. c. ptcp in Luke xix. 11, προσθεὶς εἶπεν, and c. inf. in xx. 11, 12, Acts xii. 3. In Mark xiv. 25, also, P reads οὐ μὴ προσθῶ πεῖν. Possibly these constructions were helped into use, by their possessing a sort of analogy with the Greek idioms where a verb such as λανθάνειν, φθάνειν, τυγχάνειν, formally the chief one in the sentence, expresses what most languages would express by an adv. ("he did it *secretly*," or "he did it *first*" or "beforehand," "*forte aderat*," and the like).

It is well known that αὐτὸς καὶ ἄλλοι δύο κακοῦργοι does not, in Greek, necessarily imply that the first person named was himself a κακοῦργος: see *e.g.* Xen. *Anab.* I. v. 5, οὐ γὰρ ἦν χόρτος οὐδὲ ἄλλο δένδρον οὐδέν. But ἕτερος does not appear to be so used; yet St. Luke appears so to use it in xxiii. 32, at least if we read ἕτεροι κακοῦργοι δύο. The T. R. might possibly be read as the A. V. " two other, [in modern English, " two others,"] malefactors," and then would pass: as will x. 1 ἑτέρους ο', "others to the number of 70."

But instead of assuming that St. Luke was here (as may be the case in some less important passages) attempting an elegant idiom that he could not quite manage, it may be a question whether we are not to think that he boldly wrote "two other malefactors," emphasising the fulfilment of the prophecy which he had quoted at xxii. 37. Possibly it is more reverent to think so, than either to say that his knowledge of Greek was in fault, or to say that he could not have written what the authorities (Bא and the two Egyptian versions) tell us he did write. As we have said all along, textual criticism and grammar must be servants not masters to exegesis. When the critic and the grammarian have made their report (which here is for the harder text, and against the easier interpretation), ὁ πνευματικὸς ἀνακρίνει μὲν πάντα, αὐτὸς δὲ ὑπ' οὐδενὸς ἀνακρίνεται.

INDEX.

MATTHEW.		MATTHEW (*continued.*)	
CHAP. VER.	PAGE	CHAP. VER.	PAGE
i. 2-16	46	v. 19	66
6	26	28	91
11, 12	87	29, 30	64, 178
15	27	34-36	145, 165
18	57, 172	48	115
19	54 *bis*	vi. 1	120
20	57	2	64
21	60	3, 4	54
23	150	5	115
ii. 1	139	10	36, 164
2	118	15	185
3	29	16	115
4	101	19, 20	64
5	52	24	72
8	96	25	112
9	52	26	194
12	189	28	39, 194
22	147, 179	30	127
23	142	32, 33	194
iii. 3	26	34	126
4	54	vii. 4	116, 145
11	60, 144	12	164, 177
14	62	14	68
16	64	15	145
iv. 3	177	20	181
13	142	21	73
v. 1	57, 58, 58 *n.*	24, 26	56, 87, 88
6	91	29	175
13	144	viii. 1	57
15	165	5	57
17	165	7	53

MATTHEW (*continued*)—

CHAP. VER.	PAGE
viii. 8	56, 178
19	71
20	112
22	116
23	57 *n*, 58, 59
27	174
28	57
ix. 14	83
18	71, 166
27	57
32	57
x. 5	87
14	197
16	53
19	70, 112
25	178
29	71
30	135
32	145, 198
xi. 5	79
11	94
14	60
26	76
28	62
xii. 1	38
10	192
13	34 *n*
19	89
28	181
44	180
45	195
50	60
xiii. 4	54, 194, 5
12	186
13	38
14	83, 130
30	116
38	66
56	154
xiv. 2	96
7	180
8	200
9	122
19	122
26	139

MATTHEW (*continued*)—

CHAP. VER.	PAGE
xv. 4	83
5	113 *bis*
20	120
23	29
27	138
32	69, 78, 112, 200
xvi. 14	52, 71
20	177
22	113
23	55
xvii. 2	196 *bis*
4	71
9	145
11	100
12	157
20	179 *bis*
22	57
xviii. 1	94
6	71
7	139
8, 9	92
10, 12	71
14	177
16	64
19	110
20	54
21, 22	159
24	71
25	122, 188
28	71
xix. 3	149, 192
14	62, 116
16	71
25	181
26	81
28	146
xx. 2, 13	146
15	192
18	82
20	95
21	71
22	95
23	54, 119
33	177
xxi. 1	26

INDEX. 207

MATTHEW (*continued*)—

CHAP.	VER.	PAGE
xxi.	12	50
	23	57, 135
	31	70, 138
	33	38
	42	143
xxii.	5	72
	11	187
	25, 29	188
	36	93
	41	57
xxiii.	2-12	167
	16	145
	30	38
	37	29
xxiv.	2	147, 187
	3	57
	18	143
	22	73, 184
	33	147
	40	71
	42, 43, 44	100
	48	56
xxv.	1, 3, 4, 7	64
	6	100
	8	138
	9	189
	15	200
	21, 23	39
	24	174, 180
	26	180
	27	113
	36	62
xxvi.	2	101, 162
	6, 7	57
	14	71
	18	154
	24	114, 184
	28	127
	35	112
	42	184, 6
	45	163
	50	68
	53	192
	61	139
	63	148

MATTHEW (*continued*)—

CHAP.	VER.	PAGE
xxvi.	65	88
	68	135
	69	71
xxvii.	1	119, 175
	6	80
	7	146 *bis*
	8	180
	10	80, 146
	17	180
	21	138
	23	172
	24	138
	40	140
	48	71
	49	116
	51	159
	56	27
	57	79
	58, 64	122
xxviii.	9	175

MARK.

CHAP.	VER.	PAGE
i.	7	59 *n*, 100
	9	143
	13	149
	15	144
	22	175
	34	38
	39	142
	44	152
ii.	1	139
	2	154
	16	68, 174
	18	83, 135 *bis*
	25	60
	26	47
iii.	5	34 *n*
	11	111
	14	118
	21	151
iv.	1	154, 196
	3	119
	4	195
	8	71 *n*
	10	39, 153, 195 *n*

MARK (*continued*)—

CHAP. VER.	PAGE
iv. 13	112
20	71 *n*
25	186
34, 38	60
41	174, 181
v. 4	76
11	154
21	57
23	116
26	151 188
28	170
30	135
42	173
vi. 3	154
7	72
8	122
8, 9	198
14	96
15	71
22	58
23-25	95
25	197
36	69, 112
56	111, 170
vii. 11, 19	200
27	116
28	138
viii. 1	69, 112
2	69, 78, 112
12	192
23	192
37	107
38	54
ix. 6	69, 112
11	68
12	168
13	165
17	71
19	62, 154
21	175
22	166
24	56
30	107
34	94
40	156

MARK (*continued*)—

CHAP. VER.	PAGE
ix. 43-45	92
x. 14	62, 116
17	71
27	165
33	82
35, 38	95
40	54
51	177
xi. 1	29
4	154
15	50
16	38
19	111
22	86
25	111
26	184, 5
28	135
xii. 5	52
6	180
12	163
14	182, 190, 200
28	93 *n*
32	171
38-40	77
xiii. 2	147, 187
9	143
11	70, 112
13	147
16	143
19	59
20	73, 184
24	165
25	135
29	147
32	158
35	100
xiv. 1	112
2	109
5	39, 113
8	56
11	112
19	72 *bis*
21	114, 184
24	127, 152
25	202

INDEX.

MARK (continued)		LUKE (continued)	
CHAP. VER.	PAGE	CHAP. VER.	PAGE
xiv. 36	70, 76	ii. 10	79
40	112	13	84
49	178	21	162
53	82	26	111, 189
54	154, 159	28	61
55	34	31	149
58	139	33	196
64	88	37	61
72	90	49	147
xv. 1	147	51	135
23	53	iii. 7	180
25	162	15	112
28	149	16	59 a
29	140	18	79
36	116	21	34 n
38	159	24, 29	29
40	27	iv. 10	195
44	104	14	148
47	27	15	61
xvi. 3	145	18	79, 103, 105
9	72 n	27	27
		29	175
LUKE.		36	174
		38	152
i. 1	44 n	41	195
5	47	43	79
10	84, 196	44	142
17	26	v. 1	61
19	79	5	61, 140
20	137, 188	6	84
21	195, 196	12	71
22	61	14	61, 152, 189
27	35	16	61
28	150	17	61, 71
29	52, 112	20, 23	38
30	96	33	82
33	147	47	62
35	180	vi. 9	192
37	73, 151	10	34 n
43	62, 178	11	112
60	191	12	87
66	181	17	84
79	38	18	138
ii. 4	138	20	54, 61
5	28, 35	39	72, 191

14

LUKE (continued)—

CHAP. VER.	PAGE
vi. 40	72
42	116, 187
43	188
47	88, 197
48	201
vii. 4	109
6	187
7	180
11	200
13	115
16	117
25	59 n
28	94
35	138
40	200
41	72
44	56
45	56, 201
46	56
47, 48	38
viii. 1	61, 79
2	186
5	195
9	112
18	186
22	61, 79
30	195
37	84
41	200
45	135
50, 52	115
54	76
ix. 5	198
13	110
28	78, 200
31	40
36	36, 105 n, 144
41	154
45	87, 177
50	156
52	119, 154, 175 bis
60	116
x. 1	72, 154
4	115
6	186

LUKE (continued)—

CHAP. VER.	PAGE
x. 7	151
8	197
10	198
18	123
19	113
32	148
35	147
39	65
xi. 4	38
5	113
6	62
8	173, 184
20	181
24	180
26	195
28	168
35	109
48	181
xii. 3	137
5	129
6	188, 191
8	145
10	197 bis
18	56
20	77
22	112
26	183
29	112
30	55
32	76
39, 40	100
42	119
50	56
51	166, 191
53	147
54	100
xiii. 2	93, 103
3	191
4	93
5	191
9	186, 199
11	188
19	143, 195
25	201
28, 35	111

INDEX.

LUKE (*continued*)—

CHAP. VER.	PAGE
xiv. 1	61
3	192
18	200
24	56
26	56, 62, 183
27	56
28	191
31	145, 191
32	186
49	154
xv. 7	92
8	191
14	61
25	88
31	54
xvi. 2	39
8	84, 93
9	84, 146
11, 12	183, 185
13	72
16	79, 158
20	33 n
23	98
25	39
26	179, 180
29	27, 99
30	191
31	183
xvii. 1	119
2	92
8	39, 70, 191
11	61, 142
15	56, 150
17	191
20	100
25	138
34	72
xviii. 2	188
4	184
5	173
6	84
8	191
10	72
14	92, 93
16	62, 116

LUKE (*continued*)—

CHAP. VER.	PAGE
xviii. 36	88
40	122
41	177
xix. 2	61, 129, 200
3	139
11	202
14	147
22	99
27	147
37	84, 154
40	110
42	168
43	162
48	38
xx. 1	58
2, 6	135
7	189
9	38
10	138
11, 12	202
20	121, 176
27	77
29	180
35, 36	165
xxi. 6	147, 187, 197
24	135
25	31
37	142
xxii. 1	85
2, 4	112
15	83, 130
20	127
22	168
23	42, 181
24	94
27	191
28	135
37	149, 202
42	116
49	153
53	55, 58
56	154
64	135
76	53 n
xxiii. 1	169

LUKE (*continued*)—

CHAP. VER.	PAGE
xxiii. 5	148, 159
18	46
19	130
27	84
29	100 *bis*
30	36 *n*
32	202
44	162 *n*
51	199
53	188
xxiv. 5	58, 149
11	194
14	61
18	122
20	176
21	78, 121, 166
25	148
27	158
32	191
41	58

JOHN.

CHAP. VER.	PAGE
i. 1	48, 154
3	141
5	182
6	78, 199
8	178
10	182
15	94
16	137
18	154
30	94
32	129
39	200
40	87
47	122
ii. 2	196
7	159
16	114, 115
18	174
19	140
21	85
24	64
iii. 1	78, 145, 199

JOHN (*continued*)—

CHAP. VER.	PAGE
iii. 2	150
8	89, 100 *n*
12	183
13	128
15	73, 144
16	73, 175, 178
18	182
19	167
24	188
25	145
29	83, 130
iv. 2	168
10	135
11	165
14	113
15	109
21	100
23	80, 100
25	100
34	54, 178
35	100
37	135
44	173
v. 6	191
7	178
11	52
12	135
15	135
16	182
24	100
25, 28	89, 100
29	85
32	135
37	89
40	62
42	86
45	135
47	183
vi. 2	195
9	71
13	194
22	195
24	197
26	138
29	178

INDEX.

JOHN (continued) —		
CHAP. VER.		PAGE
vi. 32		46
35		62, 113
37		62
39		73, 197
44		62
45		62, 87
46		174
50		122, 138
51		138
54-56		56
59		200
64		135
65		62
66		145
70		51
vii. 2		85
4		122
12		52
17		71, 192
22		174
26		189
32		88
33		100 n
35		174
37		62
39		200
40		84, 88
41		100
42		100, 172, 191 n
47		190
48		145
49		196
51		87
52		101, 190
viii. 6, 8		43
9		72
14		100 n
20		200
21		100 n
22		100 n, 190
25		68
38		87
39		114
40		87
44		46

JOHN (continued)—		
CHAP. VER.		PAGE
viii. 45		197
56		179
ix. 3		178
4		100
7		143
9		191
10		34 n
11		117
14		34 n
17		174
19		191
21		64
22		33 n
25		128
31		66
33 bis		114
x. 3		89
4		194, 5
5		113, 195
12		188, 195
14		195
16		89, 194, 5
27, 28		89, 195
29		197
32, 33		153
35		183 bis
37		184
xi. 1		138
6		168
9		191
14		106
18		139
19		153
20		100
21		39, 170
31		82
32		39
33		82
38		39
44		116
49		127
52		178
57		178
xii. 1		153
9, 12		46, 196

214 INDEX.

JOHN (continued)—		JOHN (continued)—	
CHAP. VER.	PAGE	CHAP. VER.	PAGE
xii. 15	100	xvi. 26	153
33	200	32	100 *bis*
40	177	xvii. 2, 3	109
42	168	6	36, 54
46	73	7	36 *bis*
47	88, 89	9	54, 153
48	66	10	54 *bis*
49	112	11, 13	100
xiii. 3	100 *n*	20	153
10, 11	191	25	163
18	178	xviii. 16	154
23	154	21	65
24	112	30	184
25	154	34	53 *n*, 63
27	94	37	89, 180
33	100 *n*	40	46
35	54	xix. 11	114, 184
36	100 *n*	12	145
xiv. 2	186	13	88
3	100, 171	17	64
4, 5	100 *n*	25	161
7	170	27, 28	195
11	186	31	194, 5
18	100	32	195
21	135	42	64 *n*
22	174, 191	xx. 11, 12	154
24	54	22	49
26	66	23	38
28, 30	100	xxi. 2	26
31	178	3	100 *bis*
xv. 3	141	6	139
5	129, 197	18	39
6	98	20	135
8	54, 178	25	189
18	94		
22	36, 114, 184	ACTS.	
24	36, 184		
25	178	i. 1	168
xvi. 2	100	3	140
5, 10	100 *n*	4	87
13	66	5	151
15	54	6	52
17	100 *n*, 145	14	28
20	143	16	76 *n*
25	100		

ACTS (*continued*)—

CHAP. VER.	PAGE
i. 18	146
24	125
ii. 10	148
12	112
18	168 *bis*
22	66, 138
23	66
25	34
30	121
33	82
38	144
45	111
iii. 1	147
2	37
11	26
13, 17	149
21	168
iv. 1	58
5	78, 147
10	65, 66, 147
11	65
16	165, 168
17	83, 130, 147
18	148
20	189
21	112
32	84
33	37
35	37, 111
v. 4	130, 174, 191
7	162, 188
9	147, 174
12	26
14	84
15	170
16	84
19	140
23	147
24	112
26	174
28	83, 130
31	118
32	84 *n*
36	143
42	79

ACTS (*continued*)—

CHAP. VER.	PAGE
vi. 2	84
vii. 4	158
5	187
8	175
20	81
21	80
34	88, 130
35	66
38	135, 159
40	197
42	201
47	34
50	191
viii. 4	79
7	196
12	79
17, 18	49
19	49, 178
22	181
25	79
27	126
30	191
31	110, 112, 172
35	79
40	79, 142
ix. 1	90
4	89
6	69, 70
7	75, 89, 90, 188
9	188
12	124
13	88
21	135
26	188
31, 42	148
x. 3	124
14	73
17	112
19	58
22	87
25	119 *bis*
28	119
36	79 *bis*
37	77, 148
42	135

INDEX.

ACTS (*continued*)—

CHAP. VER.	PAGE
x. 44, 47	49
48	142, 144, 147
xi. 7	89
11	62
13	124
15	158
18	181
20	79
28	120
xii. 3	202
8	114
14	139
19	122, 188
xiii. 2	158
10	115
12	125
13	153
17	150
22	80
24	154
25	70, 100
32	78, 79
39	158
45	130
47	80
xiv. 14	84
15	79
17	37, 64, 168
21	79
26	180
xv. 5	43 *n*
6	50
11	118
16	201
21	126
23	65, 117
27	127
35	99
xvi. 4	50, 173
9	140
10	79
16	58
19	91
33	139
36	36

ACTS (*continued*)—

CHAP. VER.	PAGE
xvi. 37	172
xvii. 2	196
4	84
6	188
10	140
11	112
13	127
18	79
19	91
20	112
21	94
22	76 *n*, 94
23	48
27	80, 168, 181, 187
28	52 *n*, 149
xviii. 14	34 *n*
17	91
21	142
xix. 1	28
2	49
5	147
6	49
22	143
27	163, 189
30	58
35	76 *n*, 172, 187
38	148
xx. 4	196
9	139
11	175
18	158
22	126 *n*
24	119, 175
xxi. 1	200
3	179
4	117
5	159
11	65
13	142
16	82, 84
17	58
21	117
28	163
30	91
33	91, 112, 122

INDEX.

ACTS (continued)—	
CHAP. VER.	PAGE
xxi. 34	122
36	84, 196
37	99
xxii. 1	88
5	180
7	36, 89
8	62
9	75, 89, 90
10	62
11	139
14	89
16	96
17	58
21	62
22	102
24	122
25	30
xxiii. 3	122
4	198
6	72
8	165, 189
9	199
14	83, 130
22	62
26	117
28	148
30	120
31	140
34	138
35	122, 200
xxiv. 5	129
11	126, 201
12	165
15	120
17	126, 139
19	62, 198
25	120
26	121
27	31
xxv. 4	143
5	200
6	122
7	58
9	31
10	94

ACTS (continued)—	
CHAP. VER.	PAGE
xxv. 11	185
13	126 *bis*
16	111
17	122, 200
21	122
22	113, 200
23	149
24	84, 112
xxvi. 3	78
4	33 n
7	120, 121, 153
10	163
14	62, 89
15	36
18	159
22	135
25	200
32	114
xxvii. 1	37
10	117 n, 120
12	172
18	200
20	187
21	168
22	80
34	154
37	38
44	147
xxviii. 3	84
13	180
14	175
16	30 n
17	187
22	87, 168

ROMANS.

i. 5	86
8	168 n
10	172
12	55
13	163, 4
15	79
17	86
25	152

INDEX.

ROMANS (*continued*)—

CHAP. VER.	PAGE
i. 26	160
ii. 7, 8	198
11, 13	151
17	39
19	121
23	50
26	80, 191
27	50, 140
iii. 2	168 *n*, 195
4	109
6	172
8	117
12	188
13	37
20	73
23	95, 105 *bis*
25, 26	155
27	105, 191
29	191, 2
30	47, 171 *bis*
iv. 1	96
2	154
11	85, 140
12	184, 8
13	86
16	148
18	120
20	125
v. 5	86
6	171
7	47, 112
8	174
11	129
12	199
13	40
14	147
18	85, 199
vi. 2	139
5	166
6	85
10	74, 81
16	164
17	167
18, 20	81
21	168 *n*

ROMANS (*continued*)—

CHAP. VER.	PAGE
vii. 1	192
5	96
6	189
7	50, 160, 170, 184
10	66
18	120
24	85
viii. 3	78
9	171, 183
15	76, 105 *bis*
17	171 *bis*
18	120
25	140
31	156
32	173, 191
33	148
39	86
ix. 3	113, 139
6	66, 174
8	80, 195
10	197
11	199
14	151
16, 18	39
20	168
22	199
25	183
27	155
29	184
33	73, 147
x. 1	168 *n*
11	147
14	88
15	79
16	166
18	166, 8
19	166
xi. 1	105, 106
2	192, 200
4	105, 106, 166, 200
6	172
7	105
13	168, 168 *n*
14	172
21	183, 5, 190

INDEX.

ROMANS (*continued*)—

CHAP. VER.	PAGE
xi. 22	172, 198
36	75, 141
xii. 1	180
5	72
6-19	129
15	116
xiii. 12	105
xiv. 5	152
9	104, 163
13	120
20	140
xv. 5	108
8	87, 156
23-28	199
24	175
25	127
xvi. 7	36
13, 19	55

1 CORINTHIANS.

CHAP. VER.	PAGE
i. 14	96
20	191
29	73
31	179
iii. 3	191
5	166
iv. 2	177, 179 *n*
6	72, 107 *n*, 145, 156
8	113
14	188
21	144, 160
v. 2	191
5	85
9	189
10	172
11	189
12	191 *bis*
vi. 1	191
2	145, 192
3	137
4	168
7	168, 191
9	165, 192 *bis*
10	165

1 CORINTHIANS (*continued*)—

CHAP. VER.	PAGE
vi. 14	163
16	200
vii. 2	72
7	164
9	185
13	129
14	172, 195
20	66
28	98
29	88
31	78
35	55, 62
37	120, 129
viii. 1	199
3	66
4	180, 199
5	171
6	75
10	191
ix. 1	191
2	166 *bis*, 184
9	91
11	191
12	55
15	145
24	175
26	187
x. 2	96
6	120
7	118
16	191
22	192
28	159
xi. 6	185
14	197
18	168 *n*
22	172
24	127
34	175
xii. 2	111, 175
6, 11	96
xiii. 3	109
13	94
xiv. 5	110, 184
10	110

1 CORINTHIANS (continued)—

CHAP.	VER.	PAGE
xiv.	11	145
	16	172
	19	92
	25	175
	33	86
	36	192
xv.	1	79
	2	184
	4	103
	12, 13	183
	15	171 *bis*
	29	172
	35	100
	36	77
	37	110, 126
	39	73
xvi.	5	100 *n*, 199
	6, 7	154
	18	55
	22	39, 185

2 CORINTHIANS.

CHAP.	VER.	PAGE
i.	6	55, 96, 156
	7	156
	8	155
	13	121, 166
	17	151
	24	174
ii.	1	120
	2	114, 163
	3	66
	4	140
	5	178
	13	104
	17	188
iii.	1	38, 191
	5	174
	8	191
	11	140
	13	120
	15	159
	18	83
iv.	8, 9	188 *bis*
	11	114

2 CORINTHIANS (continued)—

CHAP.	VER.	PAGE
iv.	12	96
	16	166
	18	59
v.	1	84 *n*
	3	171 *bis*
	6	129
	10	140
	11	121
	14	156
	15	181
	16	166
	17	74
	19	174
vi.	9	129, 188
	10	188
	13	78
vii.	4	156
	5	129
	7	55
	12	119
	15	55
viii.	7	116
	9	128
	10	158
	14	55 *bis*
	23	54, 155
ix.	2	158
x.	4	81
	8	160
	9	174
	10	200
	13, 16	118
xi.	1	34 *n*, 113
	2	118
	3	139
	4	34 *n*, 114, 168 *n*
	5	95, 157
	6	166
	7	79, 192
	16	170
	21	174
	23	157
	24	157
	25	104
	28	77

INDEX.

2 CORINTHIANS (*continued*)—

CHAP. VER.	PAGE
xii. 1, 3	184
7	45
8	156
9	104
11	95, 157, 183
12	165, 168 *n*
19	55, 65
21	124, 165
xiii. 1	100
4	166
5	63 *n*
6	121
9	55

GALATIANS.

CHAP. VER.	PAGE
i. 1	141
8, 9, 11, 16	79
18	154
23	79, 128 *n*, 135
ii. 1	139
2	114, 149, 190
4	109
5	154
8	96
9, 10	178
11	129, 149
13	175
16	73
17	191
20	86
21	170
iii. 2	49
4	171
5	96
7	66
13	125, 156
17	125
23	120
28	74
iv. 3	38, 135
6	76
7	141
8	187
11	114, 174, 190

GALATIANS (*continued*)—

CHAP. VER.	PAGE
iv. 13	79, 140
15	114, 170
17	107 *n*
20	113
24	72
27	183
30	113
v. 6	74, 96
12	113
13	140
vi. 10	181
12	109

EPHESIANS.

CHAP. VER.	PAGE
i. 11	96
13	88
17	108
20	96, 129
23	96
ii. 2	96
3	38
5, 8	22
10	55
13	128
14	61
15	83
17	79
19	181
iii. 2	171
8	32, 79, 120
19	160
20	96, 160
iv. 6	75
11	52
12	155
21	88, 171
22, 25	121
29	73
v. 4	102, 184
5	33 *n*, 73
6	100
27	178
33	116
vi. 9	151
18, 19	152

PHILIPPIANS.

CHAP. VER.	PAGE
i. 1	150 n
18	166, 172
19	55
22	119
25	55
29	120
ii. 7	125
13	96, 156
23	175
27	147
30	55, 84 n
iii. 3	188
8	166
9	54
11	172
12	105, 174
13	90, 121
16	116
18, 19	77, 198
20	55
iv. 7	87
10	118
11	174
12	163

COLOSSIANS.

CHAP. VER.	PAGE
i. 8	55
13	85
16	141
17	61
21	128
22	118
23	88, 171
26	129
29	96
ii. 1	36
5	166
8	109
14	82
19	187
20	139
23	168 n
iii. 6	100

COLOSSIANS (continued)—

CHAP. VER.	PAGE
iii. 15	87
18	102
iv. 6	118

1 THESSALONIANS.

CHAP. VER.	PAGE
i. 3	84, 5, 90
5	158
ii. 7	174
9	90
11, 12	129
13	96
18	163, 168 n
19	191, 2
iii. 5	114, 143, 190
6	79
7	55, 174
8	111
10	160
iv. 3, 4, 6	120
16	144
17	175
v. 2	100
4	177
5	86
6	181
10	110
11	72
13	130, 160

2 THESSALONIANS.

CHAP. VER.	PAGE
i. 4	62
6	171
7	85
ii. 1	43 n, 156
2	174
7	96
13	36, 86
15	181
iii. 6	36
9	178 n
10	117, 122, 185
12	122
14	66, 185
16	108

INDEX. 223

1 TIMOTHY.

CHAP. VER.	PAGE
i. 7	67, 107 *n*, 165
13	128
16	147
ii. 8	32
9	158
15	195
iii. 5	183
14	94
v. 7	122
8	183
13	32
19	158, 184
25	194
vi. 3	184
5	43

2 TIMOTHY.

CHAP. VER.	PAGE
i. 13	87 *bis*
16	34, 108
18	94, 108
ii. 2	87
14	147, 189
25	108, 189

TITUS.

CHAP. VER.	PAGE
i. 11	186
12	32
ii. 2	117
4	109
13	50

PHILEMON.

5	87, 155
10	78
13	156
18	40
19	178
22	121

HEBREWS.

CHAP. VER.	PAGE
i. 2	141
3	85
5	143 *bis*
14	191

HEBREWS (*continued*)—

CHAP. VER.	PAGE
ii. 7	93
10	125, 141
15	140
iii. 3	93
6	171
7	88, 9, 171
11	192
12	109
15	88, 9, 171
16	166
17	191
18	121
iv. 1	95
2	79
3	168
6	79
7	88, 9
12	93
v. 5	118
7	139
vi. 3	171
4, 5	87
10	90, 118
13	148
14	130, 193
16	148
vii. 1	129
5	29
9	29, 119, 175
11	26, 168, 189
27	159
viii. 5	200
8	100, 162
10	129
ix. 1	168
3	151
4	26
8	189
12	36, 96, 140
17	182, 189
22	144
25	146
26	172
x. 2	172
16	129

HEBREWS (continued)—

CHAP. VER.	PAGE
x. 22	35
25	43 n
28	158
34	35 n
39	86
xi. 1	187
4	93
9	142
17	104, 106 n
19	180
28	104
35	187
xii. 7	187
15	95
17	33 n
18	129, 199
19	31, 89
24	93
25	183, 5
xiii. 2	90
5	129
13	181
16	90
17	126

JAMES.

CHAP. VER.	PAGE
i. 1	117
13	138
17	151
19	33 n
24	104
25	84
27	120
ii. 5	81
10	110
11	184
12	175
iii. 2	66
8	77
12, 14	165
15	188
iv. 2, 3	95
5	192
13	65
15	137

JAMES (continued)—

CHAP. VER.	PAGE
v. 4	36, 138
7	201
12	39, 148
16	96
17	83, 130

1 PETER.

i. 8	167, 187
11	158
12	79
23	158
25	79
ii. 3	171
10	124, 183
14	167
17	114
18	129
iii. 1	129
3	189
8, 9	129
14	110
15	165
17	110
18	153
iv. 6	79
8, 10	129

2 PETER.

i. 1	50
5	66
9	186
18	89
ii. 4	183 bis, 185
6, 10	85
21	189
iii. 2	118
4	201

1 JOHN.

i. 2	154
3, 4	49
5	88
ii. 1	154
12	38
18	100, 180

INDEX.

1 John (*continued*) –	
CHAP. VER.	PAGE
ii. 19	. 170
21	. 73
24	. 197
25	. 78
27	. 197
28	. 171
iii. 2	. 171
10	. 195
15	. 73
24	. 61
iv. 1	. 195
3	. 100
13	61, 138
15	. 61
17	. 179
v. 6	. 140
14, 16	. 95
15	95, 110
20	109, 178

2 John.

2	. 129
4	84, 145
6	178 *bis*
10	. 183

3 John.

2, 3	55 *n*, 56
4	32, 178
6	55 *n*
10	. 165

Jude.

4	. 31
14	35 *n*
22, 23	. 39

Revelation.

i. 5	77, 144
7	. 100
10	. 89
13	. 154
14-16	. 54
18	. 104

Revelation (*continued*)—	
CHAP. VER.	PAGE
i. 19	. 194
ii. 2	. 129
3, 4	. 37
5	37, 81, 100, 186
7	39, 138
9	121, 129
10	. 145
13	. 54
14	. 80
16	81, 100, 144, 150, 186
17	. 39
18	. 129
20	38, 77
iii. 2	120, 194
8	. 59
9	40, 174
11	. 100
15	39, 113
16	. 120
20	61, 89, 147
iv. 1	34 *n*, 89
2	. 147
9	111, 147
10	. 147
11	. 141
v. 7	. 104
9	. 144
10	. 147
11	. 89
vi. 1	34 *n*
2, 4, 5	42 *n*
6, 7	. 89
8	42 *n*, 51, 157
16	36 *n*
vii. 2	. 59
7	. 29
9	59, 198
14	. 104
17	84 *n*
viii. 1	. 111
4	. 81
5	. 104
6	. 64
11	51, 143
12	. 38

REVELATION (*continued*)—

CHAP. VER.	PAGE
viii. 13	71, 145
ix. 4	73, 189
11	64
12	100
13	89
x. 4	89
7	79, 98, 161
xi. 7-11	98
9	38
12	89
14	100
xii. 4	121
6	59, 139
7	119, 150
9	51
10	89
11	142
14	59, 91
xiii. 3	84
4	80, 150
8	80
10	179 *n*
12	59
14	142
15	177
18	179 *n*
xiv. 2	89 *bis*
6	79
9	147
10	61, 162
12	179 *n*
13	89, 179
17	61
19	91
xv. 2	39, 146
xvi. 1	89

REVELATION (*continued*)—

CHAP. VER.	PAGE
xvi. 10, 11	145
15	100
18	59
20	194
xvii. 7	64
8	135
9	59, 179 *n*
11	61
14	150
xviii. 4	89
12, 13	198
21	71
23	38
xix. 1	89
3	36
6	89
10	36
11	147
13	35, 51
14	147
15	61
17	71
18, 20	147
xx. 2	51 *bis*
7-9	98
8	59
xxi. 3	89
6	36
8	128
21	72, 137
xxii. 2	30
7	100
8	89
12	100
18	89
20	100

Printed by Hazell, Watson, & Viney, Ld., London and Aylesbury.

www.ingramcontent.com/pod-product-compliance
Lightning Source LLC
Chambersburg PA
CBHW021803230426
43669CB00008B/615